Waiting for a Glacier to Move

Princeton Theological Monograph Series

K. C. Hanson, Charles M. Collier, D. Christopher Spinks,
and Robin Parry, Series Editors

Recent volumes in the series:

Paul G. Doerksen
The Church Made Strange for the Nations:
Essays in Ecclesiology and Political Theology

Lisa M. Hess
Learning in a Musical Key: Insight for Theology in Performative Mode

Jack Barentsen
Emerging Leadership in the Pauline Mission: A Social Identity Perspective
on Local Leadership Development in Corinth and Ephesus

Matthew D. Kirkpatrick
Attacks on Christendom in a World Come of Age: Kierkegaard,
Bonhoeffer, and the Question of "Religionless Christianity"

Michael A. Salmeier
Restoring the Kingdom: The Role of God as the "Ordainer of Times
and Seasons" in the Acts of the Apostles

Gerald W. King
Disfellowshiped: Pentecostal Responses to Fundamentalism
in the United States, 1906–1943

Timothy Hessel-Robinson
Spirit and Nature: The Study of Christian Spirituality
in a Time of Ecological Urgency

Paul W. Chilcote
Making Disciples in a World Parish:
Global Perspectives on Mission & Evangelism

Waiting for a Glacier to Move

Practicing Social Witness

JENNIFER R. AYRES

☙PICKWICK *Publications* · Eugene, Oregon

2011

WAITING FOR A GLACIER TO MOVE
Practicing Social Witness

Princeton Theological Monograph Series 170

Pickwick Publications
An Imprint of Wipf and Stock Publishers
199 W. 8th Ave., Suite 3
Eugene, OR 97401

www.wipfandstock.com

ISBN 13: 978-1-60899-197-6

Cataloguing-in-Publication data:

Ayres, Jennifer R.

   Waiting for a glacier to move : practicing social witness / Jennifer R. Ayres.

   x + 208 pp. ; 23 cm. Includes bibliographical references and index(es).

   Princeton Theological Monograph Series 170

   ISBN 13: 978-1-60899-197-6

   1. Theology, Practical. 2. Social justice — Religious aspects — Christianity. 3. Christian life. I. Title. II. Series.

BV3 .A97 2011

Manufactured in the U.S.A.

To Carol Jenkins Ayres

Contents

Acknowledgments

I find myself without words to adequately express my gratitude to a number of people, groups, and institutions for their support of me and my work in the research and writing of this book. Their encouragement, intellectual imagination, faithfulness, willingness to challenge me, and financial support made this project not only possible, but a joyful pursuit.

This work began during my doctoral work at Emory University. With the support of Emory's Initiative in Religious Practices and Practical Theology funded by the Lilly Endowment, I conducted ethnographic research to gather the concrete perspectives and stories that ground what you'll read in this book. Many people have read many versions of the arguments in these pages. I must thank my fantastic advisory committee who guided the design, research, and writing of the first incarnation of this project. Their contributions remain evident in the final version of the project. Tom Long was a dream as an advisor. His clarity of thought and argumentation were invaluable to me as I tried to pull together several divergent areas of inquiry in this project. I appreciate his encouragement, his friendship, and the commitments we share to both Church and academy. Committee members Mary Elizabeth Moore, Liz Bounds, and Nancy Eiesland became, through this process, friends and mentors. Nancy died in 2009. I, and many others, miss her greatly.

Two other granting institutions supported the research and writing of this book. The Louisville Institute graciously awarded me a dissertation-writing grant, and created the space for young scholars to collaborate, a wondrous gift. The Louisville Institute supports many of us who seek to stand in between church and academy, and we all are broadened and enriched by their commitment to the study of religion in America. The Wabash Center for Teaching Theology and Religion granted me a summer research and writing fellowship, which supported recent revisions of this text, particularly the chapter on hope. The Wabash Center supports new faculty as they seek to balance good teaching with quality research, and I appreciate the community of colleagues created during the Pre-Tenure Workshop for Theological School Faculty.

Other colleagues read this project in full and in part, demonstrating incredible generosity of spirit. In particular, I want to thank Michelle Voss Roberts, Andrew Radde-Gallwitz, Robert Cathey, Melody Knowles, and Cláudio Carvalhaes. Thanks to my proofreaders: Robert Saler and Martin J. Coffee; and to my research assistant, Jason Myers, who indexed a large portion of this book.

I also owe my thanks to the editors and staff at Wipf and Stock, including Diane Farley, Patrick Harrison, and Charlie Collier. I am grateful to have worked with them on this, my first book.

Of course, this book would not be possible without the willingness of the activists described herein. I must thank those activists, pastors, and denominational staffers who so graciously sat for interviews with me: Nelson and Ellen, Thurston, John, Dorothy, Caroline, Elenora, Catherine, and Carolynn.

Finally, I must express my gratitude to my family for their support and encouragement over the years. My parents, Bruce and Carol, and my brother David have alternately tolerated, cheered on, and invested in my intellectual development. During the writing of much of this book, my mom, Carol, was diagnosed with and eventually died from pancreatic cancer. During many long visits with her during those last months, she expressed to me her delight in my work and her concerns that I finish my doctoral program. She was just discovering her passion for social justice, and it is in honor of her spirit of self-discovery in the interest of justice and peace that I finally complete this book.

1

Introduction: Waiting for a Glacier to Move

ON THE SECOND TUESDAY OF EACH MONTH, 90-YEAR-OLD PRESBYTER-
ian elder Thurston Griggs gathers with a small group from Baltimore
Presbytery and takes the 8:21 a.m. train from Baltimore's Halethorpe
station to the nation's capital. The small band makes its way to the
Presbyterian Office in the Methodist Building, right next to the Supreme
Court. There, they are briefed on current legislative issues by denominational staff members before visiting the office of one of their legislators.
The group, while small, is dedicated, some of them having attended these
"Second Tuesday" briefing sessions and subsequent lobbying visits for
more than a decade. Despite their commitment to these visits, members of the group do not have grandiose expectations. As Nelson Tharp,
a regular Second Tuesday participant, describes it, "You've got a small
group of dedicated people who are in there pitching, and a few people
around the side that pay attention, and a lot of people who don't even
know there's something going on. And so you always have the feeling
that you're attacking an iceberg with an ice pick . . . But still, some people
do listen, and it does *some* good. As they say, even glaciers move every
now and then."

Waiting for a glacier to move, ice pick in hand, can be a frustrat-
ing experience. In light of these challenges, one might ask, what sustains
religious social action in the absence of large-scale support or success?
What keeps religious activists going? These same questions occurred to
me on multiple occasions over the course of several years of working
among Christian activists in peace and justice movements.

As a young seminarian, I was inspired and challenged by the stories
of lifelong activists who never gave up on human rights, peace or justice.
Some of them, like me, were Presbyterian. But as I tried to walk in the
footsteps of these mentors in Christian faith and action, I regularly found

1

myself feeling like something was missing. For a long time, I could not put my finger on it. To me, social activism felt a natural and right dimension of the Christian life; furthermore, these mentors, these inspiring leaders and grassroots workers, continually strengthened my conviction that this was so. The call to Christian social action seemed quite clear. What seemed less clear was how practices of social action are woven into the whole fabric of the Christian life. While I was intellectually convinced that social action is an essential component of the Christian life, in practice the relationship between social activism and Christian faith felt a bit strained. Sometimes, when we were deciding whether or how to act in response to broad categories of social injustice and suffering, we engaged in forms of theological discernment, seeking after God's leading for the group. It seemed, though, as if theological reflection of any sort, whether it be seeking God's guidance or reflecting upon the impact of social action upon theological knowledge, stopped once action began.

Another way to describe this phenomenon might be to say that, in most cases, theology appeared to operate as a mandate. It was as if God said, "Do it," and it was up to us humans to determine how, for how long, using what resources, and by what standards we were to measure its success. Construed this way, social action is less a theological practice than a humanistic one with a theological mandate. As such, social action becomes disconnected from other religious practices. In some contexts, the disconnect between social action and other forms of Christian practice is so sharply felt that social action is all but absent from some Christian communities. In some cases, it is completely absent. Even among those communities who sustain practices of social action over long periods of time, the practice is marked by a high degree of fragility. That is, practices of social action sometimes falter or die out, or they are sustained only in small, dedicated groups.[1]

The aforementioned challenges faced in practices of Christian social action point to two issues: (1) social action, whether it be political, cultural or economic, is often considered to be only marginally related to the whole fabric of Christian life and practice; and (2) the very component that gives the practice much of its religious character, theological

---

1. Recent research indicates that civic and political engagement are not "central" activities in the lives of most congregations. In fact, Mark Chaves notes that while such activities are significant, their prevalence might be understood as "peripheral." See Chaves, *Congregations in America*, 229.

reflection, is regularly missing or else relegated to a particular chronological moment in the life of the practice. These two issues are interrelated, and the whole tapestry of the Christian life as well as the thread of social action can be mutually strengthened by concentrated attention to the relationship between them. The relationship can be deepened and made more explicit through an intentional and sustained process of theological reflection within the context of Christian practices of social action. As the practice stands now, such theological reflection is rare. Stated more directly, the thesis of this project is: *since explicit theological reflection is a central component in Christian social witness practice, the strengthening of that component can equip practitioners to flourish in the face of fatigue, disappointment, and even perceived irrelevance. When the standards of excellence by which practitioners measure the benefit of social witness practice are informed by intentional theological reflection, characterized by a consciousness of sin and hope, participants can enter more deeply into the practice.*

Above, readers will notice a shift in my language, from describing the practice as "social action" to describing it as "social witness." This choice of terminology again points to the theological questions at the root of the project. Insofar as this book is an exercise in Reformed practical theology, one important theological assumption guiding its direction must be laid bare. In pursuing the theological character of social witness, on the whole, and the role of theological reflection within the practice of social witness, in particular, I mean to speak of the ways in which practitioners understand social witness to be practiced within the context of the divine-human relationship. Particularly in the modes of theological reflection that I propose at the end of this book, a Reformed and feminist practical theology of social witness always keeps before us the deeply embedded desire to know the heart of God and seek after it.

To call the practice a "witness" in relation to biblical literature further makes explicit its theological dimension. In New Testament Greek, μαρτυρεω means "to bear witness," particularly with regard to "the truth."[2] Witness relates to "testimony" in the judicial sense, in that those bearing witness testify to that which they have seen. Especially in the gospels, we find repeated commands to the earliest followers of Jesus that they "bear witness" to what they had seen and come to know through their relationship with Jesus. In contemporary American religious dis-

---

2. Bauer, "μαρτυρεω," 492–93.

course, "witness" often is associated with one-on-one evangelism, insofar as believers may personally testify to their experience of faith, bearing witness to their personal encounters with God. We might describe this kind of testimony as "personal witness." But Christian testimony is not only personal: it also has public and political dimensions. When Christians are called to bear witness to God's activity in the world, they are called to testify to a radical alternative vision of human community, based in theological conceptions of hope, justice, and peace. The social theological implications of this alternative vision of human community form the core of what can be described as "social witness." Social witness is practiced in response to, and in light of, the *eudaimonia* intended by God for the world and the new life promised to us in baptism.

Eudaimonia, or human flourishing, is constituted not only by physical health, but also by moral agency, education, religious freedom, and cultural development. *Eudaimonia* can be characterized as the state in which all persons participate fully in all aspects of society: educational, economic, cultural, vocational, political, familial, and spiritual. Finally, *eudaimonia* bears within it an inherently social telos, in that it entails cooperation for the common good.[3] *Eudaimonia* is the well-being of the whole person, in relationship to others and to the earth. John deGruchy has written about human well-being:

> Becoming more human has to do with the development of our capacity to love, to trust, to forgive, and to be angry when it is right to be so, even if these are expressed in ways that are different. Alongside these is the deepening of the capacity to imagine, to experience awe, to sense injustice, to recognize beauty, to distinguish wisdom from knowledge, to discover joy, to laugh, to live responsibly, and to risk vulnerability. Human well-being has to do with the development of such human capacities in each person in ways that are appropriate to that person, ways that enrich life, enable self-worth, health, restore and promote mental

3. In developing this description of *eudaimonia,* I am indebted to Rebecca Todd Peters' discussion of "What Constitutes Human Flourishing?" See Peters, *In Search of the Good Life,* 28–31. It is also important to note that the category of "common good" is contested on the grounds that it frequently is paternalistically defined by the limited perspective of the political elite. I use the category here in its broadest sense, a social context in which mutual flourishing and moral agency is realized. See, for example, Young, "Good Is Knowing When to Stop."

and bodily health, and develop a sense of connectedness to the earth.[4]

DeGruchy's description of becoming more human helps us to imagine an alternative future in which persons can flourish, both personally and corporately, and in which all can contribute to the building of the common good.

Simultaneous to this witness to God's intention for human community is a witness to all that is wrong in the world: the reality of social dynamics of sin and injustice which serve both to cause suffering and to restrain Christian action in the face of such suffering. What is to be done in response to this chasm between hope and sin? Social witness is the prophetic practice that expresses the hope of new life and just community as well as the rejection of sin and evil. Social witness requires vision to see clearly the good and impediments to the good. It also requires voice to articulate what one has seen, just as judicial witness requires an accurate recollection of events as well as a willingness to articulate clearly those recollections. Christians stand in two realities: the world as it is and the alternative world God intends. In relation to this context, we might define social witness as *the prophetic practice in which persons or communities explicitly and intentionally confront social and political systems that inhibit* eudaimonia, *with a stated goal of changing these systems, in the interest of forming a more just and empowering context for human living.*[5]

This definition is descriptive, in that it helps us to name social witness when we see it. As I have defined it, social witness bears an explicitly theological, collective, structural, and political character. In this project, social witness practice is distinguished from acts of charity in its *intentionality* in confronting the political and economic *structures* that issue in the suffering addressed in service ministries. Clearly, the distinction should not be made too sharply, as there is much overlap and a symbiotic relationship between practices like serving the homeless and confronting the systems that perpetuate homelessness. While this distinction is somewhat artificial, it does serve to specify exactly what kind of practice

---

4. de Gruchy, *Confessions of a Christian Humanist*, 50–51.

5. I elaborate on the "prophetic" character of social witness below. See Brueggemann, *Prophetic Imagination*.

we are talking about: explicit and intentional confrontations of harmful social and economic structures.[6]

We find examples of social witness being practiced in a number of communities, with varying degrees of vitality. Such witness is sometimes practiced with theological intentionality and commitment and is sustained over a long period of time. In some other cases, the practice is more fragile and less sustainable. In order to understand how social witness "works," and what might enable it to flourish, the argument that follows is inherently interdisciplinary in character and method, consulting a range of theoretical, theological, and empirical sources. The study of any Christian practice, when done thoroughly, involves consulting a wide range of sociological and philosophical theories, theologies, and lived experience. Within contemporary practical theological discourse, this kind of interdisciplinary research is increasingly common, evidence of a growing recognition that philosophical, sociological, ethical, and ethnographic insights contribute to more complex and vibrant understandings of Christian practices. This complexity stands in marked contrast to more simplistic methods of studying practices, as if they are merely applications of theological commitments.

I am making a methodological claim, then, that deep understanding of social witness practice requires ethnographic research, consulting with real people engaged in the practice. In service of this commitment, I engaged in ethnographic study of practitioners of social witness. Data gathered via ethnographic research is reported throughout this project, illustrating and challenging theoretical and theological categories. Over the course of a year, I studied two presbytery groups engaged in social witness practice within the Presbyterian Church (U.S.A.). I conducted participant observation and interviews (supplemented by documentary analysis) with participants in monthly denominational briefing and lobbying events in Washington, DC, as well as at the Greater Atlanta Presbytery's annual "Rally Day" at the Georgia State Capitol.[7]

6. Although I have stated that the distinction between charity and social justice ought not be drawn too sharply, it is also important to note the significant body of work, particularly evident in liberation theology, which criticizes an imbalanced emphasis on acts of charity as *perpetuating* injustice. Clodovis and Leonardo Boff write, "aid remains a strategy for helping the poor, but treating them as (collective) objects of charity, not as subjects of their own liberation." Boff and Boff, *Introducing Liberation Theology*, 4. See also Harper, *Urban Churches, Vital Signs*; McKnight, "Why 'Servanthood' Is Bad."

7. For a detailed description of the ethnographic research, please see the Appendix.

In the following pages, I place theories of practice and social movements, theology, and lived practice in a mutually critical conversation. By mutually critical conversation, I mean to say that the actual practice of social witness can be illumined by theory and theology, but also that the experience of participants in the practice may correct and amend both theory and theology. Similarly, both theory and theology each are nuanced by each other.[8] Rebecca Chopp has written a critique, drawing on liberation theology, of Don Browning's oft-used "revised correlation method" in practical theology, arguing that it still privileges theory over *praxis*, assumes a discernible "essence" at the root of experience and practice, and aims to help agents understand the cosmic truths which shape our existence. I find this critique compelling, because both modes of the revised correlation method, apologetics and confession, do appear to reveal a privileging of theological tradition over other sources of knowledge. Both modes assume that the desired outcome is to either express or defend already settled theological truths. In contrast, Chopp writes that liberation theology suggests a "critical *praxis* correlation" method that begins in *praxis* (the practices of agents and institutions) so that experience, and its interpretation via social analysis, is as central to practical theological reflection as are foundational or systematic theological constructs. In other words, experience and social theory are in true "mutually critical" relationship to the theological tradition.

I believe that Chopp's use of liberation theological method, as a corrective to the "revised correlation method," is a helpful lens through which to view a practical theology of social witness practice. It has a transformative trajectory, such that new understandings and, indeed, new realities are created by challenging the sometimes hierarchical, traditionalist methods of other forms of practical theology. I draw significantly on this methodological development in constructing my argument in this book, allowing practice and social theory to critique, and even transform, the theological tradition. I treat tradition as a living, evolving thing, constituted in part by sustained and meaningful arguments among those who value it as part of their own identity.[9] I fully

8. I am indebted to Rebecca Chopp for her reflections on mutually critical method. See Chopp, "Practical Theology and Liberation."

9. This definition of tradition, being constituted by sustained arguments about meaning and goods, is developed in conversation with Alasdair MacIntyre. It is not the only way in which MacInytre presents tradition, however, and I will take up MacIntyre's seemingly conflicting understandings of tradition in chapter 2. See MacIntyre, *After Virtue*, 222.

expect that through the use of ethnographic study and social theory, new understandings of Reformed theology will emerge.

At this point, a couple of clarifying remarks are in order. In conversation with Rebecca Chopp's proposals for mutually critical conversation, I understand the broader category of theology to be marked by a certain degree of groundedness. Theology, in its fullest sense, requires more than clarity and depth of (abstract) thought about God. Theological knowing is always contextual, and requires an analysis of God's presence *in history*. In seeking understanding about the nature and work of God, the fullest expressions of theology take into account how God relates to historical contingencies. Furthermore, theology is relational in that it does not rest on speculation about an abstract and distant God, but in a God whom we know to be in loving relationship with humanity and the wider creation. While theology broadly must be both concrete and relational, practical theology incorporates these realities in its method in a more formal way. Practical theology cannot be properly pursued apart from analysis of *praxis* and without the purpose of improving *praxis*. In its best sense, practical theology is a mutually critical conversation between *praxis* and theology.

Attending to the distinctiveness and interrelatedness of the components of this mutually critical conversation, I have divided what follows into three parts. The first part defines social witness theoretically, drawing together some distinctive philosophical, social, and theological categories for understanding both practice and identity. The second part places traditional theological resources in conversation with some of the categories introduced by the first part's theoretical definition of social witness. Finally, in the third part, I advocate for renewed attention to explicit theological reflection in social witness and propose a structure for doing so. I begin with two relevant, if loosely tied, families of theory: practice theory and social movement theory.

Part One: Practice Theory and Social Movement Theory

What does it mean to call social witness a "practice?" Practice theory is a broad and complex conversation that seeks to account for how "doing" influences individual and group experience and formation. Theorists interested in practice raise questions like: what knowledge is acquired through participation in practice that cannot be known in another way?

How do we know if a practice is done rightly, or if it has "worked?" How do embodied aspects of practice—how our bodies move, feel, are positioned in relation to one another—influence personal and social experience? How do practices relate to, challenge, and sustain institutions and traditions? Practice theory is better described as a field of conversation than as a discipline or subdiscipline. While the phrase "practice theory" perhaps implies a more cohesive body of work than what exists in reality, it does point us to a shared category of inquiry with relation to human and social activity. When applied to religious practice, practice theory looks for how religious experience is shaped by action as much as by thought.

In chapter 2, I address these questions, primarily engaging Alasdair MacIntyre's definition of social practice. While many scholars have, in recent years, taken up the idea of practice as a field of inquiry, MacIntyre provides a number of categories for analysis that will prove particularly salient for the study of social witness practice. For example, MacIntyre focuses carefully on what he describes as "social practices." A social practice is "any coherent and complex form of socially established cooperative human activity through which goods internal to that form of activity are realized in the course of trying to achieve those standards of excellence which are appropriate to, and partially definitive of, that form of activity, with the result that human powers to achieve excellence, and human conceptions of the ends and goods involved, are systematically extended."[10]

While critically engaging some of the implications of MacIntyre's theory, I use his definition heuristically to develop a complex account of social witness.[11] In particular, MacIntyre's definition of practice introduces the important category of "standards of excellence," a category which raises important questions about how we measure the success of social witness: by what standards of excellence do practitioners plan for, engage in, and evaluate the adequacy of their practice? What standards of excellence are appropriate to Christian social witness, and what goods do practitioners realize in their pursuit of these standards?

---

10. Ibid., 189.

11. In particular, I critically engage MacIntyre's assumptions regarding the privileging of tradition and the coherence of practices therein. Despite critiques like the one I make in chapter 2, a number of scholars, including Jeffrey Stout, acknowledge the heuristic value of MacIntyre's definition. See Stout, *Ethics After Babel*, 266–67.

Further, MacIntyre's *After Virtue* provides his definition of practice with an important larger context, a context that offers an holistic approach to the study of practices of the Christian life. The book is an argument in moral philosophy—virtue ethics, to be more precise—and part of the purpose served by the category of practice, for MacIntyre, is its role in the formation of character and virtue. For a study in Christian practice, MacIntyre's argument helps us to ask, "How does participation in this practice influence faith and identity formation?" This question is important for this project, because faith and identity formation bear much influence on human capacity for engaging in practice "more deeply." At the same time, I also challenge MacIntyre's understanding of the role of tradition in moral formation, particularly his incorporation of concept of coherence as it relates to a "tradition." As a result, MacIntyre's work on social practices provides both important categories and crucial opportunities for critical engagement that are at the heart of this book.

Above, I defined social witness as the prophetic practice in which persons or communities explicitly and intentionally confront social and political systems that inhibit *eudaimonia*, with a stated goal of changing these systems, in the interest of forming a more just and empowering context for human living. That definition helps us to identify what constitutes social witness. To that definition, we can appeal to MacIntyre and others to add categories of analysis that show how social witness is a prophetic *practice*. Borrowing from and expanding upon MacIntyre, I propose that social witness is a practice in this way: *Christian social witness practice is a complex and interrelated set of theologically, politically, and structurally-oriented activities, with standards of excellence that vary according to the prioritizing of these orientations, and with the capacity to nourish among participants the internal benefits of identity and faith formation. This set of activities is embedded and given life in the lived social patterns, historical experience, and traditions of a particular religious institution.*

By applying MacIntyre's theory of practice to the particular case of Christian social witness, we can examine not only *what* social witness is, but *how* it operates. The examination of social witness as a practice invites us to consider what constitutes *good* practice, as well as *how* the pursuit of stated political and social goals influences practitioners' identity and faith. MacIntyre's theory of practice offers us several resources to analyze social witness as a practice, accounting for its complexity, its benefits, the standards by which we evaluate it, and its connection with larger institutions.[12]

Practice theory is augmented in this book by the theoretical framework of social movement theory. Social movement theory is one current significant body of literature that accounts for religious social action. Much of the theoretical framing of religious activism is happening in this literature, and social movement theory has raised some important questions for practitioners of social witness. This theoretical school raises questions like: how, why, with what degree of success, and to what end do religious persons and groups participate in movements for social change? Social movement theorists also raise two corollary questions: how does religion influence social movements; and how does participation in social movements in turn influence religion? In chapter 3, I address the questions raised by social movement theory.

In considering social witness under the rubric of social movement theory, I join other scholars, such as Laurel Kearns, Aldon Morris, and Christian Smith, who argue that full analyses of the environmental, civil rights, and peace movements must include some account of religious participation in such movements.[13] Religion interacts with social movements at a variety of points and by a variety of means. For some theorists, the relationship between religion and social movements is largely organizational. Resource Mobilization theorists focus on how religious organizations provide innumerable resources to social movements, including leadership, communication networks, financial support, and ideology. For other, more recent theorists, however, the relationship between religion and a social movement is more complex and mutually influential than this: it has more to do with culture, identity, and discourse than

12. Of course, MacIntyre is not the only scholar who pursues questions about practice. I have noted above my rationale for choosing him as a primary interlocutor for this book, but one would be mistaken to assume that his theory would be universally preferable for any project of this sort. Particularly in practical theology, but also in sociology and anthropology, we find a number of scholars in this field of inquiry. For some practical and systematic theologians, in particular, the study of practice has been at the core of their research interests and methodologies. These scholars include Mary Elizabeth Moore, Dorothy Bass, Paulo Freire, Amy Plantinga Pauw and Serene Jones. See also Ammerman et al., *Studying Congregations*; Dykstra, "Reconceiving Practice"; Graham, *Transforming Practice*.

13. Kearns, "Saving the Creation"; Morris, *Origins of the Civil Rights Movement*; Smith, *Resisting Reagan*.

with an identifiable checklist of resources provided by religious organizations. New Social Movement theoretical literature complements practice theory with questions about the formation and expression of identity in social movements.

One such theorist is James Jasper, author of *The Art of Moral Protest: Culture, Biography, and Creativity in Social Movements.* Jasper asks, among other things, how social movements draw from, orient, and change identities. While Jasper is not concerned with religion in particular, the way in which he accounts for the construction and transformation of identities is of great use to our understanding of social witness practice. I have chosen to enter into deeper conversation with this work as a new lens through which we might view the influence of social practice upon identity formation.

Jasper argues that previous models of social movement theory depend on a tacit assumption that "protest emerges out of clear structural positions," when, in actuality, protest often emerges simply out of a quite ambiguous "shared vision."[14] Given the emergent and unpredictable character of social movements, Jasper warns that the biographies, rituals, and emotions of the participants ought not be ignored in analyzing social movements. In fact, as a movement emerges, the construction and maintenance of a coherent shared identity may be as central to the movement's work as its stated goals. Jasper's theory, accounting for the function of cultural "intangibles" in the study of social action, also asks: how do theological and biographical narratives shape participation in social movements? And how are participants in a social movement influenced and benefited by their engagement? For example, we need a way to account theoretically for the relationship between practice and identity in the case of someone like Thurston, one of the activists I interviewed, who says about his commitment to social justice, "I'm tied to these things. And my impulses, even, are governed by this sort of thing." Questions guiding my research that are derived from theoretical accounts of social movements and identity include: what about participants' biographical narratives predispose them to this particular form of social action? What self-understandings do participants develop *as* they participate in social witness and as a *result* of this participation?

14. Jasper, *Art of Moral Protest*, 89.

Part Two: Theological Orientation in Social Witness

Central to the argument in this book is the assumption that theology, both as a core commitment rooting a practice and as an activity within a practice, must have some primacy of place in the inner workings of social witness practice. That is to say that, within social witness, we might look for theology in at least two forms. First, as a core commitment rooting the practice, theological knowing provides a deep orientation for practitioners of social witness. In particular, the resources of the Reformed tradition (in conversation with process, feminist, and womanist theological traditions) can be brought to bear in inviting deep awareness of both sin and hope as core truths about human experience. Second, as an activity within the practice, theological reflection provides a method by which practitioners of social witness might intentionally examine how theology shapes their action and how their experience of action shapes their theology.[15] In both cases, I will show how, if we begin to think of theological standards of excellence, then the quality of social witness will not be measured solely by political or social efficacy.

In Part Two, I examine how theological content orients the core of social witness practice, strengthening its theological character. Two particular aspects of Christian theology orient knowledge in social witness practice: sin and hope. In *The Prophetic Imagination*, Walter Brueggemann describes the work of prophetic ministry as nurturing an alternative consciousness that both *criticizes* dominant structures (grieving that "things are not right") and *energizes* persons and communities with the promise of new life.[16] If social witness is a *prophetic* practice, as in my definition above, it must account for both of these theological realities and attend to the ways in which these realities tell us something about the relationship between God and human life.

In chapter 4, I develop the Reformed conception of sin as a relational web in which we all are implicated in the same dynamic that we seek to lay bare. John Calvin describes the human condition, in relation to original sin, as "entangled in the curse."[17] He uses this image to describe how we all are implicated in Adam's sin across time. The metaphor of entanglement, beyond Calvin's historical use of it, aptly describes how the

15. This latter claim about the role of theological reflection in social witness is addressed in detail in Part Three.

16. Brueggemann, *Prophetic Imagination*, 1–19.

17. Calvin, *Institutes*, II.I.8.

general *condition* of sin binds and shapes human life in such a way that we can hardly escape it. The Reformed trajectory contains other images that name the same phenomenon. Friedrich Schleiermacher describes the human condition of sin as alienation, going on to say that this situation conditions the totality that surrounds humanity. We are swimming in a sea of alienation, so to speak.[18] We also find Schleiermachian strands in the work of Marjorie Suchocki, who writes that interrelationality, a definitive feature of collective human life, implicates us all in a web of violence.[19]

These three figures give us a description of sin as a sticky web binding or entangling us all. Sin might be located more precisely in those dimensions of this web that result in harm to creation. Such an account of sin is an important piece of the theological orientation of social witness practice. It points to the complexity of sin in the social sphere: we should not be surprised to find a tangled mess there, and finding the right thread to pull surely proves difficult. Further, awareness of sin means that we are not fooled into believing that, while sin pervades everything "out there," things are fine "in here." By being in touch with the reality of sin, we are empowered to see rightly both the complexity of systemic sin and our complicity in it.

An honest account of the impact of sin is essential to understanding the limitations and challenges of social witness practice, created by our own sin and by systemic sin. Such an account helps us prepare for our "failures" in social action. We see the situation clearly. But what prevents us from despairing, from quitting altogether, given these realities? Awareness of sin alone will not nurture Brueggemann's alternative consciousness. It nurtures consciousness, surely, but without a hope rooted in God's coming kingdom, there is nothing "alternative" about it. The paradox of social witness, and of human vocation more generally, is that we must live and act in light of two seemingly contradictory realities that are equally true. Yes, sin has bound and entangled us. And yes, the flourishing of new life is present as God promises. We live and act in the

---

18. Schleiermacher writes this in the context of his discussion of the doctrine of original sin, which he finds inadequate in its reliance on the act of the "first pair." He does, however, acknowledge its contribution in describing the dynamics of sin which both make us *like* other human beings (sin is *in* us) and condition social realities (sin is *around* us). See Schleiermacher, *Christian Faith*, §70–71.

19. Suchocki, *Fall to Violence*, 104.

face of systemic sin and evil, "with an urgency born of this hope."[20] In chapter 5, I present the second half of the prophetic equation in relation to social witness: Christian hope.

The reason we know that structures of sin are wrong is because they stand in stark contrast to what is right and good, that which gives shape to Christian hope. Chapter 5 explores Jürgen Moltmann's concept of Christian eschatology as hope for an alternative future in the face of oppression and suffering.[21] Augmenting Moltmann's core concepts are the resources of the Reformed tradition and feminist, womanist, and process theology, marshaled to more deeply examine the object, foundation, and function of Christian hope in social witness practice. I present hope's object as defined by two core images—*basileia tou theou*[22] (frequently translated as "kingdom of God") and *eudaimonia*; and hope's foundation as rooted in the memory of God's relational faithfulness in history. The chapter concludes with some proposals for the cultivating the disposition of hope in social witness practice.

Part Three: Constructive Contributions to the Practice and Study of Reformed Social Witness

Above, I revealed my normative commitment that *active* theological reflection should be central to the inner workings of social witness practice. When practitioners of social witness do it well, they actually are *doing* theology explicitly in intentional theological reflection woven together with all of the other elements of social witness practice.[23] In Part Three, I integrate all of the resources described in this project thus far—ethnographic accounts of the practice, theoretical insights on its flourishing and identity-shaping power, and theological resources

20. In addition to the sources named here, I also incorporate the theology of Reformed creeds and confessions in Part Three. See Presbyterian Church (U.S.A.), "Brief Statement of Faith"; Presbyterian Church (U.S.A.), "Confession of 1967."

21. Moltmann, *Theology of Hope*.

22. Schüssler Fiorenza, "To Follow the Vision"; Marshall, *Though the Fig Tree Does Not Blossom*.

23. My Reformed understanding of the broad category theological reflection is that it includes a contextual seeking after God's leading. This seeking often is described as theological discernment. While the categories of reflection and discernment are not interchangeable (one might engage in theological reflection about the character of sin, for example, without a teleological purpose in seeking God's leading), *Reformed* theological reflection will always and eventually lean toward seeking God's heart.

of the Reformed tradition (in conversation with process, feminist, and womanist traditions)—to develop a constructive normative argument for the role of theological reflection in social witness practice. I argue that regular and intentional engagement in theological reflection upon *and within* social witness practice is key to its flourishing as an integral practice of the *Christian life*. I also develop concrete resources for pastors and lay leaders who seek to nurture the theological dimensions of social witness within their communities. In some of my interviews, I found that practitioners of social witness sometimes express appreciation for the opportunity to reflect on their practice, even to the point of saying, as one person did, "I feel we should thank you for letting us think about these things and express ourselves."

In the final chapter, I paint a picture of this purpose, structure, and function of theological reflection in the practice of social witness. This chapter is in large part informed by Kathryn Tanner's analysis of the role of theological reflection in Christian practice. Tanner suggests that theological reflection is "forced by the vagaries of Christian practices themselves, and is, consequentially, a necessary part of their ordinary functioning."[24] She challenges the common (mistaken) assumption made by academic theology in relation to practice, that "Christians do this or that because, as Christians, they believe this or that."[25] Theological reflection ought not to be construed as a way to understand the prescribed rules of a practice, since a practice is partly constituted by its ambiguities, inconsistencies, and open-endedness. Theological reflection does not eliminate these features from a practice, but is a critically reflective mode in which Christians deal with the problems generated by these features and enter into deeper engagement in the practice. Because the context and sometimes-complicated logistics of social witness practice are often prone to inviting such ambiguity and open-endedness, Tanner's proposals for theological reflection are particularly appropriate for our purposes.

Tanner's description of theological reflection as it relates to practice is a helpful corrective to MacIntyre's assumptions about the hierarchical role of institutions and traditions in the formation of social practices. She understands theological reflection to be a natural consequence of

24. Tanner, "Theological Reflection," 228.
25. Ibid.

practice, a consequence that affords practitioners an opportunity to reflect explicitly on the why, how, and "what next" of any given practice.

Theological reflection in social witness practice takes as its object the practitioner and all of the dynamics of practice, alongside the context in which they are situated. This means that social witness demands a degree of theological reflection upon oneself as a practitioner and upon all aspects of the practice from which theological knowing arises. Theological reflection in social witness is not "finished" with a preliminary theo-social analysis of the context. It has to take the practice and the practitioner into account, too. Is the constructive dimension of this book meant to issue in a corrected theological doctrine? Not primarily, though the kind of theological insight generated within religious practice ought to have some bearing on doctrinal formulations. Instead, I am looking for ways to invigorate the *act* of theological reflection within the practice. What happens to the larger practice of social witness when we incorporate within it new modes of theological reflection, which continually inform and infuse the practice with sapiential, divine knowledge?

Given these commitments, I conclude this book with a constructive proposal for theological reflection in social witness practice, including a definition of theological reflection, an analysis of how it is or could be incorporated into social witness, and a recounting of what needs it might address within the practice. In the end, my greatest hope is that this work will serve as a resource for those who seek deeper engagement in the practice of social witness, the kind of deeper engagement envisioned in the Presbyterian Church (U.S.A.)'s *Confession of 1967*: "God's redeeming work in Jesus Christ embraces the whole of man's life: social and cultural, economic and political, scientific and technological, individual and corporate. . . With an urgency born of (eschatological) hope the church applies itself to present tasks and strives for a better world. It does not identify limited progress with the kingdom of God on earth, nor does it despair in the face of disappointment and defeat. In steadfast hope the church looks beyond all partial achievement to the final triumph of God."[26]

---

26. Presbyterian Church (U.S.A.), "Confession of 1967," 9.55.

PART ONE

Theoretical Approaches to the Study of Social Witness Practice

2

Seeking Excellence

Social Witness as a Religious Practice

ONCE, WHEN I WAS RECOUNTING OVER DINNER WITH FRIENDS MY RE-
cent experience of participating in a political protest, I was confronted
with one of those questions that forced me to ask, "Wait, what do I *really*
think?" I had been describing a large protest organized around then-
president George Bush's 2004 visit to the crypt of Dr. Martin Luther King,
Jr. Church leaders and anti-war activists in Atlanta embraced this visit as
an opportunity to organize a protest to confront the administration with
the perceived gap between King's social policy perspectives and those of
the administration. In an op-ed piece reflecting on the protest, organizer
and pastor of Atlanta's First Iconium Baptist Church Tim McDonald
wrote, "King's philosophies could not be more different from Bush's.
King, a man of peace, was one of the first to publicly oppose the Vietnam
War. Bush, by contrast, has unilaterally and preemptively declared war
upon another country, causing hundreds of American soldiers to lose
their lives and costing the American taxpayer hundreds of billions of
dollars. You have to ask how that is consistent with the life and teachings
of King."[1]

More than one thousand people showed up for the protest, lining
the streets near the King Center with signs that expressed a wide range
of sentiments, from "Send Bush to Mars," to "America, You Must Be
Born Again." I, along with many members of my congregation, dutifully
joined the crowd with our own signs. My friend Beth and I took our
places on one street corner, and, unexpectedly, the presidential motorcade drove right past us on its way from the King Center to a fundraiser
in Atlanta. I saw George W. Bush in his car, but he did not see me. On

---

1. McDonald, "He Came Not to Praise King But. . . ."

that day, he would not see many of us because city buses were called in to block from the president's view the protestors across the street from King's crypt. He actually *could* have seen me as the motorcade passed. Instead, he turned away from the window and shielded the side of his face with his hand. If the person I wanted to challenge would not look at me, what was the point of my protest? Why was I standing there, in the cold, holding my sign, if I was being ignored? What is the point if my actions are not effective?

As if he heard my own, inner reservations, my friend Chad asked me, "How do you respond to people who dismiss protestors as extremists? Doesn't that render protest ineffective?" One might think that such a question would haunt an activist. After all, who wants to be ineffective? Instead, the question sparked for me a lengthy internal dialogue, into which I now invite you. At the time, I responded with some rambling reflections about being most interested in why protestors do what they do, how they themselves understand what they are doing, and how participation in protests particularly influences how Christian activists understand and practice their faith. In other words, while measurable effects on "powers and principalities" are most certainly central to understanding the phenomenon of protest, its effects on the protestors themselves are also important. A full understanding of the meaning and practice of protest, and of social witness in general, must account for more than its measurable results upon systems. It also must account for the complex effects of protest upon the practitioners and their social contexts as well as the admittedly open-ended character of what practitioners do and what they say *as they engage in the practice.*

To complicate matters further, I did not simply want to set aside the measurable political effects and the character of protest; I also wanted to move beyond the religious motivations of protestors. While motivations and results of social witness are key to understanding it, the complex actions and dynamics within the actual *doing* of social witness were what really grabbed my attention. Later, I would learn that these are the sorts of questions that drive the study of religious practices.

Religious practice is a burgeoning area of inquiry in the contemporary study of religion. Informed by insights from the fields of anthropology, sociology, and philosophy, the study of religious practice is rooted in the principle that religion must be studied in its lived form as practitioners engage in prayers and peacemaking, adornment and advocacy.

The study of these lived forms of religion is an important partner to the more established traditional study of religious texts. The emergence of the study of religious practice from within the fields of religious studies and practical theology has meant that religious practice has become a field of study unto itself and thus cannot be understood solely as the application of well-studied texts.

In what follows, I enter into this theoretical conversation about religious practice. I define religious practice both broadly and in critical engagement with the work of Alasdair MacIntyre. In the process, I consult other theorists of practice who present corrective alternatives to MacIntyre and develop my own theoretical definition of social witness practice, informed by my engagement with MacIntyre and the implications of the categories thus introduced.

Practice Defined

On the most fundamental level, religious practices are those things that persons *do* in relation to particular religious traditions and institutions. They complement, contrast with, and sometimes challenge those things that persons *believe* in relationship to religious traditions and institutions. To study religion in terms of *practice* invites us to examine how various forms of human activity are constitutive of religion as well as how human experiences of movement, posture, discourse, and sensory encounter shape religious identity and understanding.

Religious practices do not have a simple causal relationship with religious belief. If this were so, practices would only express those things that we already know cognitively prior to our participation in the practice, would they not? If this were the case, once a religious practitioner gains the right understanding, then the appropriate practice would reinforce or express that belief. Kathryn Tanner has summarized this oversimplified misunderstanding of practice in the following way: "Christians do this or that sort of thing because, as Christians, they believe this or that."[2] Of course, practices do, indeed, express and reinforce belief. Expressing and reinforcing, however, are not all they do. Religious practices are activities in which our participation, as Craig Dykstra puts it, extends to us knowledge that is otherwise "outside our ken."[3] They work on us through the embodied experience of them and through the

2. Tanner, "Theological Reflection," 229.
3. Dykstra, "Reconceiving Practice," 45.

meaning and traditions attendant to them. In this way, practices shape belief and knowledge.[4] Sometimes, practices are accompanied by a highly developed and articulated interpretation. In other cases, practices operate without any formal or informal interpretation. Some practices have a high degree of formality and intentionality, while others are quite informal and spontaneous.

Christianity is marked by a number of practices, no listing of which could be considered exhaustive. Practices of hospitality and welcoming include activities like sheltering ministries, evangelism, and home visitation. Meal practices include neighborhood dinners, preparing meals for the sick and the poor, and, in a very intense way, the Eucharist. One also finds practices of contemplation, study, song, and worship. In addition, we find political and economic practices. Christian practices are complex. They are carried out within the context of a dynamic interaction between such influences as personal biographies, social and institutional structures, embodied knowledge, strategic goals, and theological sensibilities. To study a practice adequately, one must consider the narratives and character of the participants, the history of the forms of the practice, the communities and institutions in relation to which the practice occurs, and the theological resources and consequences of the practice.

As noted above, practices are not made up solely by *action*, divorced from thought or belief. They are expressive of and shape belief, and their relationship to belief is more tightly woven by the fact that practices also contain within them elements of memory, liturgy, and theological conceptualization. In fact, Dorothy Bass has addressed this very dynamic, describing a practice as "a dense cluster of *ideas* and activities that are related to a specific social goal and shared by a social group over time."[5] In addition to embodied forms of activity, practices are partially constituted by their attendant meanings, interpretations, and documents.

If we return to the example of the protest at the King Center, we might identify any number of these characteristics of religious practice: embodied experience, memory and narrative, explicit interpretation, social and institutional structures, and connection between belief and

---

4. Clifford Geertz famously theorized that religion as a cultural symbol system functions both as a model *of* a particular (sacred) reality—how things are—and as a model *for* life in the world—how things ought to be. Theoretical descendants of Geertz often refer to this theory in shorthand as religion's "expressing" and "shaping" functions. See Geertz, "Religion as a Cultural System," 93–94.

5. Bass, "Introduction," 2. Emphasis mine.

practice. The president's visit to King's crypt was met with more than words. It was met with physical presence. About one thousand people came to confront him that day, walking in the cold, carrying signs, shouting chants, and joining in song. Alongside this embodied form of social action was a palpable memory, written on signs and shouted in chants, of Dr. King's identity, ministry, and activism. Organizers of the protest had established an explicit interpretation and motivation for the event. In watching the news or reading the newspaper, potential protestors and observers alike were bombarded with sound bites and op-ed pieces from Rev. Timothy McDonald, who framed the protest in social and religious terms. One could not have participated in the event without a keen awareness of the social and institutional structures and power involved, because we saw snipers atop buildings and city buses used to separate the protestors from the president's party. Finally, the actions of many of the protestors reflected a tight connection to religious belief. Many of the signs bore theological quotations from King, many of the leaders who spoke to the crowd were clergy who framed the day's gathering in theological terms, and many of the songs protestors sang were spirituals such as "We Shall Overcome" and "Lift Every Voice and Sing." Similarly, on the following Sunday, the pastor of a local congregation offered a theological interpretation of the protest within his sermon. We can discern, even from this rough sketch, that this protest and other forms of social witness are comprised of many of the elements of religious practice. To examine how these parts work together, we turn now to practice theory to ask how social witness *functions* as a practice.

How Is This a Practice?

In recent years, we have seen an increased interest in scholarly examination of the relationship between religion and political and social action. Much of the study of religious activism in social and political arenas has been conducted by scholars under the rubric of social movement theory, a conversation considered in more depth in chapter 2. Some of these scholars are also invested in the field of sociology of religion. Other studies of social and political activism have been conducted by ethicists, some of whom use ethnographic and other sociological methods. In this project, however, I offer an analysis of social and political activism as a *religious practice*. In so doing, I am making two parallel claims. First, I argue that social witness is, in fact, a religious practice and not only an outcome of other religious practices. Second, I argue that the study of social witness as a religious practice brings beliefs and "religious tradition" into a different kind of relationship to social witness. In other words, in relation to social witness, religious belief is not limited to motivation and resource for social action, but is brought into a dynamic relationship with action, so that action and belief are in creative tension, each informing the other. Considered from this perspective, a study of social witness bears implications for our understandings of faith formation and the role of active theological reflection within the practice. Thus construed, social witness is more than a fruit of the Christian life. It is a practice that, alongside others, *constitutes* the Christian life.

In the introduction, I defined social witness as *the prophetic practice in which persons or communities explicitly and intentionally confront social and political systems that inhibit* eudaimonia, *with a stated goal of changing these systems, in the interest of forming a more just and empowering context for human living.* If we take a step back and look for a broader, more foundational definition of Christian practice, we find how social witness fits into such a category. Dorothy Bass and Craig Dykstra, for example, describe Christian practices as those "things Christian people do together over time to address fundamental human needs in response to and in the light of God's active presence for the life of the world."[6] According to their definition, social witness, perhaps even a little more than any other Christian activity, falls squarely into the category of practice. With its dual prophetic vision, social witness encompasses those corporate activities that attend (on a systemic, structural level) to both fundamental human needs and God's active presence in and vision for the world. Bass and Dykstra help us to identify a practice when we see one. To develop this definition, they draw on the definition of practice from another important scholar in the study of practices, Alasdair MacIntyre. Before applying the work of theorists to the practice of social witness in particular, a preliminary examination of MacIntyre's theory of practice is in order.

---

6. Bass and Dykstra, "Theological Understanding," 18.

Alasdair MacIntyre's Philosophical and Moral Interpretation of Practice

Given that practice, as a field of inquiry, can slip into conceptual nebulosity, a clear theoretical definition serves as a heuristic device, providing us with categories for analysis and further questioning. In a case as complicated as social witness practice, the clarity of these categories assumes even more importance. Alasdair MacIntyre has developed just this sort of theoretical definition, a definition upon which practical theologians, ethicists, and even, as we shall see in the next chapter, social movement theorists, rely. In addition to the long shadow that he casts in the practices discussion, MacIntyre's work is of particular interest in this project because it centers around the concepts of ethics, moral discourse, and the development of virtue in individuals and societies.

In *After Virtue*, MacIntyre laments the decline of moral discourse in society, and lays the blame for this decline on the doorstep of what he describes as liberal individualism. In a context shaped by liberal individualism, MacIntyre argues, traditions, institutions, and social relationships no longer bear significant moral weight, and the result is an infinite degree of pluralism in which the individual perspective is irreducible. Social morality flourishes, in contrast, when a society's members are in formative relationship with a moral tradition in which *virtues* are instilled in the hearts and minds of its members. A particular tradition's concept of virtues becomes concrete in its institutions. The primary vehicle by which these virtues are taught and acquired is the "social practice," which MacIntyre defines as "any coherent and complex form of socially established cooperative human activity through which goods internal to that form of activity are realized in the course of trying to achieve those standards of excellence which are appropriate to, and partially definitive of, that form of activity, with the result that human powers to achieve excellence, and human conceptions of the ends and goods involved, are systematically extended."[7]

While MacIntyre is interested in the function of practices in the formation of social morality, the definition is also heuristically important for the close study of religious practices. The definition moves beyond what a practice is meant to do, what purpose it should serve, and what it looks like. It reveals how the practice's internal logic operates. It invites

---

7. MacIntyre, *After Virtue*, 187.

us to enter inside the practice, seeing what is gained by participating in it, by what standards it is evaluated, and what kinds of human knowledge and potential are generated within it. Below, I discuss some of the problematic implications that emerge from MacIntyre's concept of practice. First, however, we should acknowledge some of the important contributions made by MacIntyre's theory, particularly as they relate to social witness: the concepts that practices are generative of internal goods, socially established, and evaluated according to appropriate standards of excellence. Initially, examples of meal practices will serve to illustrate these categories. More detailed illustrations involving social witness practice appear below in my theoretical definition of this practice, which is a critical application of MacIntyre.

Practices Generate Internal Goods

In MacIntyre's model, practices are not only expressive of a particular worldview or belief, but they also *do* something in and among the practitioners. One thing that practices do is produce goods for practitioners that cannot be realized in any other way—they are *internal* to the practice. Participants benefit from the practices in which they take part, and these benefits are not limited to the achievement of stated goals, nor can they fully be understood by outside observers. In other words, practitioners get something unique out of the experience itself. Internal goods stand in contrast to external goods, those things that may be acquired by alternative means. In *After Virtue* MacIntyre uses the game of chess as an illustration of how internal goods work: "There are goods internal to the practice of chess which cannot be had in any way but by playing chess . . . We call them internal for two reasons: first, as I have already suggested, because we can only specify them in terms of chess . . . and by means of examples from such games . . . ; and secondly because they can only be identified and recognized by the experience of participating in the practice in question. Those who lack the relevant experience are incompetent thereby as judges of internal goods."[8]

In the case of chess, the player of the game might gain external goods, such as a monetary prize or personal prestige, but these goods can be gained by other means and are not necessary to the function of the practice itself. One may practice chess very well without attaining an

---

8. Ibid., 188–89.

external good like a monetary prize. The goods *internal* to the playing of chess are constitutive of the practice itself: the pleasure of devising game strategy, the rush of recognizing a path to checkmate, or a game well played, win or lose. If we apply the concept to a common congregational practice among Protestants in the United States, family night suppers, we can see the phenomena of external and internal goods there, too. From the outside, we see that the participants receive a meal. They eat and are nourished, but they might also achieve these goods in their own kitchens, at the drive-through window, or at a fine restaurant. These are external goods. At a family night supper, participants realize other goods, such as building relationships within the religious community and the experience of corporate servanthood as they together prepare, serve, and put away the meal. Without these sorts of internal goods, the family night supper might not qualify as a good religious meal practice.

Internal goods also work on a more pervasive level for MacIntyre. In relation to the *virtues*, internal goods show us the value of practices for human life. Practices work on us over the long term. They turn us into a different kind of people. Subsequently, the virtues developed in practice better equip us for participation in the practice and, as such, can be understood as integral to faith formation. To illustrate this formative dimension of practice, Craig Dykstra draws on another of MacIntyre's metaphors, that of the painter. Dykstra writes that an internal good gained via portrait-painting "is 'what the artist discovers within the pursuit of excellence in portrait-painting,' namely, 'the good of a certain kind of life.' That is, things of value arise through engagement in the practice itself. Some of these things are products emerging from the practice; others are the *effects of the practices on the practicing persons and their communities—including the effects on their minds, imaginations and spirits.*"[9]

Dykstra and MacIntyre help us broaden our understanding of the success of a practice. Insofar as practices help us discover the good in a way of life, they bear formative or moral power. We are changed, from the inside out, when we participate in a practice. Particularly with reference to the virtues, practices facilitate the acquisition and development of those human qualities that enable us to achieve the good.[10] In some of Dykstra's other work, one easily recognizes the influence of MacIntyre's

9. Dykstra, "Reconceiving Practice," 45. Emphasis mine.

10. MacIntyre, *After Virtue*, 191.

concept of practices on theories of religious formation.[11] Dykstra goes beyond MacIntyre's connection between internal goods and virtues to argue that practices also generate epistemological goods. Not only do practices, and participation in them, bear moral weight, but they also bring us to an "awareness of certain *realities* that outside of these practices are beyond our ken."[12] And, even more than changing our awareness, the epistemological power of practices actually may *create* new realities, new knowledge: "In the situation of faith, these new realities include a new way of life, a new form of existence, which in turn presupposes a transcendent source and ground."[13]

Practices Are Socially Established

MacIntyre's dedication to social institutions is evident in his definition of practice. For him, the communal significance of practice cannot be underestimated. His subsequent critics and interpreters consistently point out this particular element of his definition of practices. Jeffrey Stout, for example, writes that, for MacIntyre, a recovery of moral discourse "cannot succeed . . . without being embodied in the habits, dispositions, shared assumptions, and goals of a living community dedicated to the common good."[14] To participate in a MacIntyrian practice, one must accept that "its goods can only be achieved by subordinating ourselves within a practice in our relationship to other practitioners."[15] We join with a community in pursuit of shared goals, a commonly held conception of what constitutes a "good life."

Subordinating one's own ideas of what constitutes a good practice to those of the relevant community is not always easy. One local church community prepares monthly meals for a local cooperative homeless sheltering ministry. Each month, recipes are announced for members of the congregation to prepare for the meal. Once, the recipe was for an apple salad. One newer member of that congregation had reservations about apple salad for homeless men and women. In her past experience of working with homeless people, she had learned that a very large per-

---

11. See Dykstra, *Growing In The Life Of Faith*.

12. Dykstra, "Reconceiving Practice," 45.

13. Ibid., 46.

14. Stout, *Ethics After Babel*, 211.

15. MacIntyre, *After Virtue*, 191.

centage of homeless persons struggle with dental problems, and many have missing teeth. Her rule of practice had been to avoid all crunchy fruits and vegetables. In this case, however, as she joined in the social practice of this new congregation, she subordinated, for the time being, her own ideas of "good practice" to those of the congregation. She made the apple salad.

Issues of subordination to tradition and institutions are taken up in a critical response to MacIntyre below, but here it is important to note the multiple levels upon which social relationships and customs are operative in MacIntyre's practice. When we enter into a social practice, we do not enter into relationship with contemporary practitioners only. For MacIntyre, there is a strong historical component to practices. In their broad definition of Christian practice quoted above, Bass and Dykstra name as practices "those things that Christian people do together *over time*."[16] Practices are established over time, through the passing on of traditions and in the context of communities of accountability. MacIntyre writes, "To enter into a practice is to enter into a relationship not only with its contemporary practitioners, but also with those who have preceded us in the practice, particularly those whose achievements extended the reach of the practice to its present point. It is thus the achievement, and *a fortiori* the authority, of a tradition which I then confront and from which I have to learn."[17]

In other words, a practice and its practitioners can never be understood apart from their characteristic embeddedness in a tradition. The wisdom that enlivens a practice is acquired and developed through history. To enter into a practice means, *at least*, to acknowledge the weight of the tradition, and to take it seriously. Tradition, however, is not static. When it is progressing, in good order, there is always a cumulative element to it.[18] Confronting and learning from a tradition does not mean, according to MacIntyre, that one must always be in agreement with it, but that one must always acknowledge its authority before contesting it. MacIntyre expects that living traditions are shaped in part by arguments: "A living tradition then is a historically extended, socially embodied argument, an argument precisely in part about the goods which

16. Bass and Dykstra, "Theological Understanding," 18. Emphasis mine.
17. MacIntyre, *After Virtue*, 194.
18. Ibid., 146.

constitute that tradition."[19] Just the same, traditions, as they carry forth a "not-yet-completed narrative, confront a future whose determinate and determinable character, so far as it possesses any, derives from the past."[20] It is this confusing presentation of the authority of tradition that critics most often engage and is taken up in more detail below.

Practices are a means for imparting a tradition to members of the community and for inducting members into the community. By accepting the authority and achievements of the tradition, practitioners join in creating a shared identity. The social character of a practice is not limited, though, to the historical narrative and shared assumptions that serve as its context. MacIntyre also argues that internal goods are socially embedded: they are not only salutary for individuals participating in the practice, but also for the realization of the *telos*, which MacIntyre equates with the common good. External goods, such as observable expertise in performance and tangible products, are primarily identified with, even possessed by, the individual practitioners. In contrast, MacIntyre writes that the achievement of internal goods enriches the "whole relevant community."[21] Social movement theorist James Jasper, drawing on MacIntyre, writes that participation in practice surely is meant to offer the individual practitioner a "life worth living." To the criteria of individual lives worth living, he further adds that, "for a practice to be good, we must examine its effects on the entire society of which it is part."[22] In his study of protestors, Jasper offers some examples of how this might be true: "Some protestors encourage others to acquire the same virtues that the protestors enjoy: moral voice, participation, a probing of one's deepest sensibilities. They contribute to information flows, self-understanding and communication."[23]

We might identify one more way in which practices are socially established. In addition to being given shape by a living tradition over time and bearing internal goods for the entire community, practices are social in their performance. What I mean by this is that practices are corporate and collective forms of human activity, forms that, even when engaged

19. Ibid., 222.

20. Ibid., 223.

21. Ibid., 191.

22. Jasper, *Art of Moral Protest*, 342.

23. Ibid.

individually, are still understood as something we do together.[24] For example, even when a homebound member of a congregation receives communion in his home, he does not do it alone. Not only is an elder, minister or priest present with him, but the entire practicing community is symbolically present. Sometimes, this connection to the community is made quite explicit. The Book of Order for the Presbyterian Church (U.S.A.), for example, stipulates that homebound members of the congregation may receive the Lord's Supper, "*provided . . .* the elements are served following worship on the same calendar day, as a *direct extension of the gathered congregation*."[25]

Sometimes, of course, the practice in question is a group activity, yet the practitioners remain individuals. Participants individually enter into the practice with varying degrees of intentionality, regularity, intensity, and familiarity. They may even carry into the practice contradictory meanings that, for them, are attached to the practice! The minister or lay leader who plans a silent retreat, for example, may have very different expectations and interpretations for the event than a first-time participant. This particular aspect of the social character of practices makes them both fascinating and complex objects of analysis.

Practices Have Intrinsic Standards of Excellence

How do we know when a practice is done well, or poorly? What makes for a good practice? Conversely, what makes for malpractice? In his definition cited above, MacIntyre introduces a category that addresses these questions. He writes that "goods internal to that form of activity are realized in the course of trying to achieve those standards of excellence which are appropriate to, and partially definitive of, that form of activity."[26] "Standards of excellence" bear at least three remarkable characteristics: they are intrinsically derived, they are authoritative, and they are interwoven with the categories of virtue and internal goods.

To say that standards are intrinsically derived is to again point to the internal logic of a practice. An outside observer of the practice cannot evaluate its excellence by objective standards. In order to measure the

24. Dykstra, "Reconceiving Practice," 42–43.

25. Presbyterian Church (U.S.A.), "Directory for Worship," W–3.3616. Emphases mine.

26. MacIntyre, *After Virtue*, 187.

excellence of a practice, we must examine it from the inside. Borrowing MacIntyre's chess example, I might observe an experienced chess player and, not understanding the game, assume that she does not demonstrate excellence because she has fewer pieces on the board. In contrast, a standard of excellence appropriate to the game of chess would measure, among other things, her internal logic, demonstrated through her out-working of a strategy. In other words, external observers of a practice are not always equipped to judge its excellence.

Standards of excellence are appropriate to a particular form of activity and cannot be borrowed from customs, expectations, or values outside of the practice. To illustrate the concept of standards of excel-lence, let us pause here to consider a very common and familiar form of Christian practice: the shared meal. The congregation in which I grew up regularly gathered for potluck suppers. Some families became known for bringing the same items each month. For example, one family regularly brought a dish full of cheese puffs, the kind that come in a plastic bag (of course, this delighted me, as a child, to no end). Another family took great care in preparing perfect triangles of pimento cheese sandwiches. Now, if there were no intrinsic standard of excellence for evaluating good practice in the potluck suppers, by what standards would we measure contributions like cheese puffs and pimento cheese? By taste? Gourmet appeal? Cost of preparation? By all of those external standards, one might be reluctant to count cheese puffs or pimento cheese sandwiches among the excellent instantiations of the meal practice. The congrega-tion, however, did not measure them by such external standards. The families in question exhibited excellence in the practice by their faithful participation, by the intentionality of so carefully removing the crusts from the sandwiches, and by the love shown by the one who displayed her cheese puffs in her loveliest bowl. These different, intrinsic standards of excellence meant that their contributions to the shared meal were good and valued. With the building and sustaining of relationships as a valued good internal to the practice of fellowship meals, we applied a different standard of excellence to the contributions of both of these families than we might a meal served in a five-star bistro.

What sources might generate appropriate standards of excellence? We might find a number of standards of excellence operating within meal practices. The quality and quantity of food might be entirely ap-propriate standards of excellence for a catered stewardship celebration.

These standards may not be appropriate, however, for measuring the excellence of Eucharistic practice. Nor would these standards *alone* be sufficient to measure the excellence of the stewardship dinner. Because these are Christian meal practices, there are other standards of excellence in operation. As a practice of a faith community, it may be measured according to the level of intimacy and mutual support experienced among the participants. As a theological practice, it may be measured according to the theological or spiritual character of the gathering time, exhibited by distinctive forms of interaction, language, postures, or gestures. As a practice of the body of Christ, it may be measured according to its relative use of church resources and according to corresponding benevolence spending. In any given practice, standards of excellence may be derived theologically, ethically, socially, politically, economically, aesthetically, or psychologically. Each of these standards may be differently weighted or even absent, as the excellence of each practice demands unique standards.

We do not develop these standards of excellence on a whim. They, too, emerge over time, and in part make up the tradition described above. When we accept the requirement that we subordinate ourselves to the relationships constituted in practice, we accept the standards established through those relationships over time. MacIntyre writes, "A practice involves standards of excellence and obedience to rules as well as the achievement of goods. To enter into a practice is to accept the authority of those standards and the inadequacy of my own performance as judged by them. It is to subject my own attitudes, choices, preferences and tastes to the standards which currently and partially define the practice. . . . The standards are not themselves immune from criticism, but nonetheless we cannot be initiated into a practice without accepting the authority of the best standards realized so far."[27]

In this way, one subordinates the self in a practice not only to relationships to other practitioners, but also to the standards that preceded one's participation in the practice. Again, the standards established through a tradition, like the tradition itself, are not static and set once and for all, but *do* bear an authoritative weight that must be observed and challenged only with great respect and care.

Given the above discussion on standards of excellence, it is possible to imagine how we might judge a practice good or excellent. To all

27. Ibid., 191.

of these measures of excellence, MacIntyre adds the formation of virtue as the highest arbiter of what constitutes excellent practice. Virtues like courage, justice, and honesty are standards of excellence insofar as they equip practitioners to perform well and seek the internal goods of a practice. MacIntyre posits that, in striving toward excellent practice, we realize internal goods: "A virtue is an acquired human quality the possession and exercise of which tends to enable us to achieve those goods which are internal to practices and the lack of which effectively prevents us from achieving any such goods."[28]

Further, these virtues are always meant to be in service of an over-riding good, a *telos* that lends to life a narrative unity.[29] Practice is the arena in which virtues are both exhibited and defined.[30] Insofar as they are "defined" via participation in practice, they are related to the goods internal to the practice. Insofar as they are "exhibited" via participation in practice, they are related to standards of excellence. It is in this sense that we refer to a practitioner who exhibits excellence as a *virtuoso*.

Before we leap too whole-heartedly into MacIntyre's Aristotelian world, however, we are wise to pause and ask, "Do all practices in fact do this?" Might it also be possible to judge a practice to be bad or even harmful? What about historical social practices such as slavery or the Eurocentric cultural supremacy that accompanied the Christianization of peoples in Africa and the Pacific Islands? We might also ask about more current social practices, such as female circumcision or prohibitions against gay marriage. Can practices exclude, alienate, harm, or oppress? MacIntyre allows (with some reservation) that a practice may actually be evil, or, more likely, that a practice may issue in evil.[31] For example, he writes, "I want to allow that there *may* be practices—in the sense in which I understand the concept—which simply *are* evil. I am far from convinced that there are, and I do not in fact believe that either torture or sado-masochistic sexuality answer to the description of a practice which my account of the virtues employs."[32] He is reluctant to agree that practices can *be* evil because practices, when rightly conceived and facilitated, are formative of and formed by a shared understanding

28. Ibid.
29. Ibid., 202.
30. Ibid., 187.
31. Ibid., 200.
32. Ibid.

of the virtues. Tellingly, MacIntyre argues that *his* account of the virtues would preclude practices that issue in violence or oppression—an argument that reveals how difficult the negotiation of virtues and practices might be in our pluralistic context.

Challenges to MacIntyre's Theory

At this point, it is important to acknowledge some of the problematic aspects of MacIntyre's definition of practice. As noted in the introduction, MacIntyre proposes a definition of practice that is heuristically valuable, even with its problems, for developing categories of analysis for the study of religious practices in general and the study of social witness practice in particular. In order to use these categories to build a theoretical definition of social witness as a religious practice however, we must also identify those aspects of MacIntyre's definition that might prove inaccurate or inadequate when presented with the case of social witness practice. The two aspects that are most difficult to reconcile with the lived practice of social witness are the expectation of narrative coherence and the tight connection between practice and the traditions and institutions in which they are embodied.

MacIntyre writes that a social practice is a "complex and coherent form of human activity." While the activities that make up a practice are admittedly complex, they also form a coherent whole, according to MacIntyre. This coherence is framed by a tradition. Part of what gives a practice its coherence is the agreement among participants on the standards, virtues, and internal goods that constitute the practice. These values are informed, in large part, by the narrative of tradition that roots the practice. Even though MacIntyre understands tradition as an embodied argument, that argument is meant, in part, to address inconsistencies in the tradition and between the tradition and current social practices. Practices have meaning and are made intelligible by their embeddedness in the histories of traditions.[33]

Coherence may be an unattainable and undesirable ideal when it comes to corporate practices like social witness. It may be unattainable because at any given moment in any given activity of a practice a myriad of experiences, intentions, and meanings are in operation. The idea of a practice as a coherent "thing" may be an impossibility. Furthermore, we

---

33. Ibid., 222.

might also ask if such coherence is even desirable. Even if it were possible, would we actually want a practice in which each part fits precisely in its place, in which the puzzle is put together and solved?

In case these arguments about the possibility and desirability of coherence are overdrawn, perhaps we might pose one more question to MacIntyre: even if one accepts that coherence is possible or desirable, is that coherence *necessary* to the flourishing of a social practice? Or is it enough to say that the activities and ideas within a practice *relate* to each other and that the practice as a whole *relates* to a larger tradition? Is it possible that the messiness of a practice—its unpredictability, its decidedly unsystematic character—is an integral part of its character?

I believe that this is so. In fact, the demand that practices reflect coherence can be problematic in two ways. First, coherence is not a natural occurrence in the realm of practice. The complex character of a practice tends toward diversity and multivalence. For a practice to be marked by coherence requires a social institutional hierarchy that gives order to the practice; and that participants in the practice subordinate themselves to that prescribed order. Who decides what does and does not fit in the practice? Part of what makes religious practice so important is its democratic character: as noted above, participants enter into a practice with a variety of motivations, intentions, and experiences. This diversity in practice is an important complement to articles like confessions and denominational policy, which are shaped by an assumption that they reflect, to some degree, shared and common commitments.

Second, in addition to a tendency toward hierarchical influence, the demand for coherence invites reluctance toward innovation in practice. An expectation of high degrees of coherence would make it difficult for practitioners of social witness to imagine new ways of practicing, for fear that such innovations might conflict with other, historically established aspects of the practice. As time goes by, the historical narratives of a practice's meaning, purpose, and form become stronger and deeper, and a rigid expectation of coherence can bring a perhaps unintended consequence of deference to the weight of these narratives. Particularly in the context of mainline Protestantism, deference to historical narratives manifests as deference to institutions. In the deeply entrenched practices of religious institutions, innovation is not uncommonly met with raised eyebrows and objections of, "We've not done it *that* way."

This resistance to innovation is also a potential product of MacIntyre's argument that practices are always tightly tied to traditions and institutions. As noted above, to participate in a practice is to accept the authority and value of historical standards of excellence: "It is thus the achievement (of past practice), and *a fortiori* the authority, of a tradition which I then confront and from which I have to learn."[34] MacIntyre finds that practices are inextricably linked to tradition in that we, and the practices in which we participate, are inherently historical: practices have a past and a future. MacIntyre introduces his concept of tradition in the following way: "What I am, therefore, is in key part what I inherit, a specific past that is present to some degree in my present. I find myself part of a history and that is generally to say, whether I like it or not, whether I recognize it or not, one of the bearers of tradition. It was important when I characterized the concept of a practice to notice that practices always have histories and that at any given moment what a practice is depends on a mode of understanding it which has been transmitted often through many generations."[35]

For MacIntyre, the "mode of understanding" a practice is transmitted through tradition, and it is only in the context of a tradition that a practice is intelligible. Recall that MacIntyre's description of practices and tradition occurs within the context of his characterization of the decline of social moral discourse in the face of liberal individualism. The absence of a shared vision, or at least a shared language, of the common good is cause for the decay of moral discourse, MacIntyre argues. Jeffrey Stout troubles this assumption and the associated critique of liberalism and pluralism, citing the value and complexity in diverse languages of morals as well as the vision of a provisional *telos* that values tolerance.[36]

MacIntyre's understanding of tradition is problematic, in part, because it develops in two seemingly contradictory trajectories. As I noted above, MacIntyre presents tradition as both extended argument and unfolding narrative, which might leave us with the impression that the argument's purpose is to advance the unfolding narrative. If the future is wholly derived from the past, do not the arguments about the goods and standards of practices then become vehicles to eliminate inconsistency and contradiction within this unfolding narrative? To put it

34. Ibid., 194.
35. Ibid., 221.
36. Stout, *Ethics After Babel*, 291–92.

simplistically, for MacIntyre, does the argument always require a resolution that moves a coherent narrative forward? Contemporary scholars who are indebted to (and in argument with) MacIntyre disagree on this point.[37] One interesting development of the point is the possibility that MacIntyre actually presents two different concepts of tradition that give rise to a very wide range of theories of practice.

In *Democracy and Tradition,* Stout argues that MacIntyre defines tradition as "a discursive practice considered in the dimension of history."[38] Defined so broadly and fluidly, one can hardly find anything objectionable in the idea of a tradition. Stout notes, however, that this is only one concept of tradition introduced by MacIntyre. The other, more restrictive meaning of tradition veers toward *traditionalism,* in which traditions, over time, provide a unifying narrative into which all practices fit and the trajectory of which all practices serve. It is this more universalizing definition of tradition that informs the narrative theology and ethics of scholars like Stanley Hauerwas.[39]

Scholars like Stout develop MacIntyre's more lively and fluid concept of tradition in a more liberal, inclusive direction. Dorothy Bass has developed MacIntyre's interpretation of tradition as an extended argument in her analysis of the relationship between congregational life and tradition. She suggests that congregations are bearers of tradition, but not in a simplistic causal trajectory. She writes that congregations operate according to two impulses: on the one hand, they are conservative, seeking to preserve what is perceived as a "cherished inheritance;" and on the other hand, they are future-oriented, responding to contemporary contexts and incorporating new elements.[40]

Our understanding of practice also is enriched by the contributions of other scholars who introduce other categories and critiques from which we can draw correctives to and expansions upon MacIntyre. For example, we would be remiss in our examination of practice without at least an acknowledgement of the important contributions made by Pierre Bourdieu to this conversation. Bourdieu, a sociologist with ties to the structuralist conversation in that discipline, is particularly inter-

---

37. See, for example, Bass, "Congregations and the Bearing of Traditions"; Dykstra, "Reconceiving Practice."

38. Stout, *Democracy and Tradition,* 135.

39. See Hauerwas, *Peaceable Kingdom*; Hauerwas, *Dispatches from the Front.*

40. Bass, "Congregations and the Bearing of Traditions," 170.

ested in the embodied, nonrational aspects of practice. He offers to us an examination of practice that moves it away from MacIntyre's realm of practical reason and negotiation with tradition. He argues that practice is neither a product of solely individual decision-making nor structural determinism. He suggests that the power of practice lies somewhere in between these two possibilities, in the realm he calls *habitus*.[41]

Habitus is that way of acting and responding that is shaped by historical experience and practice and in turn shapes the social world in which we act and respond. It is "constituted in practice and is always oriented toward practical functions."[42] The *habitus* is made up of durable and transposable dispositions that produce a structure that adapts to the social situation, producing practices that re-generate the dispositions that make up the *habitus*.[43] *Habitus* introduces a predictability to human behavior characterized by a more relational and interactive force than the mechanistic determinism of objectivism or intellectual determinism of subjectivism. It takes seriously both social conditions and embodied experience.[44] The body, in fact, is central in *habitus* in a way that external social forces and intellectual rationality miss: "The body believes in what it plays at . . . it does not memorize the past, it *enacts* the past, bringing it back to life. What is 'learned by the body' is not something that one has, like knowledge that can be brandished, but something that one is."[45] While the *habitus* is not a product of determinism, Bourdieu is suspicious of the power of practice to shape the *habitus* and the potential that unjust social structures might be concretized via practice. It is precisely in the non-rational character of practice that this danger lies.

In contrast to Bourdieu's suspicion of *habitus,* Craig Dykstra describes the salutary role of *habitus* in the formation of a new way of life or a new form of existence. For Dykstra, the extra-rational character of practice resident in the *habitus* gives Christian practice its formative power. The *habitus* is formed by "profound, life-orienting, identity-shaping participation in the constitutive practices of the Christian life."[46]

41. For a helpful and clarifying discussion of Bourdieu's work on practice and habitus, see Jenkins, *Pierre Bourdieu,* 66–103.

42. Bourdieu, *Logic of Practice,* 52.

43. Ibid.

44. Ibid., 54–56.

45. Ibid., 73.

46. Dykstra, "Reconceiving Practice," 50.

Dykstra draws his understanding of *habitus* from the work of Edward Farley, who points to the practical wisdom of theological knowledge, informed in part by habit.[47]

While coming to different conclusions, Bourdieu and Dykstra both remind us that the power of practice derives from its comprehensive impact upon us. It shapes not only our experience, but also the *habitus* that influences how we view, interpret, and make use of that experience. The category of *habitus* enriches MacIntyre's definition of social practices with lenses through which we might construe how they contribute to the formation of faith and identity.

With these correctives to and expansions of MacIntyre's theory, let us now examine the *practice* of social witness in more detail.

Defining Social Witness Theoretically as a Religious Practice

Now, having described the phenomenon of religious practice and mined MacIntyre's definition thereof, we return to the task of applying these theoretical gleanings to social witness practice in more detail. As noted above, despite its conservative, traditionalist trajectory, MacIntyre's definition and the categories thus introduced bear remarkable heuristic value for the study of religious practices in general. In particular relation to social witness practices, the categories of analysis used by MacIntyre offer a way inside the practice, a means by which we might examine its dynamics beyond whether it politically "works" or not. MacIntyre's theory presents to us a way of studying, from the inside, what happens when religious persons explicitly and intentionally challenge harmful political and social systems.

Drawing on and correcting MacIntyre and some of his theoretical interlocutors, we can say that Christian social witness is a religious practice in that it is a complex and interrelated set of theologically, politically, and structurally-oriented activities and ideas with standards of excellence that vary according to the prioritizing of these orientations and the capacity to generate among participants internal goods related to their identity and vocation. This set of activities is embedded and given life in the lived social patterns, historical experience, and traditions of a particular religious institution. In describing the practice of social wit-

47. See Farley, *Ecclesial Man.*

ness in this way, we might divide this MacIntyrian definition of social witness into four broad categories of analysis: a complex and interrelated set of activities and ideas with varied orientations, standards of excellence varying according to these orientations, the capacity to generate internal goods related to identity and vocation, and the relationship of practice to a particular institution.

Complex and Interrelated Set of Theologically, Politically, and Structurally-Oriented Activities and Ideas

Upon first glance, it might seem that social witness practice is a unitary form of human activity that manifests itself in a number of forms. In other words, people engage in social witness practice when they protest, or when they write letters to their legislators, or when they boycott a particular corporation. Construed this way, a practice is an activity. In contrast, MacIntyre suggests that practices are complex sets of activities. We might also recall Dorothy Bass' definition, noted above, in which she describes a practice as "a dense cluster of ideas and activities that are related to a specific social goal."[48] What does this mean, to say that a practice is a set or cluster of activities? Upon closer examination, even the seemingly unitary protest described at the beginning of this chapter becomes exponentially complex. First, the protest was framed by public speech by the organizing pastors before the protest and by pastors in their congregations and in the media following the protest. Second, during the protest itself, one could hear the singing of spirituals, the chanting of slogans, and leaders preaching and exhorting over the loud speakers; one could see participants raising their arms, holding signs aloft, and climbing atop walls and city buses; and one could feel the press of the crowd as the motorcade passed. A few would even feel the clamp of handcuffs on their wrists. Finally, one could scarcely name the multitude of other background activities that surrounded and permeated the protest, from the painting of signs to the calling of volunteers, from the territory-staking in front of the Historical Center to the forming of new relationships in the streets of Atlanta.

A multitude of activities made up that protest. For example, one activity in which I took part was the extended negotiation of the placement and observance of police barriers in front of the sidewalk on which I was

48. Bass, "Introduction," 2.

standing. The police were, at first, quite disinclined to grant any grace to protestors who stood next to or in front of the barricade. As time passed, and as they made small talk with us, they moved the barriers forward a little to give us more room. As the motorcade prepared to pass by where we stood, the police again moved the barriers back, forcefully demanding that we, too, move further back onto the sidewalk. The negotiating of police barriers most certainly does not comprise social witness. As a practitioner, however, this extended and seemingly banal conversation was one logistical activity in a complex and interrelated set of activities that made up my practice of social witness that day. We can loosely categorize this seemingly infinite set of activities according to what might be described as "orientations."

In theoretically defining social witness as a religious practice, I argue that the activities and ideas comprising a practice may be oriented theologically, politically, and/or structurally. An orientation is the point of reference by which we determine the relative position, direction or attitude of something or someone. When used in relation to religious practice, we might think of an orientation as the aim of our practice, the environment in which we engage in it, and the ground upon which we stand as we do so. Orientation rings of a nautical metaphor. In the murky sea of religious practice, we gain our orientation from the place from whence we came, the lighthouse on the shore toward which we sail, and the resources (like maps and compasses) we carry with us. Along the way, any one of these orientations may take precedence over the others, and we sometimes make minute adjustments in our course.

In the study of dance, orientation is a key element for seeking excellence in the art. As a novice dancer practices her turns, balance does not come easily, and dizziness becomes almost unbearable when a vigorous instructor demands endless repetitions. The ground, walls, and mirror's reflection all spin stubbornly, refusing the dancer's desperate attempts to regain her bearings. The place from which she has come, the ground upon which she turns, and the place toward which she aims are hidden from her. Once she learns how to focus her gaze on a stable object, however, the situation changes. By starting from a firm preparation, keeping her eyes fixed on the place toward which she turns, and turning her head quickly to maintain her visual orientation, she eliminates the dizziness and, over time, develops a deep awareness of the relative position of her body. She is grounded but moving, directed but fluid.

Certainly, in both the nautical and dance metaphors, there is a teleological source of orientation: the place toward which we are heading. While our origins and current environments are significant in determining our course of action, a dynamic and purposeful practice requires an end that is valued enough to keep us moving. For Christian social witness, this end is largely theological in character, envisioning what Jürgen Moltmann describes as an alternative future that stands in contradiction to present reality.[49] In chapter 4, I address the relationship between Christian eschatology and social witness in more detail, but it is important to note the role that a theological *telos* plays, even implicitly, in the formation and practice of social witness.

Such is the nature of strong and deep orientations. They make it possible for us to dance by establishing a *telos* toward which to move and points of reference along the way by which to mark our journey. In social witness, any number of discourses and value systems might serve to orient our practice: political process, economic justice, theological and social ethics, structural analysis. At any given time, we might sense one orientation more keenly than another. An orientation may be foregrounded in a particular moment or activity of the practice. For example, large portions of the Presbyterian rally day at the Georgia State Capitol were oriented around political process. Participants received a brief primer in the distinctions between a bill and a resolution and discussed the intricacies of arranging visits with public officials. At noon, however, orientations shifted dramatically. We gathered, slowly, on the steps in the rotunda of the capitol building and, after some awkward standing around, we were led in a hymn-sing. In this moment, our practice was primarily oriented by theology.

While the practice in the long term is oriented toward a theological and ethical *telos*, it is also, as practitioners participate in it, oriented by political and social realities that shape its form. Of course, theological, structural, and political orientations are not discrete. The very existence of Presbyterian social action, for example, is dependent upon a distinct set of theological and ethical commitments that teach practitioners that Christian discipleship requires political participation. John Calvin himself expressed his disdain for those who would believe that Christian faith nullified civic commitments: "Still the distinction does not go so far

---

49. Moltmann, *Theology of Hope*, 85–86.

as to justify us in supposing that the whole scheme of civil government is matter of pollution, with which Christian men have nothing to do."[50]

These orientations not only give shape and direction to the content and meaning of the practice, but also provide a myriad of languages that aid the discursive character of the practice. Thus, the practice of social witness is quite public and relies on the ability of practitioners to articulate their motivations, goals, meanings, and hopes in a variety of contexts. In some respects, the practitioner of social witness quickly must become multilingual, utilizing a number of forms of discourse to communicate with a number of diverse actors. The practice of social witness requires a high degree of flexibility and an ability to move quickly between political, structural, and theological orientations. In some moments, the practice might, in fact, embody all three.

Social witness is guided by a political orientation in its interaction with governmental polity. Practitioners of social witness know, to varying degrees, how legislation is created, how to contact government officials from school board members to the president of the United States, and the workings of the judicial system. They visit with and write letters to congressional representatives, they observe court proceedings, they organize voter registration drives, and they gather in the streets and on the national mall to demonstrate objections to U.S. foreign policy and unjust budget proposals.

One might even be surprised by the political savvy exhibited by these decidedly amateur political actors. Immediately following a briefing session in the Presbyterian Washington Office, for example, the group from Baltimore presbytery gathers in the lobby of the Methodist building to strategize their next visit with a representative whom they expect to be quite resistant to their requests regarding federal funding of domestic programs and environmental policy. As they huddle there, just in front of the door, one woman suggests, "I think we should start by thanking him for his support of internet child pornography legislation. We actually agree with him on that." The group has learned, over the course of the fourteen years that they have been making such visits, that beginning by expressing gratitude and acknowledging points of agreement is a good strategy for opening conversation. Participants also quickly develop working knowledge of important bills and resolutions,

---

50. Calvin, *Institutes*, IV.XX.17.

asking the staff of the Washington Office such detailed questions as, "Catherine, what is the status of the McCain amendment on torture?"

Social witness does not always directly address governmental polity, however. Sometimes, practitioners intentionally confront other social structures, some of which might bear less obvious connections to governmental polity. For this reason, efforts to describe the orientations guiding social witness must account for more broad-based activism than explicitly political tactics and goals. Other structures, such as economic systems and cultural institutions, have been the subjects of religious social action too. For example, in recent years, religious groups have worked with the Coalition of Immokalee Workers to organize large-scale protests and boycotts of restaurants and institutional food service providers, actions that resulted in small per-pound wage increases for tomato pickers.[51] Some denominations, including the United Methodist Church and the Presbyterian Church (U.S.A.), supported the efforts financially. Economic activities such as boycotts, divestment, and purposeful investment are common elements of social witness practice. This is so because injustice results from more complicated factors than unfair legislation or enforcement thereof. While, if traveling far enough up the ladder of accountability, social witness practitioners might find an applicable governmental policy to confront, practitioners often seek out more immediate contexts in which to pursue change. For example, while Christian activists might aim, finally, to change federal or international law so that multinational corporations are restricted in their labor practices in other countries, they do not focus solely on these large-scale legal changes. They also challenge corporations directly through boycotts and demonstrations, with hopes that economic and social pressure will encourage them to change their practices even when governmental legislation does not demand it. Similarly, activists might pursue more cultural aims, like changing or supporting diverse forms of media and entertainment. Beyond calling for changes in Federal Communications Commission regulations, activists may appeal directly to networks and advertisers to encourage the portrayal of particular cultural and social values and to discourage that of others. A full definition of social witness requires the flexibility to account for action that is not polity-oriented. At the same time, even witness that primarily is aimed at changing govern-

51. For more information about the Coalition of Immokalee Workers movement, see their website. "Coalition of Immokalee Workers (CIW)."

mental policy usually also contains other cultural and economic dimensions. To account for these realities, we can say that social witness bears a structural orientation, in that participants engage various structures and systems of power beyond institutional government.

Finally, as noted above, social witness that is oriented only by political and structural values and aims is not, as described in the introduction, a theological practice of "witness" at all, but social action. This is not to say that social action stands in contradiction to social witness. In fact, practitioners of Christian social witness may often choose to mute their theological language as they collaborate with nonreligious partners in their pursuit of social change. Just the same, insofar as it is a practice of *witness*, it is propelled and sustained by a theological vision that may, at any given point, remain implicit or be made explicit.

Martin Luther King, Jr., for example, regularly made explicit the theological vision of brotherhood at the core of his understanding of both the civil rights movement and the larger human rights movement: "We must all learn to live together as brothers. Or we will all perish together as fools. We are tied together in the single garment of destiny, caught in an inescapable network of mutuality. And whatever affects one directly affects all directly . . . This is the way God's universe is made; this is the way it is structured."[52] King's concept of brotherhood would inform and shape his practice of social action in response to a variety of structural and political issues: segregation, disenfranchisement, the Vietnam War, the plight of the American poor.

Sometimes, the theological orientation of the practice is understood as a foundation or root of the practice. Sometimes it functions as a resource for the practice, a tool that practitioners use to work toward their goals. Sometimes we find the theological dimensions of the practice in its public language (such was certainly the case in King's activism) and sometimes we hear theological language only among the practitioners themselves. Sometimes, theology may give rise to social action, and other times social action necessitates theological reflection. In any case, what distinguishes social witness from the broader category of social action is its theological orientation and the fact that even its political and structural goals are shaped by the theological and teleological character of the practice. The nature and function of theology within social witness is taken up in more detail in the second half of this project.

52. King, Jr., "Remaining Awake," 269.

It is not difficult to appreciate the exponentially complex and varied nature of the kinds of activities that make up social witness. The political, structural, and theological orientations that characterize the myriad activities are not discrete, however. As much as it is complex, the practice also is marked by the way in which its activities are *interrelated*, woven together in a complex practice. In religious activists' support of gay and lesbian rights, for example, social witness may consist of marches and lobbying visits in opposition to proposed legislation defining marriage as exclusively heterosexual, prayer vigils and worship services, and communication both with the media and within religious communities aimed toward the full support of gay and lesbian persons. These activities overlap, inform each other, and work together within this complex practice.

As noted above, MacIntyre describes a practice as a *coherent* and complex form of human activity. The difference between coherence and interrelatedness is, of course, not merely semantic. For MacIntyre, coherence demands a fit among complex parts and, in particular, a fit between practice and tradition. While coherence entails interrelatedness, it surpasses it, requiring that pieces not only relate to one another, but also are in neat agreement. In its broadest sense, coherence might be understood as interrelatedness. This, however, is not MacIntyre's usage, so another term is more suitable to reflect both the independence *and* interdependence of the components of a practice. Therefore, we might say that the components are *interrelated*.

Standards of Excellence Vary According to the Prioritizing of Orientations

Given the need to account for such diverse components as letter-writing, prayer vigils, media communication, and protest, establishing what makes for good practice is certainly a complicated process. How do we know if we have practiced well? The answer to this question can shift dramatically according to what standards we use to measure the quality of the practice.

When I was teaching a summer academy course on Christian political action for Emory University's Youth Theological Initiative, the significance of standards of excellence became apparent when one seventeen-year-old scholar voiced his objections to such practices. He said, "We are already at war. I don't understand why Christians would want to protest it. It won't make any difference. Peace is not realistic." Implicit in his objection, one might discern, is that, for him, the operative standard of excellence is the political efficacy of a practice. Not only is the practice unsatisfactory if its political goal is not attainable, but it is not even worth doing. (Incidentally, as the academy wore on, we learned that other standards of excellence were in operation for him, such as the criterion that religious practices ought not be political in the first place.)

MacIntyre calls standards of excellence those means by which we judge the benefit, performance, or value of a practice. In MacIntyre's example of portrait-painting as a practice, we might imagine a number of standards of excellence that the apprentice painter must acknowledge and strive to meet. As noted in the discussion of MacIntyre above, different instantiations of a practice might demand different standards of excellence or that standards be prioritized differently according to variations in context, purpose, and form.

The theoretical definition of social witness as a religious practice proposed here integrates the category of standards of excellence within a practice's theological, political, and structural orientations as described above. In other words, a full measure of the excellence of the practice can be ascertained only if the standards by which we judge the practice also are theological, structural, and political in character. Externally derived standards are inadequate for measuring the practice according to its own purpose, function, and character. Standards of excellence are intrinsic to a practice or, as MacIntyre holds, appropriate to and partially definitive of a practice.

The young man quoted above who objected to the Christian protests against the second Iraq war measured the excellence of the practice according to its political orientation. This standard is not inappropriate as a measure of the value of the practice: the activities, after all, have a strong political orientation. One might raise, however, generative questions about the acknowledgement and ordering of standards of excellence. First, is it appropriate to evaluate a practice *solely* according to one, in this case political, standard of excellence? Second, even when structural or theological standards of excellence also are consulted in measuring the performance and benefit of a practice, what difference does it make to *prioritize* standards of excellence?

In my theoretical definition of social witness practice, I propose that the means by which we prioritize political, structural, and theological standards of excellence influence our perceptions of excellence. If only one standard, or even multiple standards developed according to a singular orientation, are used to determine what makes for a good practice of social witness, then the resulting estimation of the practice does not account for the rich complexity and diversity of the practice. No, standards of excellence, to be truly appropriate to the practice of social witness, must attend to the theological, structural, *and* political dimensions of the practice. Taking the protest at the King Center as an example, let us identify the contrasting and complementary standards of excellence that are generated according to the political, structural, and theological orientations of the practice.

According to *political standards of excellence*, the protest might be judged inadequate, because none of President Bush's policies, from his investment in the Iraq war to his plans for exploration of Mars, apparently changed as a result of the protest. Further, protestors were not granted access to the president or his staff, so their position in relation to the political power was quite distant. At a more fundamental level, the protestors perhaps did not have explicit political outcomes in mind as they planned and executed the protest. Given this situation, the practice might be judged as a failed practice because it was not even oriented by political goals, strategies, and outcomes; or, it might be determined that the political orientation of the event was given a low priority, and thus political standards of excellence ought not be the first standards by which we measure this instantiation of the practice.

Instead, the protest is perhaps better evaluated according to *structural standards of excellence*. The structural orientation of the protest was evident in the planners' use of public media; in the intentional gathering of one thousand Atlantans across class, race, and social lines; in the negotiation between police, city officials, Secret Service, the transit authority, and the citizens; and in the symbolic and literal message that President Bush's agenda directly conflicted with the vision of Dr. King. If we were to measure the adequacy of the practice according to these structural dimensions of the protest, we might come to a different conclusion about the value of the practice than if we measured it according to political standards alone. The planners used the media and shaped the protest to reflect broader concerns than a specific political issue. The protest reflected the broader cultural, economic, and social commitments of the participants. And the outcomes of the protest, for some of the participants, had more to do with social relationships and shared commitments than with political process.

Finally, the protest can be analyzed according to *theological standards of excellence*. We cannot forget that the protest was organized by Tim McDonald, pastor of First Iconium Baptist Church and president of Concerned Black Clergy. In his call for the protest, McDonald made clear what was, at least in his mind, the theological orientation of the protest. To analyze the protest according to theological standards of excellence, we might ask whether McDonald named a theological dynamic that was already implicit within the practice and in the motivations of those who would join the protest; whether he was imposing one theological orientation on top of others that other protestors may have held; or whether he was supplying a theological narrative to a largely political practice.

Theological standards of excellence can be tricky, however, since "theology" connotes such an ideational dimension of the practice. Who determines the theological ideas inherent in a practice, or how they are both articulated and understood by participants? These all are questions related to the theological ideas woven throughout a practice. Theology, however, is not only present in social witness in ideational form, but also has a functional role in the practice. To oversimplify, theology is both idea and activity in social witness. In the interest of grasping fully the complex role of theology in social witness, theological standards of excellence must address both of these dimensions of the theological orientation of social witness.

Some theological standards of excellence that help us to judge the ideational role of theology in social witness practice are important, but we also need standards that account for the functional role of theology. Functionally, we might ask whether or not practitioners reflect theologically on their actions and how this reflection happens. For example, we might ask who participates in theological reflection; in what context they so reflect; whether they engage in discussion, listening, and/or silence; and how they make use of resources like biblical texts, denominational creeds and statements, and their own experience of witness. Even when we consider the role of theology in social witness from a more ideational perspective, however, we do not leave behind questions of theological process: we might ask whether a particular theological doctrine is appropriate to an instantiation of social witness practice, or whether the particular ideas contained therein contribute to theological reflection. For example, while preparing for a meeting with legislators in Washington about proposed federal budget cuts to domestic aid programs, practitioners may consult the Sermon on the Plain.[53] Certainly, the topic at hand bears strong theological connections to Jesus' words, "Blessed are you who are poor . . . Blessed are you who are hungry now." But the adequacy of these biblical images might be measured not only according to relevance, but also according to what resources they contribute to theological reflection among participants.

Asking a question about the appropriateness of a theological idea assumes that part of what it means to practice with theological excellence is that practitioners should reflect a sort of *phronesis* in the practice. Practical theology, Bernard Lee has suggested, requires a step in between theory and practice in which we develop "knowledge of the kind of world we should be making together," which he describes as *phronesis.*[54] Lee argues that the importance of phronetic reflection, which is characterized by theological and ethical reasoning, is expressed when participants in a practice ask, "Is this of a piece with the kind of world (or church, or city, or corporation) we would want to call to life?"[55] The challenge and promise of theological reflection in social witness is taken up in more detail in chapter 6.

Intentional reflection upon all standards of excellence—political, structural, and theological—is essential to the flourishing of a complex practice like social witness. In reflecting upon our standards, we ask: what is important to us in this practice? What is *most* important? What constitutes failure or success? How do we know if we have practiced well? Reflection upon standards, in MacIntyrian terms, demands our participation in tradition, that long-standing argument about the goods being sought in this practice or any other. This argument has many participants: lay practitioners and clergy, local congregations and denominational divisions, voices of the relevant traditions and voices of the times. In social witness, standards are also negotiated in conversation with practitioners outside our religious communities, such as other religious groups, political entities, media outlets. Together with other

53. Luke 6:17–31; cf. Matt 4:24—5:12.

54. Lee, "Practical Theology as Phronetic," 1.

55. Ibid., 14.

practitioners, we discern what matters most in the practice and its intended consequences. By engaging in the negotiation and discernment of the things that matter in practice, we deepen our experience of and commitment to the practice and thereby gain more from participation in it. MacIntyre describes these gains of a practice as *goods*.

Capacity to Generate Among Participants Internal Goods Related to Identity and Vocation

In the discussion of MacIntyre above, I explained the theoretical distinction between internal and external goods. Internal goods take on particular significance in the practice of social witness, since few external goods may be attained. The company continues to underpay its workers. The anti-immigration bill passes. The stay of execution is denied. In the absence of the realization of its stated goals, is social witness judged a failed practice? If we borrow MacIntyre's category of internal goods, we can say, with confidence, "By no means!"

Even when instantiations of social witness practice bear no obvious political or structural goods, participants still benefit from the practice in other ways. MacIntyre illustrates this phenomenon with the example of a child learning to play chess: "But, so we may hope, there will come a time when the child will find in those goods specific to chess, in the achievement of a certain highly particular kind of analytical skill, strategic imagination and competitive intensity, a new set of reasons, reasons now not just for winning on a particular occasion, but for trying to excel in whatever way the game of chess demands."[56]

It very well may be true that, for many practitioners of social witness, the external goods of changed policy or increased wages are *the* reasons for engaging in the practice. Over time, however, some other reasons must also sustain the practice. In the case of the Baltimore Presbyterians who visit their legislators monthly, one would be hard pressed to find immediate, explicit political gains made by their visits. If their practice of social witness is deemed of value only if particular political goals are clearly met, we face two problems in appreciating the full picture of the practice. On one hand, even when particular political goals are met, measuring how much of the success is attributable to the practice is a nearly impossible task. Some members of the Baltimore group

---

56. MacIntyre, *After Virtue*, 188.

acknowledge that, on many of their visits, they find themselves across the table from officials who already agree with them. The legislator may already have held a position amenable to that of the practitioners, or may be facing economic or political pressure from other sources to vote in a direction that happens to match that of the practitioners. In other words, the external goods of changed policy might be had apart from the words and actions of the group from Baltimore.

On the other hand, when the group's practice is not met with immediate change, how can we know that political change is not happening, albeit slowly? As elder Nelson Tharp put it, "You always have the feeling that you're attacking an iceberg with an icepick." The group from Baltimore meets monthly with legislative aids, asking for political changes that they are unlikely to see in the near future. For example, after discussing the official agenda in one meeting, a member of the group added, "I have something to add. I think we are in agreement that we all want universal health care. We feel this is very important." Pragmatically speaking, these practitioners do not expect immediate, measurable change. Hence the iceberg metaphor. For Nelson Tharp, however, the stubbornness of the iceberg is not the end of the story. He continues the metaphor, saying, "But, still, some people *do* listen, and it does *some* good. As they say, even glaciers move every now and then." Occasionally, the stated goals of social witness are achieved. For example, Eleanora Giddings Ivory, past director of the Presbyterian Church (U.S.A.) Washington Office, points to President Bill Clinton's signing of the 2000 international debt relief bill, for which she was present, as a gratifying moment in her advocacy work, one that took years to bring to completion. From the time an issue is first raised in the political consciousness, Giddings Ivory notes, it usually takes ten years for Congress to deal with the issue.

Given the political reality that the external goods of political change are both slow to come to fruition and difficult to attribute solely to religious social witness, a theory of the practice of social witness must account for other gains, which sustain practitioners in their work. Sometimes, activists are loath to acknowledge any benefits aside from political and social change, perhaps because they are resistant to the implication that they engage in these practices for their own benefit. MacIntyre's concept of internal goods, however, is misused if we think of them as individual and self-satisfying. No, MacIntyre insists that the goods internal to a practice enrich the whole relevant community and that the effect of these goods is the realization of the good of a certain kind of (virtuous) life. Dykstra applies these MacIntyrian qualities of practice to his theory of Christian formation, pointing to the formative "effects of the practices on the practicing persons and their communities—including the effects on their minds, imaginations and spirits."[57]

What is gained when we take a broader view, when we look deeper into the practice at its formative power? What sorts of goods do we find there? While we might find many goods internal to social witness practice, I will consider just two related ones here: identity and vocation. Practices have the capacity to "make us better people or involve us in a kind of life that is itself good," Dykstra interprets MacIntyre to say.[58] The narratives retold by participants in social witness bear out the claim that practices are partly constitutive of one's life. For example, one Presbyterian activist recounted to me numerous stories of his activism, including his experience as a conscientious objector during the Second World War, connecting these sorts of practices to his perceived identity and calling as a peacemaker and social justice-seeker. Identity is a complicated phenomenon in any case, and is especially so in relation to practices of social witness. Does identity motivate social witness, or does social witness form identity? Of course, the answer is *both*. In the next chapter, I will consider theoretical constructions of identity, but here I would like to at least name the theological and moral dimensions of vocation and identity as they relate to social witness.

Vocation comes from the Latin, *vocare*, meaning "to call." John Calvin wrote that the Christian life is lived in multiple spheres of calling, contexts in which Christians hold responsibilities: "The last thing to be observed is, that the Lord enjoins every one of us, in all the actions of life, to have respect to our own calling."[59] These spheres include the social and political context. Activists often describe their work in the political sphere as a kind of calling. Importantly, practitioners of social witness sometimes grow in their theological and vocational identity. This sort of theological vocational awareness emerged more often in my conversations with pastors and others who are very invested in the theological framing of social witness. They talk about how they have come to understand themselves as the voice of the body of Christ in the world,

57. Dykstra, "Reconceiving Practice," 45.

58. Ibid., 44.

59. Calvin, *Institutes*, III.X.6.

issuing prophetic calls for equality, justice, peace, and hospitality. Over time, some come to see their witness as an embodiment of Jesus' own description of his ministry in the world, bringing good news to the poor, proclaiming release to the captives, and letting the oppressed go free.[60]

Even where this explicit sort of theological articulation of identity is not at the fore, however, practitioners may demonstrate a more general sense of vocation and identity in relation to social witness. The ways in which they tell their stories of witness reflect, to use MacIntyrian categories, an acquisition of virtues related to moral formation. Over time, as they have participated in various forms of religious practice, including social witness, they have developed moral sensibilities that demand that they intervene where others are suffering.[61] Ellen Tharp, for example, describes her own formative experience during temperance movement: "To me, I feel that social action is part of religion. I think I grew up feeling that religion very much was how you dealt with all these things. Maybe originally, it was anti-drinking, but that wasn't the only thing . . . It seems like throughout the biblical teachings (there is) pro-concern about the least, the hungry, the enslaved, and everything else."

Of course, Tharp did not come to these conclusions in isolation. She grew up in a church and family for whom these commitments were core faith values. In particular, she found inspiration in her own family's participation in the prohibition movement as well as in a Mennonite youth director who, in the 1940's, was himself a participant in a burgeoning peace movement. Throughout her adolescence, Tharp's identity was formed in part by her participation in relationships and practices which encouraged in her a particular way of understanding her place in the world. And so, a full definition of social witness practice must take into account its social and institutional character.

Activities Are Embedded and Given Life in Particular Religious Institutions

Practices do not occur in a vacuum. One of the critiques often levied against MacIntyre and some of his interlocutors is that the social context in which they imagine these practices taking place has a rootless

60. Luke 4:16b–21.

61. Both James Jasper and Christian Smith discuss the development of moral voice and moral outrage in social movements. I discuss the implications of social witness for moral development more fully in chapter 2.

feeling about it, that it looks very little like any actual social institution. An analysis of the social, cultural, and economic contexts of social witness are central to a full understanding of this complex practice. The very example cited just above illustrates the importance of contextual analysis. In Ellen Tharp's case, the practice of social witness was born and nurtured in a particular institutional and familial context.

A tradition is living insofar as it is socially embodied in the practices of an actual community. Institutions, such as congregations, presbytery groups, and even ecumenical issue-oriented groups sustain those practices that enliven traditions. A full definition of social witness practice requires some attention to this contextualization of practice within institutions. Institutions can be described and defined in a number of ways, but at the very least, we might name three components of institutional life that are particularly relevant to religious practice: lived social patterns, historical experience, and traditions.

The lived social patterns of an institution include a variety of components: the construction and maintenance of collective identity, the structure and dynamics of relationships between members, and the relationships an institution has with other institutions. In their paper on Presbyterian congregational identity types, Jackson Carroll and David Roozen use a national survey of Presbyterian session members to measure "shared perceptions of members about themselves," as well as shared perceptions of congregational tasks and programs.[62] From the data thus collected, they develop a "cluster" typology that includes six Presbyterian identity types, including: Sojourner, Activist, Evangelical, Civic, Old First Presbyterian, and Family.[63] They conclude that identity types (along with church size and community context) help to explain differences both in how congregations rank tasks in importance and in the programs that congregations offer.[64] Since Carroll and Roozen were primarily concerned with ideational constructions of congregational identity, the types that they develop are ripe for testing in relation to the effect of practices on congregational identity. Nancy Ammerman places congregational identity in conversation with congregational *culture*, suggesting that culture "is who we are and all the ways in which

---

62. Carroll and Roozen, "Congregational Identities," 352.

63. Ibid., 355–57.

64. Ibid., 362.

we reinforce and recreate who we are.[65] She argues that a congregation's culture and identity are shaped by its activities (what its members *do*), its artifacts (what they *make*), and its accounts (what stories they *tell*).[66] Ammerman's framework complements the congregational identity work of Carroll and others by suggesting that what a congregation does, its practices, impact the institution's identity just as much as identity shapes a congregation's practices.

An important nuance in understanding institutional culture, especially with respect to practices, has to do with just who the practitioners *are* as well as how they relate to one another. With regard to social witness practices, it is entirely likely, *especially* in larger congregations, that activists form a *very* small minority of the membership. Penny Becker, in her book *Congregations in Conflict*, develops four models of institutional environment that are arranged according to core tasks and "legitimate ways of doing things."[67] These include "house of worship," community, family, and leader models, each of which reflects "different bundles of ideas, ways of doing things, discourses, and taken-for-granted assumptions about 'who we are' and 'how we do things here.'"[68] The models are distinguished by how decisions are made, how members relate to each other and how the congregation relates to its broader context. Becker offers some help for considering how members occupy varying roles and exhibit varying degrees of participation in practices. For example, a community model congregation is likely to be more democratic in its decision-making (and thus diffuse in mission) while a leader model congregation operates "more like branches of a social movement organization, with a strong mission."[69]

Religious institutions, whether they are local congregations, denominations, ecumenical bodies, or small study groups, are shaped by the ways in which their members relate to one another, by their histories, and by their activities. Practitioners of social witness come from a

---

65. Ammerman et al., *Studying Congregations*, 78. It is just a bit confusing that Ammerman seems to neither equate congregational culture with congregational identity, nor draw a sharp distinction between the two, frequently using both terms together in her argument.

66. Ibid., 84.

67. Becker, *Congregations in Conflict*, 7.

68. Ibid., 13.

69. Ibid., 14.

variety of congregational institutions with a variety of understandings about leadership, identity, relationships, and goals. Furthermore, in the Presbyterian Church (U.S.A.), these practices are often facilitated by other denominational institutions: presbyteries and national offices. Each of these institutional contexts bears some impact upon the practice, and the practice impacts the life of the institutions. Do the institutional leaders draw the parameters of the conversation? Or is the agenda more democratically established? Who plans social witness events: individual congregation members, leaders, committees, or external institutions? And how do participants in a practice draw on their relationships with one another to engage in and reflect upon social witness practice?

Of course, as MacIntyre rightly points out, when we participate in a practice, we do so not only within the contemporary context of an institution but also in relation to the historical experience and traditions of that institution. An institution's history—the events that have marked its life, its pastors and memorable leaders, and the stories that the members tell about the past—is very much a live force in its present life. As Dorothy Bass writes, "congregations, as tradition bearers, are arenas within which individual and collective identity can be discovered, in all the local particularity that enables people to experience a deep sense of belonging. At the same time, they are places where the conflict that characterizes living traditions takes place, and where the larger tradition's challenges to restricted local forms of individual and group identity are encouraged."[70]

While the role of history and tradition is an important piece of institutional life and bears much influence on religious practice, the definition of social witness practice that I have developed proposes a significant revision on MacIntyrian deference to tradition. I have described this revision above as a shift from the concept of coherence, as MacIntyre understands it, to the concept of interrelatedness. Of course, practices are related to the historical experience and traditions of an institution. But they are not prescribed by them. Because the practice of social witness, like other Christian practices, involves diverse participants with varying degrees of familiarity with and reverence for tradition, practitioners are in a relationship of reciprocal influence with history and tradition. As Bass theorizes, institutions such as congregations are not only shaped by tradition but also innovate tradition. A congregation who participates

---

70. Bass, "Congregations and the Bearing of Traditions," 174.

in the advocacy work of Bread for the World may develop a new and deeper understanding of the gathering at the Lord's Table. As a congregation or other religious community lives and participates in practices, it is formed by both the tradition that gives birth to those practices and the continually changing context in which it engages in them.

Conclusion

In the preceding pages, I have drawn upon and challenged Alasdair MacIntyre's important definition of social practice to describe how social witness functions as a religious practice. The foregoing description facilitates our study of social witness practice by complexifying the levels of analysis by which we understand the practice. It raises many new questions about the dynamics of social witness, some of which are addressed in the pages that follow. These questions help us to deepen our understanding of what we see when we look at particular instantiations of social witness practice, identify gaps or opportunities for new developments of the practice, and reflect broadly and critically upon the significance and benefits of the practice. More specifically, this theoretical description invites us to consider religious social action not only in terms of its political effects, but also in terms of its inner logic and theological and social significance. It places social witness squarely within the context of institutional life, complicated as that may be. And it introduces new categories of analysis such as internal goods and standards of excellence.

The categories of internal goods and standards of excellence nudge this project in new and interesting directions. If new perspectives on identity are goods gained via participation in practices, how exactly does this happen? Interestingly, newer strands of social movement theory have taken up this question in relation to how participation in social movements relates to personal and collective identity, and this conversation is addressed in the following chapter. Similarly, if standards of excellence are theological as well as political and structural, what sorts of theological questions might we raise that would complement or challenge our prevalent ways of evaluating the practice? In "A Brief Statement of Faith," the Presbyterian Church (U.S.A.) confesses,

But we rebel against God; we hide from our Creator.
>   Ignoring God's commandments,
>   we violate the image of God in others and ourselves,
>   accept lies as truth,
>   exploit neighbor and nature,
>   and threaten death to the planet entrusted to our care.
>   We deserve God's condemnation.
> Yet God acts with justice and mercy to redeem creation.
> . . . Like a mother who will not forsake her nursing child,
> like a father who runs to welcome the prodigal home,
>   God is faithful still
>
> . . . In a broken and fearful world
> the Spirit gives us courage
>   to pray without ceasing,
>   to witness among all peoples to Christ as Lord and Savior,
>   to unmask idolatries in Church and culture,
>   to hear the voices of peoples long silenced,
>   and to work with others for justice, freedom, and peace.
> In gratitude to God, empowered by the Spirit,
>   we strive to serve Christ in our daily tasks
>   and to live holy and joyful lives,
>   even as we watch for God's new heaven and new earth,
>   praying, "Come, Lord Jesus!"[71]

In its confessions, the denomination sets the practice of social witness squarely between the dialectical poles of sin and hope. How can the theologies of sin and hope thus inform, shape and measure the excellence of such practices? Chapters 4 and 5 address these questions. First, however, let us augment the rich conversation of practice theory with the resources of social movement theory to examine how social witness practice shapes religious and moral identity.

71. Presbyterian Church (U.S.A.), "Brief Statement of Faith," 10.3–4.

3

Goods Internal

Social Movement Theory and the Construction of Identity

"I'm Tied to These Things"

PRESBYTERIAN ELDER THURSTON GRIGGS, IN THE TENTH DECADE OF HIS life, describes his commitment to social justice in the following way: "I'm tied to these things. And my impulses, even, are governed by this sort of thing." What leads activists to describe their commitments on such a gut level? They say that their beliefs and actions are a part of them, even exerting a sort of force upon their lives. But what are the "things" to which activists like Griggs are tied? Are they personal characteristics? Are they experiences? Are they beliefs? In any case, "these things" are more than objective or strategic decisions or actions. They operate on a level deeper than any one isolated circumstance; they are, in part, products of repeated ways of being in the world. They are generated within and among us as we participate in practices. Griggs, for example, recounts how his life has been affected by many forms of social witness, from his parents' activism in the temperance movement to his own work as a conscientious objector during World War II, as a peace activist during the nuclear freeze movement, and now as an advocate with legislators during his monthly visits to Capitol Hill with other members of Baltimore Presbytery. From a very early age, participating in social activism has shaped Griggs' understanding of himself. In other words, his *identity* has been formed by his practice.

How is this so? Certainly, it is easy to imagine how Griggs' identity predisposes him toward social activism. One's self-understanding has everything to do with whether or not one chooses to participate in this kind of activity. But Thurston Griggs and other activists tell a more complicated story than this. They weave their experiences of activism and their developing sense of themselves together in a way that makes it clear that identity and practice shape each other. To use our MacIntyrian categories, in social witness practice, *identity is a good realized by participants as they engage in a practice.* In other words, practitioners become different kinds of people via social witness.

MacIntyre offers us the category of internal goods for thinking about the creation of identity. In this chapter, I turn to the resources of social movement theory to develop the concept of identity further, asking, "How does social witness generate among participants internal goods related to identity?" First, I will delve into the role of internal goods in social witness practice, demonstrating how identity fits into this category. Then, I will argue that recent theoretical accounts of the role identity plays within social movements complements our MacIntyrian assertion that social witness practice has the capacity to generate internal goods related to identity. Finally, I will discuss the varying levels upon which identity has been construed in social movement theory, engaging in primary dialogue with theorist James Jasper. I conclude the chapter with some reflections on the kinds of identity that might be constructed in the practice of social witness.

Practice Theory and Lives Worth Living

Just by participating in a social practice, MacIntyre argues, we receive certain goods, some of which are tangible, and some intangible. He makes this argument via an extended consideration of the practice of portrait-painting. In the practice of portrait painting, he writes, two kinds of goods are generated internal to the practice. First, when portrait-painting is practiced with excellence, it produces products marked by excellence. Each portrait reflects the quality of the practice, as does each painter. A virtuosic performance and a flawless portrait are produced when portrait-painting is practiced with excellence. These goods can be acquired only by participating in the practice of portrait-painting and not by any other way.

The second kind of good generated internal to the practice of portrait-painting is perhaps less measurable, but even more significant in MacIntyre's perspective. As one engages in the practice of portrait-painting over time, a different sort of good emerges: the discovery of the value of "a certain kind of life."[1] As a painter endeavors to achieve progressive excellence in the art, she also learns the joy of *being* a painter, of *being* an artist. It is a sort of identity discovery, in which one internalizes the virtues of portrait-painting. As noted in chapter 1, Craig Dykstra also points to this character-forming power of practice. He says about internal goods: "Some of these things are products emerging from the practice; others are the effects of the practices on the practicing persons and their communities—including the effects on their minds, imaginations, and spirits."[2] The conviction that a practice might shape the minds, imaginations, and spirits of participants is a significant claim, one that warrants deeper analysis. Particularly in service of a deeper and more rounded understanding of religious activism, we must examine social witness in its formative capacity, and this demands an account of its identity-forming potential. What exactly does it mean to "discover the good of a certain kind of life?"

One response to that question comes from James Jasper, who concludes *The Art of Moral Protest* with a section called "Lives Worth Living." He ends with an ode to the creative aspects of social movements, describing activists as "more like poets than engineers," and movements as sources of moral vision and voice.[3] He writes, "Entire lives can be artful creations, as protestors try to fit their convictions into their daily routines. They epitomize Socrates' call for 'the examined life.' Protestors often find new ways of living, new modes of applying moral visions in everyday life . . . Protest offers many virtues to its practitioners, giving meaning to their lives. Their moral sensitivity, often painful but also deeply satisfying, is precious to them as well as being their greatest gift to the rest of us."[4] Jasper's theory is that the development of moral virtue, an essential product of social movements, gives meaning to human life. Similarly, the exercise of moral reflection has transformative power, so that practitioners understand themselves and their witness in deep and satisfying ways. Jasper's theory and the narratives of activists both point to the capacity of social witness to generate transformation in human life.

1. MacIntyre, *After Virtue*, 190.
2. Dykstra, "Reconceiving Practice," 45.
3. Jasper, *Art of Moral Protest*, 379.
4. Ibid., 340.

For many practitioners of social witness, activism is underestimated if we consider it a hobby or a phase. Many of the activists I met in this study have been engaged in social witness for decades. They have, to use Jasper's language, crafted lives of meaning and moral sensitivity. One woman's story began with her pacifist youth minister, while her husband's story began a little later, with the anti-nuclear movement. Another man recounted his experience as a conscientious objector during the Second World War. Their stories are echoed by many of the activists Christian Smith interviewed in his study of activists in the 1980s Central American peace movement. One such activist is Phyllis Taylor, who goes so far as to say, "People's lives were profoundly transformed."[5]

The political activists found great meaning in their travels to Central America, and the moral sensitivity they acquired there would lead them to pursue political change upon their return to the United States. Another activist Smith interviewed, Mike Clark, admits, "You *thought* you were going to Central America to offer solidarity and moral support, then you discover that your *life* had been changed. That's what happened. Thousands of people fought Reagan for years because Central America changed their lives."[6]

What is it that happens when one's life is said to be changed by participating in a social movement? It means something different, or at least *more*, than a changed mind. While changes in thoughts, perspectives, and ideas are significant in their impact on something as complex as U.S. foreign relations, MacIntyre, Jasper, and Smith all describe a far more comprehensive change in self-understanding. Activists' experiences affect them emotionally, spiritually, even bodily. If we maintain a holistic understanding of identity, as developed below, we are talking about identity when we talk about lives transformed.

Why Social Movement Theory?

How can we explain how these activists' practices transform their lives, creating in them new self-understanding? We might turn to any of a number of identity theories, which are in ample supply in contemporary psychological, narrative, sociological, and cultural theory. For an analysis of the role of identity in Christian practices of social action,

5. Smith, *Resisting Reagan*, 374.
6. Ibid.

however, social movement theory (and *new* social movement theory, in particular) is best suited to account for the public, political, and social dimensions of identity formation in Christian social witness.

To illustrate the complementary relationship between MacIntyre's theory of social practices and social movement theory, I plumb the resources of social movement theory in order to discover how the conversation about identity and social movements has emerged. I show how the most recent theoretical literature (nebulously named "new social movement theory") has made the greatest contribution toward the project of understanding identity in the context of social movements. I also discuss the challenges inherent in studying aspects of culture (including identity) in relation to social movements. Having shown the contributions offered by social movement theory in general to the study of social witness practice, I argue that new social movement theorist James Jasper is a compelling interlocutor for MacIntyre's theory, because he offers the most complex analysis of the *construction* of identity as one of the most important outcomes of social movements. Jasper's work is complemented by several other scholars in the new social movement theoretical school, perhaps most notably by Christian Smith, whose study of Christian participation in the Central American peace movement of the 1980s also attends to the construction of identity.

A Brief Evolutionary Tale of Social Movement Theory

Any study of Christian social witness that takes seriously current literature on political activism must deal with social movement theory. Social movement theory is the primary collection of scholarly literature accounting for religious social activism. This conversation has developed over the past half-century, and is a fertile place in which to explore the connections between religion and social change. Scholars of social movements have theorized about the material and ideological resources contributed to social movements by religious persons and groups; about how religious groups offer pre-existing communication networks, leadership and tactics; and, most recently, about how religion affects the culture of social movements and, conversely, how participation in social movements influences religious life. Practice theory, in its present iteration, bears only partial explanatory power for the peculiar character of religious political activism. Given this gap in practice theoretical literature, a full definition of the practice of *social witness* requires that we also consult social movement theory.

An appeal to social movement theory is rooted in more than a salute to previous scholarship. A clear affinity exists between MacIntyre's internal goods and accounts of the production of identity in social movement theory. Some of the most recent social movement theory makes a fine complement to MacIntyrian practice theory because it accounts for the *creation* of culture, reminiscent of MacIntyre's conviction that participation in social practices *creates* goods that can be had only via participation in a practice. In our theoretical definition of social witness, the construction of identity, as an outcome of social movement participation, correlates with the generation of internal goods within a social practice. Just as practices create new realities within and among practitioners, social movements generate new self-understandings within and among participants.

Social movement theorists have not always taken such a nuanced view of the mutually influential relationship between religion and social movements, however. In fact, until the last third of the last century, sociological accounts of social movements largely were confined to theories of collective behavior, in which movement participants were understood to be influenced by crowd interaction, collective excitement, naïveté, or diverse sources of social strain.[7] In 1972, Ralph Turner and Lewis Killian defined a social movement as a "collectivity acting with some continuity to promote or resist a change in the society or group of which it is a part."[8] By attributing strategic and organizational characteristics to social movements, their definition crystallized a theoretical approach that had emerged, challenging analyses that belied cultural fear of social movements and relatively simplistic readings of collective behavior. Instead of understanding social movements as strategic, meaningful, and good for societies, early theoretical work reveals an interpretation of social movements as irrational and reactionary. Even more charitable accounts of social movements attributed very little intentionality or deliberation to their participants. Social movements were understood to be collective, decidedly non-strategic responses to experiences of social strain. Since social movements were not considered strategic or purposeful collec-

7. For a reliable summary of developments in social movement theory, see Jasper, *Art of Moral Protest*, 19–42, 69–99.

8. Killian and Turner, *Collective Behavior*, 246.

tive action, the question of how religious groups would participate in an organized effort toward social change was not of prevailing theoretical concern. If anything, the positive forces of religion to sustain peace in society would serve to restrain the irrational actions of the crowd.

Eventually the prevalence of religious persons and groups in seeking social change would render moot this theoretical dismissal. As large numbers of religious actors entered the labor movement, the civil rights movement, and the women's movement, their intentional participation demanded a new kind of theoretical analysis. In the 1960s, the theoretical literature on resource mobilization began to describe participants in social movements as rational actors.[9] Resource mobilization theorists construed social movements as strategic and highly organized efforts to influence institutions in response to challenges and opportunities in the political structure. Although Marxist assumptions about the restraining function of religion would persist, some scholars began to argue, with the advent of resource mobilization theory, that some social movements cannot be adequately studied without attention to religion. Religious groups, like other organizations, can contribute leadership, monetary support, communication networks, and physical space to nascent social movements. Resource mobilization theorists explain the role of religious groups in social movements as organizations with resources to offer to the movement. Aldon Morris, for example, describes religious organizations like the Fellowship of Reconciliation as "halfway houses" for the civil rights movement, providing space, access to networks of activists, leadership, and other tangible supports in the movement's earliest stages, despite their own marginal roles relative to national political life.[10]

Despite its tremendous contributions to the study of religion and social movements, however, resource mobilization theory is also limited. For example, one critique is that the theory offers accounts for clearly defined, tangible resources contributed to social movements by religious persons or groups, but does not offer accounts for other categories of analysis with regard to social movements. How can we analyze the role of ideology, biographical narrative, collective identity or social psychol-

9. For examples of resource mobilization theory, see McCarthy and Zald, *Trend of Social Movements in America*; Morris, *Origins of the Civil Rights Movement*; Oberschall, "Mobilization, Leaders, and Followers in the Civil Rights Movement"; Zald and Ash, "Social Movement Organizations."

10. Morris, *Origins of the Civil Rights Movement*, 139–73.

ogy in social movements if we focus only on tangible resources contributed by clearly defined religious organizations? Similarly, resource mobilization theory does not equip us to address how participation in social movement activism affects religious persons or groups. These gaps in resource mobilization theory were addressed by the development of "New Social Movement" theory in the 1980s and 1990s.

New social movement theorists seek to account for these more fluid, cultural dimensions of social movements. "New social movement" theory is a somewhat misleading classification, because it relies upon a false division between older, class-based social movements for rights and more recent, identity-based social movements for cultural change. In other words, "new" social movements are thought to be less about immediately experienced social strains (such as discrimination or low wages) and more about broader cultural values (such as environmental protection or peace). Of course, this distinction falls apart when one examines, for example, the discrimination at the heart of the gay rights movement, which often is classified as a "new" social movement, or the cultural aspects such as modes of dress that supported the French Revolution. James Jasper, among other theorists, has pointed out that the contributions of new social movement theory toward understanding the cultural dimensions of social movements actually address gaps in theory that would enhance the analysis of *all* social movements, not just the most recent ones. Certainly a fuller picture can be painted of the civil rights movement if we attend to its cultural aspects, such as ritual, identity, ideology, and biographical narrative, both among its individual participants and among its constituent religious groups. Imagine the impossibility of describing the civil rights movement without attention to the significance of song and ritual within the movement!

In addition to legitimizing new categories of analysis for the study of social movements, new social movement theorists develop a more nuanced relationship of mutual influence between religion and social movements. In other words, identity becomes exponentially more complex when we think of it as more than a resource contributed to a movement by religious organizations. In relation to social movements, culture, which includes identity, is *both* a resource and an outcome. At the risk of oversimplifying the distinction, we find in traditional models of resource mobilization theory cultural elements explained in a static way, as a resource to be *used* by the social movement, rather than as dynamic phenomena which also are affected and even created by social movements.

New social movement theory holds that social movements both influence culture and produce their own cultures, which sometimes stand, even intentionally, in marked contrast to dominant cultures. Social movements produce what might be described as oppositional cultures, and participants in social movements find what they sometimes describe as great fulfillment in the oppositional character of these cultures. In some cases, social movements may even produce their own alternative cultural institutions, as was the case with the radical lesbian feminist movement in the 1980s.[11]

To put it mildly, the relationship between culture and social movements is rich with potential for thinking about religious practices of social action. James Jasper writes, "Culture and morality are important to me because they make life interesting and meaningful. Culture is unavoidable, but meaningful morality is often hard to come by . . . Protest movements are a good place to look for collective moral visions, with the good and the bad they entail. In modern society, they are one of the few places where we can see people working out new moral, emotional, and cognitive sensibilities."[12] Culture and morality, in relation to social movements, are what generate "lives worth living." They form a nexus where participants work out new moral, emotional, cognitive, and *theological* self-understandings. Below we turn, in more detail, to the construction of identity in social witness. Before doing so, however, it behooves us to note some of the methodological difficulties related to researching cultural dimensions of social movements.

A Methodological Note on the Cultural Aspects of Social Movements

Like the study of a practice, the study of the cultural aspects of social movements is both complex and ambiguous. Just as we asked, "What are we studying when we study a practice?," we also might ask, "What are we looking for when we look for the cultural aspects of a practice?" Confusion on this point is a result of two related issues with regard to so-

---

11. Taylor and Whittier, "Analytical Approaches," 170–71.

12. Jasper, *Art of Moral Protest*, xii–xiii.

cial movements and culture. First, what exactly do we mean by "culture"? Second, once we know what we mean by it, where do we find it?

As noted above in the brief tracing of developments in social movement theory, one might loosely categorize as cultural those elements of social movements ignored for a time by theoretical accounts: ideology, biography, emotion, aesthetics, personal relationships, and media. Cultural theory is a broad and inclusive scholarly tent, and merely naming, by way of family resemblance, those things about which scholars of culture might theorize hardly gives us a sharp definition. James Jasper suggests that the category of culture has become overextended and that scholars sometimes use it to account for too divergent a collection of social movement components.[13] In response to this problem, Jasper defines culture as "shared understandings (emotional, moral, and cognitive) and their embodiments."[14] Of course, the idea of shared understandings as a resource or component of social change shows us just how far we have moved from Marx's verdict that ideology is, in every case, a tool used to silence opposition.[15]

Even if we develop a clear and concrete definition of the cultural aspects of social movements, studying them still presents challenges. Jasper writes, "Cultural components . . . are not, foremost, physical things like resources (although they may be embodied physically). They are ideas and enthusiasms and sensitivities. Sometimes they are graciously explicit, but often they are implicit and subtle and difficult to measure, or even to observe clearly."[16] When we observe Christian activists as they engage in practices of social witness, or as we invite them to reflect upon their experience of participating in such practices, the reality of this methodological dilemma becomes palpable. What is culture, and into what are we digging when we study it? Further, on what level of analysis do we study culture? Are we speaking of broad, social values, ideas, and practices, on a macro-level? Or is culture understood on a closer, meso-level, residing within such organizations as congregations or presbytery groups? Or, finally, on a micro-level, are we looking for how individuals

---

13. In fact, Jasper does not include biography in the broad category of "culture," since it relates to the "inner, subjective world," rather than the intersubjective world of relationships. See ibid., 54–55.

14. Ibid., 44.

15. See, for example, Marx, *German Ideology.*

16. Jasper, *Art of Moral Protest,* 97.

are formed by and participate in the formation of culture? Of course, culture operates on all of these levels, but methodological questions like these clarify what level of cultural processes are at the root of any particular research question.

As Jasper notes, the promise and problem inherent in the analysis of culture is that it cannot be cordoned off and treated alongside other categories of analysis. Instead, it actually "consists of discrete, measurable items, but it is also a filter through which all action occurs."[17] In another effort to clarify some of these issues, Verta Taylor and Nancy Whittier organize the current study of culture and social movements into four broadly construed conceptual frameworks. They include: group development of emergent norms and interpretive frames in the process of defining issues of concern and goals; construction and maintenance of collective identity from the shared interests and experiences by which a group defines itself; the expression of solidarity and evocation of shared feelings in ritual; and the development of forms of discourse that articulate new symbolic codes in contrast to the texts of the dominant group discourse.[18]

Each of these ways of approaching culture in relation to social movements are ripe for further analysis. In service to our theoretical definition of social witness practice, let us focus upon the category of identity and particularly the production of identity in social witness. If we take Jasper's definition of culture as shared understandings and their embodiments, we can see how identity becomes central to the study of culture and social movements. Particularly in relation to religious groups, the shared worldviews and practices that express and shape these perspectives and values have everything to do with who practitioners understand themselves to be. Like other aspects of culture, however, identity is not easily studied. Nor is it easily defined. Jasper writes, "Identity is a tricky concept, often a crude label for a collection of other things. When possible, we must try to specify its content. It may include cognitive images of a collective actor, boundaries perceived or drawn among social groups, affective solidarities to certain abstract or concrete groups and individuals, moral institutions and principles, even tastes or styles of ac-

---

17. Ibid., xi.

18. Taylor and Whittier, "Analytical Approaches," 164–65.

tion. . . The term identity is a recognition that actions are filtered through some sense of self."[19]

The category of identity in social movement theory, Jasper argues, has been simultaneously overextended and limited. Like culture, it has been overextended in that it is a diffuse category, used to describe a motley assortment of attributes. At the same time, when social movement theorists *have* sought to define identity more clearly, they have limited identity to a particular way of *thinking* about the "self." Jasper points out that identity has been "often treated simply as a matter of cognitive boundaries," but that the study of identity requires a far more comprehensive view: "Emotions, morals, and cognition—embodied in practical know-how—are equally important components of culture."[20]

Into these complicated, multivalent self-understandings, these conceptions of identity, we now immerse ourselves, turning primarily to Jasper for elucidation.

James Jasper, Internal Goods, and the Construction of Identity in Social Action

Jasper makes plain his indebtedness to MacIntyre and the concept of internal goods for his theory of the creativity and artfulness of social movement outcomes. He uses MacIntyre's definition of social practices and, more specifically, MacIntyre's category of internal goods to describe the deep, internal satisfaction that protestors find in their practice. He writes, "In a way that eludes rationalistic models, we often engage in practices for their intrinsic rewards, the satisfaction of the activity itself, rather than for extrinsic rewards such as remuneration. This is one of the key ways that unpaid protestors regularly differ from the paid state and corporate spokespersons opposed to them."[21]

While Jasper draws heavily on MacIntyre, we should not rely too much on his interpretation of internal goods, since his description is a bit limited in places. In the citation above, Jasper uses "rewards" and "satisfaction" as if they are interchangeable with MacIntyre's "goods," which they are not. Furthermore, he introduces MacIntyre in a chapter entitled, "Culture and Biography: The Pleasures of Protest." For MacIntyre goods

19. Jasper, *Art of Moral Protest*, 90.

20. Ibid., 98.

21. Ibid., 219.

internal to practice are far broader and deeper than personal satisfaction. They have to do with the formation of virtue within practitioners and the enrichment of the "whole relevant community."[22] Just the same, Jasper develops such a complex account of identity that his theory bears deeper connections with MacIntyre's fullest sense of internal goods than he himself names.

Despite its complexity and the methodological challenges introduced by it, Jasper holds that we must, when possible, specify the content of identity. In what follows, I examine the levels upon which identity functions (personal, collective, and movement); the moments at which identity might appear in social action (recruitment, strategy, and outcome); and the kinds of identity that shape and are shaped by social witness (political and theological).

The Function, Appearance, and Character of Identity in Social Witness

Personal, Collective, and Movement Identity

Through their participation in social action, activists like those I met and those interviewed by Smith find that their understandings of themselves are challenged, deepened, and confirmed. These self-understandings are not simple and discrete categories, however. Practitioners of social witness understand themselves as individuals as well as members of a number of communities. In order to account for these varied levels of identity, Jasper identifies three divergent categories: personal, collective, and movement identity.[23] In every case, identity is not adequately theorized as a static resource contributed to a social movement; instead, as a cultural construction, it is negotiated in relationship to other persons, groups, and institutions. In other words, an activist is not always and everywhere the same. She changes according to her experiences, her relationships, and her position in social contexts. She experiences herself as an individual, as a participant in a social movement, and as a part of many other, more diffuse, groups.

Individual personal identities emerge from the biographies of participants, while movement identities are formed "when a collection of

22. MacIntyre, *After Virtue*, 191.
23. Jasper, *Art of Moral Protest*, 85–90.

groups and individuals perceive themselves (and are perceived by others) as a force in explicit pursuit of social change."[24] Finally, collective identities consist of "perceptions of group distinctiveness, boundaries, and interests, for something closer to a community than a category."[25] Collective identities find their sources in faith communities, civic organizations, political affiliations, neighborhoods, and families, to name only a few. An activist is simultaneously influenced by personal and biographical identity, movement identity, and any number of collective identities.

In the case of Christian social witness, with what kind of identity are we dealing? Using these three categories of identity, we can see how identity appears in some of the contemporary instantiations of social witness. Many participants in practices of social witness have long-standing personal identities that compel them to engage in such activities. These identities exhibit rootedness, but they also develop over time. As these activists continually engage in practices of social witness, their identities and commitments become more pronounced. Recall that Thurston Griggs, the Presbyterian activist, notes that his whole life has been affected by a number of forms of social witness, from his parents' activism in the temperance movement to his own work as a legislative advocate. Of course, Griggs did not come to this understanding of himself in a vacuum, but in relationship to numerous collectivities: his family, the church of his childhood and youth, the American Friends Service Committee, his present congregation, and the presbytery group with whom he now travels monthly to Washington. Each of these groups has its own history, set of practices, and worldviews that make up who they understand themselves to be.

Rev. John Fife tells a similar story about the development of his own self-understanding. When asked in an interview whether his work

24. Ibid., 86.

25. Ibid. Another new social movement theorist, David Snow, defines collective identity in this way:

"Although there is no universal definition of collective identity, discussions of the concept invariably suggest that its essence resides in a shared sense of 'one-ness' or 'we-ness' anchored in real or imagined shared attributes and experiences among those who comprise the collectivity and in relation or contrast to one or more actual or imagined sets of 'others.' Embedded within the shared sense of 'we' is a corresponding sense of 'collective agency.' This latter sense, which is the action component of collective identity, not only suggests the possibility of collective action in pursuit of common interests, but even invites such action." See Snow, *Collective Identity and Expressive Forms*.

in the 1970s with the denominational Mission Responsibility Through Investment committee helped shape his understanding of the Church's call to social justice and his later work with the Sanctuary movement, he responded:

> No, I think I came out of (Pittsburgh) seminary with that . . . Let's see, I was in seminary from '63 to '67—which is the guts of the civil rights movement . . . And then, from '67 to '70, . . . my first job out of seminary was just doing street ministry. They had three of us. Seven big downtown cathedral churches of different denominations hired three of us to just work the streets in the community around them and begin to relate them to what was going on . . . So, my first job out of seminary was to organize African-American and Appalachian communities in there. And be on the streets. And that was a better education than seminary.

Fife's relationships with a series of communities—seminary, the downtown churches of Pittsburgh, the neighborhoods in downtown Pittsburgh, the Presbyterian denomination, and, finally, Southside Presbyterian Church and the larger community of Tucson, Arizona—expressed and shaped his developing identity as a Christian activist. Some of these communities were themselves involved in social movements, and sometimes Fife participated as an individual in social movements, such as the time he marched from Selma to Montgomery in 1965. In sum, discrete social movements, as well as communities that supported or participated in them, influenced his identity.

John Fife's life history is an illustration of what Christian Smith describes as a significant outcome of social movements: the formation of activist identities.[26] Furthermore, movements construct their own identities in the place where internal movement culture and the broader culture intersect.[27] When we are talking about Christian activists, the distinction between personal, collective, and movement identity is not always clear. Especially in the case of the Sanctuary movement, the very mission of the movement was, from the perspective of the members of Southside Presbyterian, a Christian imperative and thus associated with collective identity. Christian Smith describes the religious identity of the Sanctuary movement in the following way: "The group, excited now,

---

26. In his research for *Resisting Reagan*, Christian Smith also interviewed John Fife, an interview subject for this study. Smith, *Resisting Reagan*, 372.

27. Jasper, *Art of Moral Protest*, 86–87.

then had the idea of declaring Southside Presbyterian a sanctuary for refugees. The ancient Hebrews, Fife remembered, declared entire cities sanctuaries of refuge for accused criminals."[28]

Personal, collective, and movement identity are all relevant to our definition of social witness. The categories introduced by Jasper shed some light on our definition, however. Recall that our definition claims that social witness practice has "the capacity to generate among participants internal goods related to their identity and faith formation." MacIntyre's theory accounts for the development of *collective* identity via social practices within the context of institutions and *personal* identity insofar as it is derived from the collective identity embodied in practices and tradition. But when we consider the case of Christian social witness, we find that individuals may also connect with a *movement* identity, characterized by the pursuit of social change, sometimes apart from aspects of their collective religious identities. Thurston Griggs, for example, describes himself as somewhat isolated within his own congregation in his concern for social justice. At the same time, he has found another religious community and source of collective identity in the presbytery group, which shares his commitments to social justice.

In the end, we return to the production of identity as the key category for construing identity in our definition. In other words, the self-understandings of activists are not wholly formed before they engage in social witness practice. Their participation in social witness also forms identity in all three arenas: personal, collective, and movement. Here is a key point: while movement identity is certainly a product of Christian social witness insofar as Christian activists bring their collective religious commitments with them as they participate in social movements, it is not the identity at the heart of our questions. Movement identity is tied specifically to a particular social movement and its specific goals and strategies. It does not transfer intact to personal and collective identity. *Instead, we want to know how practices of social witness impact Christian activists* qua *Christians, both personally and collectively.* The salutary point of theological reflection in witness practice, for example, is to equip participants to enter into the practice more deeply and consciously. In this project, identity works hand in hand with faith formation. Without suggesting that movement identity and broader culture are irrelevant, the production of religious personal and collective identity is at the fore.

28. Smith, *Resisting Reagan*, 66–67.

Identity and Movement Recruitment, Strategies, and Outcomes

Much ink has been spilled on the question of how and where identity appears in social movements. In addition to classifying identity according to its personal, collective, and movement instantiations, we also ask: is identity that which prepares us for, and predisposes us to, the practice of social witness? Is identity the source upon which we draw *as* we practice social witness, or is it constructed in our practice of social witness? While our definition is attentive to the construction of identity in social witness, the honest answer to these questions is, of course, "yes." In the pages that follow, let us examine how identity appears and functions in recruitment to social action, the development of goals and strategies, and the outcomes in the life of a social movement. Along the way, we will see clearly that identity and movement participation mutually reinforce one another as evidenced in the stories of activists and in the theoretical literature.

Recruitment

First, we are open to recruitment by social movements because we hold particular comprehensive self-understandings that predispose us to these sorts of practices. For example, Presbyterian elder Ellen Tharp describes how she was recruited into the nascent peace movement during World War II:

> I had already been a little bit influenced to have rather strong pacifist tendencies, I think, from a youth minister from our church. . . . (T)he minister hired a young man who was going through Garrett seminary, which is a Methodist seminary there, who had grown up as Church of the Brethren, and he had rather strong pacifist thinking. And so in high school, he was in charge of the youth group at church, and I think I was strongly influenced by him. So that in college, as the war was kind of looming I remember having strong feelings, and we used to discuss it a lot there.

Tharp's story illustrates the decidedly not-neat narratives that activists tell about how their self-understandings contribute to their recruitment into social action. We find in such narratives a number of relational and experiential influences that reveal an extra-rational dimension to social action recruitment. Jasper challenges resource mobilization theory and the political process model in their tacit assumption that "protest emerges out of clear structural positions." He goes on to say that protest often emerges simply out of a sometimes vaguely-defined "shared vision."[29] As it relates to collective religious identity, this shared vision is influenced by relationships and experiences like those described by Tharp, as well as by other practices such as acts of charity and worship.

When, in the 1980s, the time came for Southside Presbyterian to discern whether or not they would join the Sanctuary movement, the collective identity of that congregation influenced their decisions in important ways. When asked if the proposal to act as sanctuary to Central American refugees—illegally—was met with much resistance, John Fife says:

> No, but that was due to the refugees themselves. We started by doing a legal aid project, trying to help people apply for politi-cal asylum who were in detention centers. And when we bonded them out, they stayed in the church or they stayed with people in the church and they came to worship, and we asked them to tell their story, in worship. So, over a year, a year-and-half's period of time, people got connected with their suffering—and it was compelling. It's just compelling. And so, when the question of Sanctuary came up, we took a vote—we did a secret ballot, so nobody felt coerced. And people had to vote, really, what their faith indicated to them. And there were only two negative votes in the whole congregation . . . It blew my socks off.

The members of Southside Presbyterian did not arrive at the decision to become a sanctuary congregation based only on rational deduction or political goals. Over time, that congregation had developed a shared nar-rative comprised of relationships with refugees, corporate worship expe-rience, encounters with the suffering of refugees, and a changing political situation. All of these factors informed the congregation's shared vision and its work together; it also predisposed them to take the next step and co-found the Sanctuary movement. This identity would continue to be an operative force in the goals and strategies that the congregation would develop as their work in the sanctuary movement continued.

GOALS AND STRATEGIES

Just as identity contributes to the recruitment of activists, it contributes to the activities and ideas that develop within the movement, too. The

29. Jasper, *Art of Moral Protest*, 89.

numerous influences in the construction of identity exert similar influence in the construction of a social movement's goals and strategies for action. Furthermore, some of the work of participants in a social movement is devoted to constructing and maintaining a coherent shared identity. Identity is, at the same time, a resource for the work of social movements as well as partial content for the work of social movements.

Christian Smith argues that religion is advantageous to social movements in its provision of identities: "Religion, as a pre-existing collective identity that can be conferred upon or coopted by a movement, represents a valuable resource for the task of collective identity construction and maintenance."[30] Smith claims that an essential task of social movements is the construction and maintenance of "collective identities that signify to themselves and the world who they are, what they stand for, and what kind of society they hope to create."[31] When religious participants bring their shared visions and experience to social movements, these serve as resources for the construction of a new movement identity.

The personal identities brought by participants, together with the identities being constructed within the movement, serve as resources for movement goals and tactics. For example, some scholars have noted that religious activists participate in the peace movement in a peculiar way. In his essay, "The Political Behavior of Faith-Based and Secular Peace Groups," Ron Pagnucco focuses on the tactics of faith-based peace groups, finding that "faith-based peace movement organizations, because of their religious identities and moral claims, are more likely than secular PMOs (peace movement organizations) not to use conventional tactics of political bargaining, but to use more unconventional, unruly tactics of 'moral witness.'"[32] While Pagnucco's study reveals different tactics than the ones under consideration here, the connection that he draws between the religious identity of the groups in question and their strategies fits with the claim that personal identity, movement identity, and movement activities influence each other.

In addition to preexistent identities, religious groups may also provide ritual and symbolic resources that support and shape movement activities, thus contributing to the construction of movement

---

30. Smith, "Correcting a Curious Neglect," 17.

31. Ibid.

32. Pagnucco, "Political Behavior," 210.

identity. Jasper writes, "Collective rites remind participants of their basic moral commitments, stir up strong emotions, and reinforce a sense of solidarity with the group, a 'we-ness.' . . . In many forms, rituals are vital mechanisms keeping protest movements alive and well. They pull together, in an emotional format, many of a movement's cultural processes. They not only reinforce pre-existing feelings, but help to construct new ones . . . (They) finally are a crucial component of what we will examine in this chapter: the collective emotions and identities generated within a movement."[33] In practice, ritual continues to function in social movements in much the same way as it does in worship. It both shapes and expresses who we are. Rituals generate identity. Participants in social movements and their rituals describe how their perceptions of themselves were changed beyond their participation in the movement. The rituals also create movement identity, which becomes a resource for the continued vitality of the movement.

Another manner in which identity forms and is formed by social movements is in the development of discourse. By necessity, social witness is a highly verbal practice. Activists use nonverbal communication in their work for social change, but this must be accompanied by discourse with political and governmental figures, business leaders, and other persons and groups who share their concerns. In the process of this discourse, identities are both expressed and shaped, just as they are in the employment of ritual in social action. In *Faithful and Fearless*, Mary Fainsod Katzenstein describes the discursive route taken by feminists seeking to alter the identity and status of women in the American Roman Catholic Church in the last quarter of the twentieth century.[34] When the institutional choices for handling dissent are presented as a polarization between loyalty to the institution and exit from it, claiming voice within and in relation to the institution represents activism, she argues.[35] By discursive politics, Katzenstein means "the politics of reflection and reformulation. Much of this politics involves words and images."[36] Activists seek to infuse the Catholic Church with resources drawn from their collective identity as feminists, and their work, via symbol and text, also shapes their identity: "(O)ne must understand

33. Jasper, *Art of Moral Protest*, 184–85.
34. Katzenstein, *Faithful and Fearless*, 107.
35. Ibid., 134.
36. Ibid., 107.

both opportunities for activism and the sources of identity-formation that shape what feminist activists imagine for themselves."[37]

While Katzenstein's analysis is of a discursive activism *within* a religious institution, her definitions are relevant to religious social witness in the larger political and structural context as well. In the imaginative work of feminist discourse, activists both challenge oppressive structures and generate new self-understandings. In Katzenstein's model of discursive activism, identity mobilizes activists, contributes to the formulation of strategic discourse, and is *created* anew as the imaginative work of discourse shapes the practitioners as well as the broader context. In the case of discourse alone, we can see the interdependence of different types of identity and different stages of a social movement.

Similarly, above, I quoted two of Christian Smith's interview subjects, Mark and Phyllis, who reflected on how their lives were changed, transformed even, by their work with the Central American peace movement. Their self-understandings were radically altered by their experience of witness. It is important to remember, however, that while some practitioners admit that they brought very few ideas about the connections between faith and activism, most participants in the Central American peace movement brought with them certain commitments to justice, peace, economic rights, and welcoming the stranger. These commitments were galvanized and given further content and embodiment in these practices of witness.

Outcomes

To conclude this section, let us turn to the construction of identity as the final point in this analysis of the appearance and function of identity within social action. Just as collective and personal identities help to birth social movements, and rituals and discourse function to construct and maintain movement identity as a resource, social movements also function to generate long-lasting effects upon personal and collective identities. Identity is an outcome of social movements.

In fact, Jasper writes, protest is a "rich breeding ground for new understandings of the world and new patterns for action. Learning . . . lies at the heart of social movements."[38] In another essay written with Francesca

---

37. Ibid., 134.

38. Jasper, *Art of Moral Protest*, 98.

Polletta, Jasper posits, among other things, that changing identities is often a movement goal, that participants' identities are in fact changed in social movements, and that changed identities may bear long-term impacts on the cultural and political terrain.[39]

How are participants in social witness impacted and benefited by their engagement? The way in which I have sketched the relationship between identity and social witness above challenges the order of influence as it traditionally has been worked out in research on both religious identity and identity and social movements. It seems that in much of that literature, when collective identity is considered in relationship to practice, ideology and religious belief are are construed in a somewhat simplistic causal relationship to identity and religious practices. This happens particularly when identity is construed in an excessively cognitive way, as Jasper describes, and is closely associated with belief. At the risk of oversimplifying this formula, I will describe it in this way: We assent to a particular ideology, which forms our identity, which then determines our practice.[40] This way of understanding identity continues to carry explanatory power. Literature on the theory of practice, however, paints a slightly different picture: while identity surely bears influence on how we act in a particular community or in the world, the reverse is also true. Participation in practices actually influences identity. We are changed by what we *do*, not only by what we believe. Furthermore, what we do also changes what we believe. Due to practices' power in this regard, theorists from diverse perspectives study this aspect of practice with varying degrees of suspicion and admiration. Some laud the power of practice to create moral persons, deeply faithful religious communities, and the good society.[41] Others are wary of the dominant class wielding the extra-cognitive power of practice to maintain unjust power

---

39. Jasper and Polletta, "Collective Identity and Social Movements," 296–97.

40. See, for example, Carroll and Roozen, "Congregational Identities"; Peek, Konty, and Frazier, "Religion and Ideological Support for Social Movements." This may be a legacy of Geertz and his use of symbol in interpreting "meaning." James Jasper and Nancy Ammerman have complexified the relationship between practice and identity in interesting ways that will be taken up later in the proposal. See Ammerman et al., *Studying Congregations*; Jasper and Polletta, "Collective Identity and Social Movements."

41. See, for example, Bellah, *Habits of the Heart*; Bass and Dykstra, "Theological Understanding"; MacIntyre, *After Virtue*.

structures.[42] In both cases, we might imagine ways in which the *practice* of social witness forms identity, both personally and collectively.

Formation of Political and Theological Identity in Social Witness

In conclusion, let us examine the kind of identity that is constructed in the practice of social witness. More specifically, let us explore how the formation of identity matches MacIntyre's "discovery of the good of a certain kind of life."[43] The discovery of a certain kind of life casts new light on what constitutes movement success. Barbara Epstein writes that the success of the peace movement, especially for religious participants, might best be measured according to changes in personal and collective identity: "Unlike the more conventional wing of the movement, which was most concerned with bringing about immediate changes in policy, the direct action movement wanted to change public attitudes, and it wanted to create a community within which activists could *change their ways of thinking and of living, and which could serve as a magnet to others, a living demonstration of alternatives.* Judged by these standards, the direct action movement was often quite successful."[44]

In what way might activists' ways of living and thinking be changed? Of what alternatives might their practice be a living demonstration? We might identify two dimensions of life that are often described as being transformed via social witness practice: political life and theological life. Transformation of political and theological identity is often named as an outcome of social movements. In the context of religious practice, the outcome of changed identity can be described as a significant good attained within the practice of social witness.

For many activists, part of what is created in their participation in a social movement is the awakening and development of what Christian Smith describes as an "insurgent consciousness," formed when movement participants judge unjust circumstances in relation to a moral *telos* of how the world ought to be. In the case of the United States' exacerbating role in the Central American crisis of the 1980s, Smith writes that the situation "was so noxious, so morally reprehensible, so contrary to their

42. Bourdieu, *Logic of Practice.*
43. MacIntyre, *After Virtue*, 190.
44. Epstein, "Politics of Moral Witness," 109.

convictions that they felt compelled to mobilize a political movement to stop these things from happening."[45] John Fife describes how personal interactions with Central American refugees instilled in members of Southside Presbyterian a willingness to confront, even at the risk of imprisonment, political structures. Their legal aid work with the refugees in the months preceding the inauguration of the sanctuary movement created in that community a new collective self-understanding: "So, over a year, a year-and-half's period of time, people got connected with their suffering—and it was compelling." Sanctuary was born.

Southside's experience of being compelled to political action illustrates Smith's description of insurgent consciousness. Smith writes, "But absolutely nothing ignited in United States citizens the fierce insurgent consciousness for activism more than personal encounters with the traumatized victims of the United States-sponsored war in Central America."[46] This growing political self-understanding informs persons and groups as they participate in social movements, with the cumulative effect of creating "activist identities" which live long after movement participation has ended, perpetuated by subsequent activism.[47] Smith argues that individuals gripped by insurgent consciousness are likely to embrace the longer-term activist identity, as well.

Southside Presbyterian Church's story is not fully told by recounting stories of individuals who developed activist identities, however. The congregation also developed a collective identity that reflected the "we-ness" of a congregation who welcomed strangers, who sheltered the homeless, and who spoke a risky truth to the federal government. For James Jasper, the development of individual identities does not tell the full story. While activists may pursue "lives worth living" personally, they also pursue it collectively. Jasper, once again appealing to MacIntyre, writes, "MacIntyre insists that humans face two fundamental moral questions: What is the good for me, and what is the good for humankind? And he asserts that 'it is the systematic asking of these two questions and the attempt to answer them in deed as well as in word which provide the moral life with its unity.'"[48] Jasper describes lives worth living in terms that reach beyond Smith's activist identity. He describes the reflection

45. Smith, *Resisting Reagan*, 134.

46. Ibid., 151.

47. Ibid., 372–73.

48. Jasper, *Art of Moral Protest*, 338–39.

upon the individual and common good as what gives shape to the moral life. When Christian activists seek to make sense of their lives, reflection upon political identity is surely a part. But how does the practice of social witness also impact theological identity? We find activists like Ellen Tharp, whose prohibition-movement parents taught her that "religion was the way you dealt with these things." And we also find activists like John Fife, who name the centrality of corporate worship as a lifeline to social action.

But what would we be able to say about the creation of new theological identities in social witness if we took seriously the role of theological reflection throughout the practice? What if we reflected upon ourselves as caught up in the same web of sin as those structures we seek to change? What if we reflected upon Christian hope in the imagination of an already-but-not-yet "alternative future," to use Jürgen Moltmann's phrase? To these theological questions, we now turn.

PART TWO

Theological Perspectives on Social Witness: Sin, Hope, and Social Change

In sovereign love God created the world good
    and makes everyone equally in God's image,
        male and female, of every race and people,
    to live as one community
But we rebel against God; we hide from our Creator.
    Ignoring God's commandments,
    we violate the image of God in others and ourselves,
    accept lies as truth,
    exploit neighbor and nature,
    and threaten death to the planet entrusted to our care.
    We deserve God's condemnation.
Yet God acts with justice and mercy to redeem creation.

. . . Loving us still,
    God makes us heirs with Christ of the covenant.
Like a mother who will not forsake her nursing child,
like a father who runs to welcome the prodigal home,
    God is faithful still.

. . . In a broken and fearful world
the Spirit gives us courage
    to pray without ceasing,
    to witness among all peoples to Christ as Lord and Savior,
    to unmask idolatries in Church and culture,
    to hear the voices of peoples long silenced,
    and to work with others for justice, freedom, and peace.
In gratitude to God, empowered by the Spirit,
    we strive to serve Christ in our daily tasks
        and to live holy and joyful lives,
    even as we watch for a new heaven and new earth,
        praying, "Come, Lord Jesus!"[1]

1. Presbyterian Church (U.S.A.), "Brief Statement of Faith," 10.3–4.

"Bound Together in a Delicate Network of Interdependence"

The Complicated Character of Social Life

In the Brief Statement of Faith, like in so many other confessions in the Reformed tradition, the role of sin in human life and society is juxtaposed alongside work toward, and anticipation of, the coming of a new heaven and new earth. In its brevity, this particular confession expresses in sharp relief what Reinhold Niebuhr called the paradox of the Christian life.[1] In one and the same moment, we are both bound and free, both sinful and hopeful. Our lives are defined by our unlimited capacity for sin and by God's unlimited capacity for grace and peace. At every turn, human life is shaped by a dual reality of sin and hope. When we view this dual reality in terms of its social implications, as does the Brief Statement of Faith, we recognize its influence in our efforts toward social change. In light of this influence, the following two chapters take up the relationship between sin and hope as well as the relationship of sin and hope to social change.

Before taking these two aspects of theology on their own terms, however, let us examine how they together shape both the context in which social witness is practiced and its form. Together, sin and hope emerge out of the depths of an inarticulable complexity, depths of complexity that in the same moment give rise to powerful connectedness and vast, knotty systems of suffering. As Desmond Tutu put it, "(W)e are indeed members of one family, bound together in a delicate network of interdependence."[2] This delicate network of interdependence bears within it both great promise for connectedness and great peril for sin and suffering. The connectedness itself is the way that the world and the world's relationship to God are structured. That structure can either exacerbate suffering or communicate grace.

1. Niebuhr, *Nature and Destiny*.
2. Tutu, *No Future Without Forgiveness*, 274.

Sometimes, the increasing frustration of activists is almost palpable as they encounter new sources of injustice, new resistance to change, and new iterations of the same old stories. The brokenness of the world seems to have a life of its own, and despite sincere human striving, situations of injustice and suffering sometimes get worse, not better. The seemingly insurmountable character of social evil leads even the most committed activists to frustration, and sometimes weariness, fatigue, or even numbness.

In the face of these realities, we might ask, Is this what God truly intends? To this question, Walter Brueggemann offers an emphatic "no!" In the introduction, we encountered Brueggemann's argument for the development of prophetic imagination, by which Christians expose the "deathliness" of dominant culture *and* imagine new forms of community.[3] The message of both the prophets and Jesus is this: things have gone wrong, and in contrast, we are to direct the work of our lives toward a different future, which God promises and brings about and in which God invites us to participate. It is in this contrast that social witness takes place.

According to Brueggemann, the voice of the dominant community works to numb human consciousness, a numbness that we accept in the interest of avoiding painful confrontations with death and suffering. The role of the prophetic community, however, is to reject the structures as they are, its critical task being to break through the untruths of the dominant community. Brueggemann also points out that this new alternative community has a "variety of relationships with the dominant community."[4] The relationship seems at points to be defined almost entirely contrarily. The new social order imagined is, for Brueggemann, everything that the current social order is not. The mistake of liberals, he argues, is that they accept the current structures, assuming that the new creation promised will entail "merely a moving of the pieces into a new pattern."[5]

If we place Brueggemann in conversation with other theological descriptions of the structure of human life and its relationship to God, we find a more complex portrait of the relationship between dominant

3. For a helpful summary of Brueggemann's argument, see Brueggemann, *Prophetic Imagination*, 115–16.

4. Ibid., 117.

5. Ibid., 14.

structures of sin and the new life promised by God. In some variations of process theology, for example, we read that the way that things "ought to be" is, in fact, the way that they structurally already *are*. While Brueggemann concentrates on the "not yet" dimension of the new reality, scholars in process theology see the "alreadiness" of new realities resident in the interwoven shape of life.[6] Instead of understanding current reality as being in wholly contrary relationship to the new, promised reality, process theologians describe alternative futures in ironic relationship to current structures. The connectedness that gives rise to immense and compounded injustice and suffering is the very same connectedness by which creation is meant to flourish. God already has structured life on earth in an interdependent manner, so that one person's flourishing is tied to another's flourishing, and an injury to one is an injury to all.

In her book, *Fall to Violence: Original Sin in Relational Theology,* Marjorie Suchocki writes, "We presume that the influence of God is toward interrelated communities of well-being. Violations of well-being most certainly occur, and these violations constitute a rebellion against the well-being of the world."[7] Suchocki describes a God whose greatest hope for creation is that it be intricately woven together in a structure of interdependence that cooperates toward visions of human flourishing.

The concept of interdependence and its role in social structures, while clearly central to process theology, is not a new idea. It is reminiscent, for example, of another twentieth century theological ethicist, Dr. Martin Luther King, Jr., who so famously exhorted listeners to brotherhood: "We must all learn to live together as brothers. Or we will all perish together as fools. We are tied together in the single garment of destiny, caught in an inescapable network of mutuality. And whatever affects one directly affects all directly. . . This is the way God's universe is made; this is the way it is structured."[8] These words from King would res-

6. This distinction, in fact, may be one of the more significant breaks between process and Reformed theology. To anticipate a coming new creation that is, in some respects, unimaginable reflects Reformed theology's traditional emphases on God's mystery and transcendence. To anticipate a coming new creation that is, in some respects, already visible in the world reflects process theology's characteristic emphases on God's immanence. Of course, both schools of thought contain the full spectrum of the doctrine of God, but perhaps this distinction in emphasis reveals possibilities in how the two families might complement one another. In this project, process theology serves as a corrective conversation partner to the broadly construed Reformed tradition.

7. Suchocki, *Fall to Violence*, 60.

8. King, "Remaining Awake," 269.

onate, some 20 years later, in one of the greatest human rights struggles of our time: the defeat of apartheid in South Africa. In his reflections on the experience of apartheid in South Africa and the resulting Truth and Reconciliation Commission, Desmond Tutu describes the African concept of *ubuntu* as central to the work of social reconciliation: "To work for reconciliation is to want to realize God's dream for humanity—when we will *know* that we are indeed members of one family, bound together in a delicate network of interdependence."[9] In *No Future Without Forgiveness*, Tutu does not describe God's dream for humanity as that social structure in which we *will be* bound together by networks of interdependence, but as the situation in which humanity *recognizes* that this is already the case. To recognize *ubuntu*, Tutu writes, "is to say, 'My humanity is caught up, is inextricably bound up, in yours.' We belong in a bundle of life . . . Harmony, friendliness, community are great goods. Social harmony is for us the summum bonum—the greatest good . . . What dehumanizes you inexorably dehumanizes me."[10]

This theme of interdependence and its implications for the complex shape of sin has deep roots in the Reformed tradition, as well. Friedrich Schleiermacher famously described the root of Christian faith as "God-consciousness," or the religious awareness of God, the perfection of which is constant communion with and dependence upon God. Christian piety is marked by this God-consciousness and involves the whole person—feeling, knowing, and doing. We are in relationship with God, and our consciousness of this relationship is what makes us unique creatures. In our self-consciousness, we recognize the character of human life as dependent and free, a recognition that induces in human consciousness a sense of reciprocity between the self and the world. The feeling of *absolute* dependence, however, is reserved for the human-divine relationship experienced via God-consciousness.[11]

This framework, which Schleiermacher develops at the beginning of *The Christian Faith*, is central to our discussion here and to many subsequent incarnations of liberal, open, and relational theologies. We might identify three major contributions in Schleiermacher's framework that make him a fine Reformed conversation partner for process theologians like Marjorie Suchocki. Likewise, these contributions are central to

9. Tutu, *No Future Without Forgiveness*, 274. Emphasis mine.

10. Ibid., 31.

11. Schleiermacher, *Christian Faith*, §4.4.

assumptions of interdependence upon which the two following chapters are constructed.

First, Schleiermacher describes the development of the God-consciousness in *relational* terms. As the God-consciousness develops and advances, it moves us *toward* God, toward the perfection of the God-consciousness, which is constant communion with God. We have seen the perfection of the God-consciousness in the person of Jesus Christ. At the same time, when the development of God-consciousness is arrested, we are further alienated from God. We call this condition of alienation "sin."[12] Both sin and hope for a new life are thus rooted in humanity's relative relationship to God.

Second, the God-consciousness drives us to seek *fellowship* with other persons who recognize the experience of absolute dependence. In this fellowship, which comes to expression as "Church," we find "an ever self-renewing circulation of the religious self-consciousness."[13] We need these communities in order to express faith. Redemption and reconciliation are achieved wholly through the new, divinely-effected corporate life of blessedness, which stands in contrast to the corporate life of sin.[14] In these communities of fellowship, we strive together toward God's alternative future, the *basileia tou theou*, in which God establishes just relationships of power which make possible the flourishing of all.

Finally, even apart from the God-consciousness, Schleiermacher identifies the antitheses of *dependence and freedom* as constitutive of human life in relationship to others. He describes the human situation of existence and co-existence in this way: "For we have a feeling of freedom (though, indeed, a limited one) in relation to the world, since we are complementary parts of it."[15] As Walter Wyman has helpfully interpreted, "That is, the self-world relationship is a reciprocal relationship of activity and receptivity: the self can act to some extent upon the world, and the world influences the receptive self."[16] Human relationships with the world are marked by both freedom and dependence, a characterization that might be described fairly as a condition of *interdependence*. This condition of interdependence, as noted above, means that we might

12. Ibid., §63.

13. Ibid., §6.4.

14. Ibid., §87.

15. Ibid., §4.4.

16. Wyman, "Sin and Redemption," 131.

act upon the world in ways that either encourage or inhibit *eudaimonia,* and that our own flourishing is also influenced by the world.

Indeed, even in our striving and watching, we are "bound together in a delicate network of interdependence."[17] All of life should be understood as bound together, as if in a web. The web is sturdy, and very strong strands connect those things held by it. At the same time, the web can become tangled, in which case its strength becomes constricting, even deadly, instead of supportive and life-giving. In this context of a web of interdependence, with the dimensions of sin and hope that give it shape, we reflect upon the practice of social witness.

17. Tutu, *No Future Without Forgiveness,* 274.

4

Entangled in the Curse

Sin and Social Action

FOR CHRISTIAN ACTIVISTS, AND PERHAPS EVEN MORE SO FOR *PRESBY-terian* Christian activists, the pervasiveness of sin is never far from consciousness. The vulnerable suffer as a result of human sin. When human greed results in the exploitation of entire groups of persons, when a brutal dictator orders the torture of outspoken citizens, when a sex trafficker dupes young and desperate teenage girls with promises of economic security for themselves and their families . . . when these things happen, we are quite comfortable naming greed, torture, and exploitation as sin. In such cases, the connection between sin and suffering is immediate. Sin is a clear and compelling theological category for describing these situations.

In other contexts, however, the connection may be more ambiguous. Where exactly is the sin in poverty, in political unrest, in insufficient healthcare? The complexity of human suffering, human sin, and human agency makes sin difficult to sift out and examine. The assignation of blame becomes exponentially ambiguous when we consider the stockholder in the company raking in profits on the backs of exploited workers, the initiation of military action against an oppressive regime, or a sexualized culture in which even children are learning the economic value of exploiting their bodies.

In part, this is due to the structures of interdependence outlined in the beginning of Part Two. My actions affect the lives of others, and the actions of others shape me. The situation is complicated further by the fact that, by purchasing certain products or eating a certain kind of fish, I unknowingly contribute to systems that result in harm to another person or the earth. How can my consumption of a taco implicate me in a web of sin?

97

If the practice of social witness is, as described above, meant explicitly and intentionally to confront social and political systems that inhibit *eudaimonia*, then the theological orientations of such a practice must have some way to account for the myriad ways in which this inhibition takes place as well as the myriad ways in which we seem unable to change it. A theology of sin that takes seriously the interconnectedness of creation teaches us that we can, in fact, be unwittingly implicated in this web of sin, even through the seemingly most mundane of activities. Sometimes, a spider's prey may not fully understand the vastness of the web into which it has flown. One of the great contributions made by Reformed theologians toward understanding such ignorance resides in its stubborn insistence that sin always surrounds and infects us. Contemporary feminist and process theologies augment this substantial doctrine of sin with complex accounts of power and violence.[1]

Sin and the Practice of Social Witness

The practice of social witness needs a healthy theology of sin that elucidates its complicated and stubborn context, as well as the inner workings and limitations of its practitioners. It needs this theology because a healthy and complex doctrine of sin can serve as a source of freedom in practice, so that we are not bound by expectations of perfection. This freedom is further supported by a strong theology of grace and hope, by which we recognize God's work for good in the world, work into which we are invited to participate.

Practitioners of social witness seek to confront and change those structures that inhibit *eudaimonia*, but they themselves are bound by these structures. The focus of this chapter will be on sin as those aspects of the web of interdependence that cause or perpetuate harm.[2] This injurious dimension of the web of interdependence is what social justice ac-

---

1. Of course, the relationship between feminist, process and Reformed theology cannot be described as entirely harmonious, particularly when it comes to the doctrine of sin. I take up some of these challenges below.

2. It is important to note that I am not arguing that my definition of sin as that which causes harm should be understood as an identification of the root of all sin. Many a theologian has sought the universal aspect of sin, only to be challenged later by all that is left out of these supposedly universal descriptions. For our purposes, I am here proposing *a* definition of sin that is particularly relevant to the practice of social witness. While it might, in fact, be far more generalizable, I have phrased this definition in a way that is particular to social witness practice.

tivists seek to change and in which they are, at the same time, entangled. A few implications of this way of understanding sin will become apparent in the pages that follow, but here just receive preliminary comment.

First, I define sin as the causation or perpetuation of harm, in conversation with feminist amendments of traditional doctrinal understandings of sin. I also describe sin as both act and condition, drawing on classical theological formulations and contemporary critiques. While sin is easily identified with those things that we do or fail to do, we also need an accounting of how the condition of sin so binds us that we cannot help but participate in structures of sin, even unwittingly. To describe sin as an *aspect* of the web of interdependence means that sin is far broader, more ambiguous, and more constitutive of the human context than any one particular action. In the second section, I examine how sin shapes the context in which activists work, the issues they seek to change and the limitations of human action. A healthy doctrine of sin in the context of interdependence can help us to reflect theologically upon the complexity of structures of sin, as well as human complicity in these complex structures. The chapter concludes with a challenging question: if, indeed, sin so totally conditions the human experience, then why and how should we act at all? What is left to say about human agency if sin so completely binds us?

The proposed theology of sin here employed in relation to the practice of social witness is largely informed by the work of Friedrich Schleiermacher, Marjorie Suchocki, and Serene Jones. Along the way, I will introduce other important voices on these questions, but these three will guide our path. The many reasons for these choices will become evident in the coming pages, but I will note a few reasons at the outset. As noted in the preceding pages, Schleiermacher and Suchocki are helpful to us in conceiving creation as an interdependent, interrelated web as well as the implications of this description for theologies of sin. Suchocki is indebted to Schleiermacher's concepts of God-consciousness and absolute dependence as sources for her own thesis that humanity and creation are woven together in interdependence.[3] All three scholars also help us to reconsider what we mean when we describe sin as the "human condition," giving it a complex social meaning that traditional doctrines of original sin sometimes miss. Finally, they all offer resources for examining how, despite "entanglement" in the human condition of

3. Suchocki, *Fall to Violence*, 85–89.

sin, the spiritual freedom of humanity allows us to transcend ourselves both to recognize this entanglement and to strive for the good, for God's aims for creation.

Getting a Grip: Defining Sin

One need not be a genius or sage to know that all is not well with the world. Nightly, we are barraged with video footage and sometimes even live images of incomprehensible suffering, violence, and hatred. Some of these images come from far away, thus seeming removed from us. Some of the images come from across town, however, and still seem removed from us because they appear from within the same distant medium—television. Even when we are touched by otherwise distant suffering, what is the emotional and moral shape of that encounter? We might feel sympathy (perhaps even empathy), pity, righteous anger or helplessness. But do we feel responsible, culpable, or even guilty? Why should we feel these things, as innocent bystanders in the global tragic drama? In an interdependent world, however, these circumstances do have something to do with *us* in the broad sense (meaning humanity) and even in the more narrow sense (meaning that *I* somehow may be responsible for this suffering).

We need a theology of sin complex and strong enough to sustain social witness in the face of stubborn and tangled systems of suffering. Given the pervasive character of social suffering and social evil, we must now ask ourselves: what is this thing called sin? Looking back at my description of sin—"those aspects of the web of interdependence that cause or perpetuate harm"—we can find three useful theological categories introduced therein. First, we see again the centrality of the "web of interdependence." In the pages above, I described in detail the theological and social significance of that image. Within this web of interdependence, sin operates as those aspects that cause or perpetuate harm, introducing two additional important categories for thinking about sin. First, sin is that which causes or perpetuates *harm*. Naming harm as the content of sin requires a reexamination of traditional Reformed commitments that define sin *entirely* under the rubric of rebellion against God. In the following pages, I explore how harm constitutes a sort of "living against God," to borrow a phrase from Reformed feminist theologian Serene

Jones.[4] Second, sin is described as *aspects* of the web of interdependence. In other words, beyond human action, sin has worked itself into the very fabric of life. Sin is not *only* action or choice, but also a component of an intricate system that tells us something about how sin functions. I will take each of these categories in order, after a preliminary word about the language of sin.

The Problem with "Sin"

To consider questions of social evil through the doctrine of sin is a bold enterprise that, understandably, makes more than a few Christians uncomfortable. I might be quite comfortable in confessing those things that I have consciously *done*, which are limited in number and scope; but those things that I have left *undone* are seemingly infinite and not even identifiable in many cases. It is easy to think theologically and ethically about my actions as a perpetrator of harm, or about my status as a victim. But how do I understand my place when the roles are not so clear: when I am a beneficiary of a sinful structure of which I may not even be aware; when I am a bystander, either across the street or across the ocean, a distant and sympathetic observer; even when I am an activist, seeking to change these seemingly infinite structures of harm; even when I am one of the "good guys?"

Now, contemporary theologians find themselves in the unenviable position of trying to account for mind-boggling levels of human atrocity, on the one hand, and trying to reinterpret or retrieve theologies of sin with care and sensitivity to their tenuous position on the other. In this regard, Alistair McFadyen asks in *Bound to Sin* whether, when tested, the doctrine of sin bears any "explanatory power" in dealing with concrete pathologies in the world: "If it could be shown that theological language was incapable of bringing the core pathological dynamic to expression, of naming and identifying it, then that would be sufficient for it to fail the test."[5]

In what follows, I examine the discourse of sin to evaluate its explanatory power. Sin presents a problem in three senses of the word. First, it is a problem in the sense that violence, oppression, abuse, poverty, imperialism, suffering, and systemic corruption continue to plague

---

4. Jones, *Feminist Theory and Christian Theology*, 113.

5. McFadyen, *Bound to Sin*, 53.

societies. As a result, theologians and ethicists have, for the most part, rejected naïve theories of progressivism. In order to account for the rampant violence and suffering in the world, contemporary theology must take theodicy seriously, and since the violence and suffering is almost always, finally, traceable to human actions, we also must take sin seriously.

Sin is a problem in a second sense as well. Traditional efforts to define the roots of sin have reflected the particular social biases of people in power. As the task of theology has come to include women, scholars from the two-thirds world, and scholars of color, the Christian community can no longer presume that those social biases represent the universal human condition. For these reasons, sin-talk has a well-earned reputation of being at least irrelevant and, at worst, damaging for people who are already marginalized. In fact, some of the earliest and most influential feminist critiques of systematic theology were on exactly this point. In light of this critique, much of feminist and liberation scholarship has sought to refine, expand, and challenge traditional definitions of sin.

Valerie Saiving, for example, famously critiqued Reinhold Niebuhr's misplaced emphasis on pride as the primary form that sin takes—an emphasis that did not originate with him, but began as far back as Augustine. She wrote:

> For the temptations of a woman *as woman* are not the same as the temptations of man *as man*, and the specifically feminine forms of sin . . . have a quality which can never be encompassed by "pride" and "will-to-power." They are better suggested by such items as triviality, distractibility, and diffuseness; lack of an organizing center or focus; dependence on others for one's own self-definition; tolerance at the expense of standards of excellence; inability to respect the boundaries of privacy; sentimentality, gossipy sociability, and mistrust of reason—in short, *underdevelopment or negation of the self.*[6]

Saiving's identification of the chink in classical theology's armor would offer, to many theologians who followed her, entrée into theological conversations about the nature and meaning of sin. She does not identify negation of self as the universal root of all feminine sin, but uses the category to demonstrate that "pride" is inadequate. While the sin-as-

---

6. Goldstein, "Human Situation," 108–9. First and second emphases in original, third emphasis mine.

pride formulation has not diminished in influence, we find feminist, process, liberal, and liberation theologians who broaden the tradition with accounts of sin as negation of the self, violence, refusal of gifts from a beneficent God, oppression, and harm.[7] This broadening has aided theologians who seek to account for the social dimensions of sin, moving the discussion beyond the bounds of personal piety.[8] Below, I explore in more detail the debate over whether sin must be defined in every case as over and against God, or if violence against another aspect of creation qualifies as sin, irrespective of its connection with the divine-human relationship.

Finally, sin-talk presents problems in a third sense that relates particularly to social witness. As I noted in the beginning pages of this chapter, to consider problems of social suffering under the rubric of sin can arouse suspicion among Christians, because some problems seem simply too big, too insurmountable, to be attributed to human action or inaction. Among progressive Christian activists, sin-talk is rare, and one senses that many activists feel that theologies of sin are better suited for other contexts. When sin-talk *does* emerge, it is usually in reference to the social suffering activists seek to change, which is a necessary and powerful component of social witness practice. But what difference does it make for the practitioners to reflect on their own relationship to structures that injure creation? And why would they be loathe to engage in that kind of reflection?

One reason for this disconnect may be the prevalence of what McFadyen describes as "moral" interpretations of sin, which are guided by a set of assumptions: "I may only be held responsible for that which I am the cause of; which I could have willed to do otherwise; which is a product of my own freedom in action and not an outcome of determining conditions."[9] He finds this popular formulation to be problematic, because even those actions that directly issue in violence or suffering can rarely be attributed solely to free and rational personal choice. If the doctrine of sin is to bear continued explanatory power in accounting

---

7. See, for example: Jones, *Feminist Theory and Christian Theology*; Suchocki, *Fall to Violence*; Tanner, *Jesus, Humanity and the Trinity*; Ray, *Do No Harm*.

8. Saiving herself focused on the personal in her analysis of feminine forms of sin. The point in naming her here is to show how her critique revealed that, for too long, sin-talk had "assumed an audience of men socialized to value autonomy and having social power." See Jones, *Feminist Theory and Christian Theology*, 111.

9. McFadyen, *Bound to Sin*, 20.

for how we may be complicit in comprehensive problems, such as gross economic disparity, segregation, and genocide, it must move beyond the simple definition of "bad action" to help us understand how the human condition is actually bound by sin. On the one hand, many activists already have sophisticated analyses of complex social problems, and thus are not particularly susceptible to simplistic moral interpretations of the doctrine of sin. On the other hand, when activists move beyond moral interpretations of sin to reflect upon how they, too, are bound by sin, will they be discouraged from participating in the practice at all?

Is sin-talk, in the end, too problematic to be of benefit to the practice of social witness? Does its explanatory power collapse under the weight of global systems of suffering and domination, traditional interpretations that work to further oppress the marginalized, and the seemingly awkward relationship that activists have with the discussion on the whole? This need not be the case. In fact, the problems just laid out actually point the way forward for practitioners of social witness to embrace theological reflection on the character and function of sin. In particular, these problems invite new ways of thinking about sin in the social context, demanding that we broaden the categories that identify the *content* of sin to include more than pride and also deepen our understanding of the manner by which sin *functions* to include more than bad action.

If we take the interdependence proposed by Suchocki, Schleiermacher, and others seriously, and if we imagine that treating this web of life with reverence and care is God's intention for human and global life, then we need the language of sin to account for the myriad means by which we fall short. Without the theological language of sin, we are left with a tragedy in relationship to which we are reckoned helpless participants. The language of sin, particularly as harm to the interdependent web of life, helps us to identify those deliberate acts or failures to act that result in suffering; name as sin those structures that result in suffering, as well as unknowing participation therein; and acknowledge our own entanglement in structures of sin, even to the degree that our work for good is limited.[10]

---

10. Critics have faulted both feminist and process theology for what they sometimes describe as an atheological concept of sin. This challenge is addressed below, in the section subtitled, "What Have We Done? Sin as Human Action."

Sin as Harm

As noted in the introduction, practitioners of social witness confront those political and social systems that inhibit *eudaimonia*, which means, literally, "well-being of spirit." In common philosophical and ethical discourse, it is translated as human flourishing. Wherever *eudaimonia* is violated or stifled, harm has been perpetuated. This harm is sin. By calling it harm instead of injury, we acknowledge the fact that some dimension of culpability is involved in the suffering of human beings or of the earth. This culpability may not always be locatable; however, awareness of it reminds us that, if one is unable to flourish, it is incumbent upon us to seek out and address the sources of such incapacity. The Germanic origins of *harm* include grief or sorrow, in addition to injury or wrong, in the meaning of the word. The addition of grief and sorrow reminds us that harm includes not only physical violence, but also the undue causation of emotional suffering. It also invites us to examine value distinctions with some sophistication, for example, the distinction between swatting a mosquito, which might cause physical injury to the mosquito, and razing acres of rainforest, which might cause less immediate, but more extensive environmental and economic suffering and human sorrow. To account adequately for the vast degrees and means of human and environmental crises, the doctrine of sin must include a significant discussion of the concept of *harm*.

In conversations with practitioners of social witness, one can expect to be met with impatience upon trotting out dogmatic theological constructs. At the same time, one can expect to encounter great passion and compassion when asking questions about suffering, exploitation, oppression, violence, or poverty. Are these not theological categories? In my brief introduction to feminist critiques of traditional theological conceptions of sin, I noted that much feminist scholarship has questioned the adequacy of traditional definitions of sin to account for these contemporary problems. In traditional discourse, sin has been defined primarily in relation to personal piety—how do my actions constitute a rebellion against God? While some feminist theologians choose to reject traditional categories, finding them completely bereft of meaning when confronted with the vast and virulent human capacities for harm, other scholars seek to reclaim traditional categories in a way that helps explain the social ills that plague our common life.[11] Even this vibrant debate about whether Christian concepts of sin are adequate to account for vast social problems points to its significance in understanding such issues.

Marjorie Suchocki rightly identifies the awkwardness introduced by traditional constructs that argue that violence is a sin only insofar as it is derivative of more primal sins like pride and unfaithfulness. She rejects the tradition on these grounds, arguing that violence is itself the root *and* effect of sin, without qualification.[12] She writes that God's creative influence upon the world cannot be reduced to particular aims, so to define sin wholly as a violation of God's aims misses the point.[13] Suchocki argues that to limit sin to the violation of God's aims restricts our understanding of God's creative work in the world and assumes that such aims are without ambiguity, even in complicated social contexts. She posits that something else is needed—the violation of the criterion of well being—in order to call violence, oppression, and exploitation sin.

Suchocki makes a good point about what sometimes feels like woodenness within the Reformed tradition. Can we not agree, however, that God's aims *are* for the well-being of the world, for the flourishing of Tutu's delicate network of interdependence, without assuming that these aims are rigid? Is it necessary to add an adjunct criterion?

The Reformed tradition, in its insistence upon the divine-human relationship as the context for theological knowledge, resists such adjuncts. In the case of sin as harm, an adjunct criterion is not necessary. In the Genesis accounts of creation, the psalms, prophetic literature, Jesus' words, Paul's admonitions to the churches, and even in the liberatory words of Revelation, we are confronted by image heaped upon image of God's intention for the flourishing of the earth. We read that this was God's original intention and is the future toward which God is calling us. In the perpetuation of harm and the inhibition of *eudaimonia*, we find a direct contradiction of God's intentions. The causation of harm denies the flourishing of not only the one harmed, but also the one culpable for that harm. As noted in the introduction, flourishing includes the ca-

---

11. Alistair McFadyen, for example, retrieves Augustine's category of "bondage of the will" to explain the human situation. See McFadyen, *Bound to Sin*, 67–99, 129.

12. Suchocki, *Fall to Violence*, 29.

13. Ibid., 57–59.

pacity for imagination and living responsibly.[14] As Christians who stand in relation to God, both individually and collectively, we are called to participate in God's intentions, as we can best discern them. This is not to say, of course, that God's intentions for flourishing are always clear to us, or that we all will agree on the best way forward toward flourishing.

God's activity for good in the world calls us toward deeper connection with God and the world, not retreat. Thus, our human relationships, our social contexts, our relationships with the earth—all of these are understood within the frame of God's activity in the world. Serene Jones, reflecting on her conversations with a women's circle from her church, calls on Calvin's primal definition of sin as unfaithfulness, or "living against God." Unfaithfulness instigates a way of living in contrast with God's purposes in creation:

> (I)t is a way of living in which women do not flourish but instead experience (and participate in) oppressive forces . . . The "sin" of unfaithfulness not only refers to persons who harm others or to institutional and cultural forms that perpetuate the systemic deformation of identity but also describes the brokenness of persons who suffer such harm and whose identities are deformed by destructive cultural and institutional forms. . . . (I)t includes, in different ways, those who are harmed and their perpetuators as well as the material and cultural relations of power that form the nexus within which such harm occurs.[15]

Jones describes sin's all-encompassing character, which comprises an entire way of living. We all are entangled in it, in all dimensions of life. All of these aspects of harm—its intentional causation, structures that perpetuate it, even the brokenness that consequently defines human life—have everything to do with God's intention for and activity in the world. I neither propose that harm is the universal root of human sin, nor endorse Jones' naming "unfaithfulness" as the root concept. While Jones and her Tuesday night women's circle decided that they were helped by a "root" definition, many theologians have expended far too much energy arguing what they identify as the universal "root" of sin. While I do not dispute that a universal root concept may exist, I argue that identifying it does not work like a magic key, unlocking and solving the mysteries of human suffering. In fact, the search for a universal root

14. de Gruchy, *Confessions of a Christian Humanist*, 50–51.

15. Jones, *Feminist Theory and Christian Theology*, 113.

of sin sometimes presents more theological problems than it solves. We can say with confidence, however, that sin has everything to do with the mysterious character of the human condition, shaping our relationships with God, other persons, and the creation.

Describing harm and the inhibition of *eudaimonia* under the rubric of sin, though, amplifies the relevance of sin discourse to the practice of social witness. It speaks to practitioners' deep concerns for human suffering and injustice. By describing as sin the causation and perpetuation of harm, social activists can come to understand their own complicity and entanglement under the framework of sin. Identifying harm as sin also points to the supple character of the web of interdependence that serves as the context for social witness. When a strand is pulled, broken or weakened, it influences other dimensions of the web. Whether or not we are the ones who break a strand, we are all caught in the same damaged web. Let us now turn to these aspects of harm, both those for which we are actively culpable and those that are, in part, constitutive of the human condition in general.

What Have We Done? Sin as Human Action

Certainly, our local, national, and global contexts are filled with evidence that acts of sin are rampant and that there is no shortage of human choices that result immediately in harm to another person or to the earth. Marjorie Suchocki precedes each chapter in *The Fall to Violence* with a brief clipping recounting a violent incident: rape, murder, police brutality, torture, and ethnic cleansing.[16] In such cases, we can identify specific *acts* that we name as "sin." Certainly, without what Schleiermacher calls "actual sin," the acting out of corrupt nature, suffering and injustice would drop dramatically.[17] Likewise, Calvin reminds us that Adam's sin not only bound us via an inherited corruption, but that "this perversity never ceases in us, but continually bears new fruits—the works of the flesh that we have already described—just as a burning furnace gives forth flame and sparks, or water ceaselessly bubble up from a spring . . . For our nature is not only destitute and empty of good, but so fertile and fruitful of every evil that it cannot be idle."[18] In sum, no account of sin in relation to

---

16. Suchocki, *Fall to Violence*.

17. Schleiermacher, *Christian Faith*, §73.1.

18. Calvin, *Institutes*, I.II.8.

social suffering is complete without attention to the actual sin that makes for so much of the trouble.

What constitutes an actual "sin," though? Even among those who would agree that an act of violence is, in fact, sin, we would find a number of rationales for describing it as such. Suchocki defines sin as participation in violence, wreaking ill-being.[19] Schleiermacher, in contrast, describes sin as the subordination of the spirit to the lower nature, or a "positive antagonism of the flesh against the spirit."[20] The spirit, for Schleiermacher, is the place where the God-consciousness resides. So is sin an offense against another strand in the web of life, or is it an offense against God? This contrast illustrates a point of agreement between process theology and Reformed theology: sin cannot be reduced to a violation of an impersonal moral law. It is *always* relational. Relatedly, if we keep in mind what sin *does*, according to Schleiermacher, we are reminded that "whatever alienation from God there is in the phases of our experience, we are conscious of it as an action originating in ourselves, which we call Sin."[21] Sin always is born out of and results in our being alienated from God.

Can sin be directed toward another human being, toward a collective, toward the earth? Or is sin in every case directed toward God? In the Reformed tradition, there is little debate about the locus of actual sin. Beginning with Calvin, we read that the root of every actual sin is unfaithfulness, a failure of *pietas* in relationship to God. The human condition, which Calvin lays out so forcefully (an explication of which appears in the next section), is such that "once we hold God's Word in contempt, we shake off all reverence for him."[22] Ambition, pride, and ungratefulness follow from this failure of *pietas*, and we name them as sin *because* of the break in the God-human relationship that they represent.

As noted above, Suchocki, in her definition of sin as the act of participating in "unnecessary violence that contributes to the ill-being of any aspect of earth or its inhabitants," rejects the Reformed tradition of defining sin always and in every case as being against God.[23] Following a sympathetic reading of the feminist critique of traditional theologies of

19. Suchocki, *Fall to Violence*, 12.

20. Schleiermacher, *Christian Faith*, §66.

21. Ibid., §63.

22. Calvin, *Institutes*, II.I.4.

23. Suchocki, *Fall to Violence*, 12.

sin, Alistair McFadyen writes, "In its lack of clarity concerning the sense in which sloth and pride are sins against God and not just against self or 'right relation', one wonders whether sin is here a functioning theological language. Or is it retained only because of the communal location of this particular discussion, out of habit or for rhetorical flourish?"[24] McFadyen names in particular the work of Mary Daly, Carter Heyward, Rita Nakashima Brock, and Sharon Welch as exemplars of the "right relation" thesis.

Does defining sin as a violation of right relation, however, *necessarily* require that we define it solely in social or moral instead of theological terms? Suchocki would argue that it does not. In fact, she writes, "(T)he interpretation of sin as being against God becomes less what one has done with the aim of God, and more what one has done *to* God as God receives the effects of one's deeds into God's own experience. Sin is the unnecessary violation of well-being, and its occurrence in creation has an effect upon God. Because of this, sin against creation is also against God."[25]

Given Calvin's description of sin as a lack of trust in God and Schleiermacher's description of sin as a turning away from God, one might argue that, by so emphasizing the immediacy of sin's violation *of* God, Suchocki actually offers a more robustly theological doctrine of sin than do some Reformed formulations![26] Suchocki demonstrates to us, among other things, process theology's contribution of the categories of interdependence and violation to our discussions of the structure

---

24. McFadyen, *Bound to Sin*, 165.

25. Suchocki, *Fall to Violence*, 57.

26. At the same time, however, process theology's proposition that God is *affected* or *changed* by events in history, even hurt by them, runs contrary to much of Reformed theology's traditional emphasis on the sovereignty of God. This disagreement has to do with how the two schools define "power," and whether power is determined by independence. For Reformed theology, God's power is at least partly defined by God's *otherness*. God does not *need* humanity, and by grace condescends to be in relationship with us. In process theology, God's power is marked by God's creativity, receptivity and ability to persuade humanity "toward the best possible future." As feminist process theologian Lucinda Huffaker writes, "If the future is open and creatures make decisions freely, how then can we think of God's unboundedness or ultimacy? For feminists concerned for the just treatment and self-determination of people who have been marginalized and disempowered, God is unlimited in providing for the flourishing of all. God's is the ultimate inclusivity—nothing and no one is wasted or lost or left out." See Huffaker, "Feminist Theology in Process Perspective," 179–80.

of sin. Placing these process categories in conversation with Reformed theology, then, let us define actual sin as any act that results in harm to a part of creation, resulting in injury and sorrow. Suchocki suggests that deviation from the aims of God must be augmented with *another* criterion, the violation of well-being, in order to name something as sin. I suggested above that such actions are called sin because to violate the well-being of another person, community, or the earth *is* to violate the aims of God. God's vision of *eudaimonia* is developed in more detail in the next chapter. What would cause us to actively reject God's gift of flourishing and relationship? To answer this question, we now turn to an explication of the human condition.

Who Are We? Sin as Human Condition

In order for the language of sin to make sense in the context of social injustice and suffering, it must describe more than wrong action. If social injustice were caused exclusively by wrong action, two problems arise. First, why have we been unable to change our actions, to choose otherwise, in the interest of promoting the flourishing of the earth? Second, how can large-scale problems such as genocide, oppression, and environmental degradation be attributed simply to bad choice? The language of sin must explain why we continue to commit acts of sin, as well as why injustice persists even in the absence of an obvious act of sin.

Serene Jones presents a compelling illustration for how she understands original sin to be at work in the world. She describes the birth of her daughter and her deep unrest as the hospital staff quickly placed a pink hat on the infant girl. Images raced through her mind of all that the pink hat signified, of all the assumptions about gender roles that the hat represented. Quite literally, she says, she was confronted by the tangible ways in which we are "born into sin." Before the baby could even open her eyes, she was drawn into complex webs of social and systemic expectations for what kind of person she would be, as a wearer of the pink hat. For Jones, this picture was not good.[27]

Can we attribute the pink hat incident to some actual sin? Shall we blame the nurse who placed it on the baby's head? Shall we lament the company who would likely pay significantly less to the grown-up wearer of the pink hat than to the wearers of the blue hats? Shall we pre-

---

27. Jones, *Feminist Theory and Christian Theology*, 117.

emptively condemn those who would inflict violence upon the wearer of the pink hat? Pink is not inherently sinful. What Jones recognized in that moment was the social web of meaning attached to the pink hat. It signifies a myriad of implications, many of which are harmful, associated with gender roles in the United States. Few of these implications could be attributed to a specific, actual sin. In all likelihood, neither the nurse nor the baby consciously, at that moment, agreed to participate in the structure of sin that we call patriarchy. Just the same, they are caught in the web of sin. This web of sin so binds the human condition that we can hardly move in this world without encountering another of its strands.

While intentional and even unintentional *acts* of sin are important to consider in the context of social witness, defining sin *solely* as a freely chosen act ignores the ways in which sin impacts the totality of human experience. We read among a diverse group of theologians a shared assumption that freely-chosen "bad action" cannot account for all of the unnecessary suffering in the world. To Jones' pink hat illustration, we might add Cornelius Plantinga's Jim Bob illustration. In the first chapter of *Not the Way It's Supposed to Be*, Plantinga takes up the case of Jim Bob, who grows up in a racist culture only to absorb it and claim racism as an adult. If Jim Bob apparently had no choice for an alternative worldview, is it right to call such a seemingly inevitable outcome "sin"?[28] Plantinga says "yes":

> Still, we know perfectly well that human pride, injustice and hard-heartedness weave the web of social evil in which people like Jim Bob get caught and that this is true even when we cannot state with certainty whose pride, injustice and hard-heartedness have produced the sticky strands. . . . (T)hat new and derived racism is often called sin because it is the fruit of sin and because it is morally evil . . . The paradigm case is the doctrine of original sin. All traditional Christians agree that human beings have a biblically certified and empirically demonstrable bias toward evil. We are all both complicitous in and molested by the evil of our race.[29]

Marjorie Suchocki tells a different yet corresponding story, in which she tries to make sense of a news report of school violence. She describes

28. Plantinga, *Not the Way It's Supposed to Be*, 23–25.

29. Ibid., 26. Plantinga's sweeping generalizations about "all traditional Christians" aside, I find his description of the doctrine of original sin as a "bias toward evil" to be a helpful contemporary interpretation of Calvin.

how aspects of American culture—violent cartoons and video games, youth-oriented films that portray violence as an answer to problems, and tiny replicas of instruments of war manufactured as toys for the youngest children—create an environment that encourages acts of violence. She then writes, "Throughout these and other modes, violence is shown to be the norm for dealing with the problems of life . . . Given the presence of weapons of violence, norms that sanction their use, and the presenting occasion of perceived violation of their own well-being, the children in the news report murdered or attempted to murder. The culture creates the conditions within which children become murderers."[30] To these illustrations of sexism, racism, and gun violence, we might add Alistair McFadyen's illustrations of the sexual abuse of children and the Holocaust to demonstrate how freely-chosen action cannot fully account for such totalizing structures of sin.

Preceding the theological writings of Jones, Plantinga, Suchocki, and McFadyen, we find in the roots of Reformed theology a number of means by which we might construe the situation of sin in which we all are implicated. John Calvin is perhaps the most prolific imaginer of metaphors for sin. Schleiermacher, too, addresses the realities underlying these metaphors.[31] To their metaphors and Suchocki's development of them, I now turn.

Entangled Yet Alienated: The Legacies of Calvin and Schleiermacher

Calvin understands the condition of sin to be the status of total depravity, by which the whole person is infected by the poison of sin. This disease afflicts not only the appetites or the flesh, but the whole person—so that

---

30. Suchocki, *Fall to Violence*, 124.

31. Once I was in a seminar in which a Schleiermacher scholar said, with a grin, that "Schleiermacher considered himself a good Calvinist." The implication was that Schleiermacher actually did not carry over many of the concepts and structures from John Calvin, and this, in her estimation, was a good thing. Walter Wyman, for example, has described Schleiermacher's account of the condition of sin as "dramatically revisionist . . . Schleiermacher revises the doctrine to show how sin can be both universal and inevitable without being an inheritance from a particular act that changed human nature." Wyman, "Sin and Redemption," 134. I argue that Schleiermacher was indeed a good Calvinist, representing important refinements and developments of his thought, a lineage that sometimes is overshadowed in the North American context by the dominance of Barthian interpretations of Schleiermacher.

the person is overwhelmed, "as by a deluge."[32] Even when we think that our intentions are good, even when we think we've done our best—our actions reflect this blind and directionless depravity: "Therefore let us hold this as an undoubted truth which no siege engines can shake: the mind of man has been so completely estranged from God's righteousness that it conceives, desires and undertakes, only that which is impious, perverted, foul, impure and infamous. The heart is so steeped in the poison of sin, that it can breathe out nothing but a loathsome stench."[33]

Incorporating Calvin's total depravity, we might say that, in Schleiermacher, the development of the God-consciousness is arrested by the human condition of total depravity. For Calvin, total depravity's grasp on us is, well, total. The idea of total depravity bears within it many related metaphors, including these three: deluge, contagion or defect, and entanglement. Total depravity is like a deluge in that it overwhelms the human person, drenching her mind and will. Sin overturns the whole person.[34] Total depravity is like a contagion that corrupts every part of us, spreading without abatement. The contagion of total depravity ravages the human soul in its very depths, infecting every part of us with a wound in need of healing. This defect also acts as a disease in human nature as a whole, spread via inheritance.[35] And finally, total depravity entangles us all, so that no one escapes its grasp. Even babies, sadly, before they see the light of this world, are soiled and spotted with sin. Before they actualize this sinful condition in an act of sin, they function as seedbeds of sin.[36] In these images of deluge, contagion, and entanglement, we begin to see that the condition of sin is something within us, spread through us, and surrounding us.

Schleiermacher, too, understands the force of the condition of sin to operate by a variety of means. He writes, "We are conscious of sin partly as having its source in ourselves, partly as having its source outside our own being."[37] The inward and outward sources of sin in Schleiermacher roughly correspond to Calvin's metaphors of contagion and entanglement, respectively. About the inner source of sin, Schleiermacher writes,

32. Calvin, *Institutes*, II.I.9.

33. Ibid., II.V.19.

34. Ibid., II.I.9.

35. Ibid., II.I.5.

36. Ibid., II.I.8.

37. Schleiermacher, *Christian Faith*, §69.

"In this sense, therefore—but only because there exists a living seed of sin ever ready to burst forth—there is such a thing as an abiding consciousness of sin, now preceding the sin itself as a warning presentiment, now accompanying it as an inward reproof, or following it as penitence."[38] In both Calvin and Schleiermacher, the condition of sin is something *in* us.

For Schleiermacher, however, the inner force of sin is largely driven by the lower nature, the senses, which work against the higher nature, the spirit. Sin appears when the lower nature, which Schleiermacher calls the "flesh," triumphs over the spirit. At every turn, the flesh seeks to do so. In contrast, Calvin warns against associating sin solely with the flesh: "I have said that all parts of the soul were possessed by sin after Adam deserted the fountain of righteousness. For not only did a lower appetite seduce him, but unspeakable impiety occupied the very citadel of his mind, and pride penetrated to the depths of the heart. Thus it is pointless and foolish to restrict the corruption that arises thence only to what are called the impulses of senses. . . ."[39]

Whether in the senses or in the spirit, Calvin and Schleiermacher agree that we know sin, in part, "as an action originating in ourselves."[40] Both also point to the condition of sin as exerting an external force upon us. Calvin writes, "(W)e are to understand it not as if we, guiltless and undeserving, bore the guilt of his offence but in the sense that, since we through his transgression have become entangled in the curse, he is said to have made us guilty."[41] Being "entangled in the curse" means that we are bound so tightly that we cannot help but sin. In recent theological constructions of sin, writers like the ones named above—Suchocki, Jones, McFadyen, and Plantinga—have looked to the doctrine of original sin to account for the ways in which we are bound from the outside, by forces such as political institutions, cultural values, economic arrangements, and even family life. Schleiermacher and Calvin's assessment of the condition of sin working from the outside in, entangling us all in a web of sin, provide ample resources for considering the sources of sin.

For Schleiermacher, the social character of the condition of sin cannot be overestimated. In many places he reiterates this point, including his critical discussion of original sin: "Now if the sinfulness which

38. Ibid., §66.1.
39. Calvin, *Institutes*, II.I.9.
40. Schleiermacher, *Christian Faith*, §63.
41. Calvin, *Institutes*, II.I.8.

is prior to all action operates in every individual through the sin and sinfulness of others, and if, again, it is transmitted by the voluntary actions of every individual to others and implanted within them, it must be something genuinely common to all."[42] All of us "who depend on a corporate life from the outset" are caught up in this web of sin, so much so that Schleiermacher finds it difficult even to identify an "individual" sin.[43] Not only is sin in us, but it conditions the totality that surrounds us. This is a significant and helpful development of Calvin's concept of entanglement: an explicit statement that sin is not only in us, but around us. This means that Schleiermacher can avoid some of the more contrived genetic accounts of original sin that bogged down Calvin and his theological ancestor Augustine. He can focus energies on the experiential reality that there is something external to us, something that we did not choose and into which we are born, that both implicates us in sin and damages our relationship with God.

As noted above, several contemporary theologians have sought accounts for social sin by retrieving and/or reinterpreting the traditional doctrine of original sin. Calvin and Schleiermacher disagree on the meaning and content of the doctrine of original sin, but both do appeal to its use as a means for conceiving the universality of sin. In both of Calvin's descriptions of total depravity as defect and entanglement, the language of inheritance is central.[44] Although Adam earned this curse, we all are deservedly implicated.

Unlike Calvin's account of total depravity's transmission, Schleiermacher does not propose a complete identification between the condition of sin and a hereditary understanding of original sin. For Schleiermacher, the language of "original" and "actual" sin is problematic; he points instead to an experiential sense that sin finds its source both inside and external to us.[45] Original sin is real in that it gives birth to acts of sin. In this regard, we might more accurately describe it as "originating sin," Schleiermacher suggests.[46] Since we experience originating sin

---

42. Schleiermacher, *Christian Faith*, §71.2. For further references to the corporate character of sin, see §69–72, §75–78.

43. Ibid., §82.3.

44. Calvin, *Institutes*, II.I.7–8.

45. Schleiermacher, *Christian Faith*, §71.

46. Ibid., §72.6.

as a relatively external compulsion arresting the God-consciousness, we experience it as a component of the alienation we feel from God.

Alienation from God is how Schleiermacher describes the experience of the condition of sin. Walter Wyman, placing *The Christian Faith* in conversation with one of Schleiermacher's sermons, writes,

> Sinfulness would be an inability to "join the thought of God with every thought of any importance," an absence of conscious relation to God in one's everyday existence. The problem of sin is a religious, not a moral problem; it is, as he says, "God-forgetfulness" (§11.2). By the experience of *Unlust,* Schleiermacher apparently means a sense of incompleteness, mental discomfort, of things somehow out of joint, of the world lacking in religious meaning. It would make sense that this experience of "pain" would arise within the Christian community where the expectation of a pious consciousness is cultivated.[47]

Humanity has forgotten God. We are no longer connected with God's thoughts or intentions; we do not have a sense of the continuity of God's aims. We are swimming in a sea of alienation, so to speak. The theme of interdependence and solidarity in sin is clear, "for the sinfulness of each points to the sinfulness of all alike in space and time, and also goes to condition that totality both around him and after him."[48] Upon this legacy, contemporary theology has continued to build.

Contemporary Developments of the Concept of Sin as Human Condition

David Kelsey has sought to show how, if we dismiss Calvin's idea of total depravity, we lose something.[49] Likewise, Alistair McFadyen argues that the doctrine of original sin, construed as the will bound by idolatry, helps us to account for some of the most troubling atrocities in our historical context.[50] Their appeals to the retention of traditional categories that make sense of the condition of sin are compelling. If theologies of sin are to continue to offer explanatory power for contemporary human experience, they will have to guard against moral interpretations of sin which attribute all violence, suffering, and sin to consciously chosen action.

47. Wyman, "Sin and Redemption," 133.
48. Schleiermacher, *Christian Faith,* §71.2.
49. Kelsey, "Some Kind Words for Total Depravity."
50. McFadyen, *Bound to Sin,* 221–26.

If sin is to be rightly understood in a more complex way than as "bad action" and thus make accounts for how we may be complicit (though perhaps not intentionally involved) in comprehensive problems such as gross economic disparity, segregation, and genocide, we must have some way of understanding sin as a force that binds the whole human condition. This is what Calvin and Schleiermacher's work on total depravity and alienation offers us: a sense in which the human person is shaped by conditions outside her immediate control. Whether these binding dynamics come from external, social forces, or internal, psychological dispositions, they offer explanatory power for the experience of human life.

Suchocki, like Schleiermacher before her, revises the doctrine of original sin, reinterpreting the tradition in the contemporary context. She describes the condition of sin as propensity toward violence, the mediation of violence through the web of human solidarity, and the perpetuation of violence through the social formation of conscience.[51] Like Schleiermacher's contention that sin's source is both inside and external (in time and space) to us, Suchocki argues that we bear within us a propensity toward violence, but interrelationality and social inheritance condition our context beyond and before our individual experience. Sin is universal in that everyone is implicated not only individually, but also relationally, "We are, then, no matter how personally in control of our own violent tendencies, surrounded by and invaded by a vast amount of violence . . . It is mediated not simply through the bent toward violence built into our humanity, but by an interrelated solidarity that mediates the effects of violence throughout the race."[52]

This description of sin as reverberating through the web of interdependence can be likened to Schleiermacher's contention that sin conditions the totality *around* us. Similarly, Schleiermacher's corollary contention that sin also conditions the totality that historically precedes us is echoed in Suchocki's description of the social inheritance of sin:

> Individuals raised within such a society internalize the norms, thus supporting them and ensuring their continued perpetuation. Since it is the individual *self*-consciousness that is so formed, it becomes constitutive of the self, and difficult to transcend. One's

51. These arguments are detailed in Part 2 of *The Fall to Violence*, but also are summarized in the book's conclusion. See Suchocki, *Fall to Violence*, 162–63.

52. Ibid., 109.

actions from the center of consciousness will then actualize the norms, perpetrating them relative to one's own position and perspective within the grid of the intersubjective society at large. By definition, the inherited norms cannot be questioned prior to their enactment: one is caught in sin without virtue of consent. Original sin simply creates sinners.[53]

In the end, both Reformed and process theologians pay far more attention to the conditions of sin that bind human life than to the content of actual sins, or catalogues thereof.

What can be culled from these emphases, particularly as they relate to the practice of social witness? Let me name just three themes that might guide us in the coming pages. First, Reformed and process understandings of the condition of sin and interrelatedness make it not only impossible, but perhaps even undesirable, to focus solely on actual sins in the social sphere. Second, Schleiermacher and Suchocki's emphases upon interrelatedness remind us of the complexity of sin and its relation to the social context—reminders that simplistic solutions rarely will heal complex systems of suffering. Third, the universality of sin invites participants in social witness to engage in practices of self-reflection as they seek to change structures of sin, structures in which they also are implicated.

Social Witness and the Condition of Sin

One may have noticed that the actual activists interviewed for this book have yet to make an appearance in this chapter. There is a reason for their absence, and it is not because they are free from sin! As I noted above, sin-talk rarely emerges in the forms of social witness practice that I have studied. We do hear it, from time to time, in sermons preached at events like the Montreat Conference Center's 2005 Reclaiming the Text conference, whose theme was "Telling the Truth in a World of Denial." Even then, however, sin-talk is sometimes cast in two molds: that structural sin "out there" and the actual sin of ignoring these structures. Rare is the acknowledgement of the complexity of sin and its stubbornness in response to human pursuit of the good. Rare also is confession of our complicity in structures of sin, *particularly* within the social witness practice, itself. Perhaps such rarity is due to a fear that acknowledgement

53. Ibid., 126. Emphasis in original.

of sin's aspects of complexity and complicity will immobilize those who otherwise would persevere in the quest for flourishing.

Among the activists I met in researching for this project, I heard a common objection that focusing on the complexity of social problems provides an excellent excuse to hesitate in action. Even in the media, on both sides of political debate, we hear claims that the gospel is "clear and unambiguous" on issues of personal morality, social justice, and economics. Is it true, however, that acknowledging the complexity of sin in a global economy, and also our complicity in it, necessarily impedes social action? One would hope not. In fact, one compelling counter-example is detailed in the documentary advocacy film, *The Corporation*. The film seeks to demonstrate the myriad means by which corporations diminish human rights, environmental sustainability, and political and economic stability. Along the way, viewers are introduced to Ray Anderson, president and CEO of Interface Carpeting. He describes the process by which he came to commit the company to 100 percent environmental sustainability by the year 2020.[54] He says:

> For twenty-one years, I never gave a thought to what we were taking from the earth, or for what we were doing to the earth, in the making of our products. . . . (Reading *The Ecology of Commerce* by Paul Hawkins) was the point of a spear into my chest. And I read on, and the spear went deeper and it became an epiphanal experience, a total change of mindset for myself and a change of paradigm . . . One day early in this journey it dawned on me, that the way I'd been running Interface was the way of the plunderer, plundering something that's not mine, something that belongs to every creature on this earth.[55]

For Ray Anderson, an acknowledgement of his own complicity in environmental degradation prompted a desire not only to change his own practices, but also to advocate for just practices throughout the carpet industry. Anderson is not free from entanglement in the systems of economic and environmental injustice that continue to impact the global community, but neither has he been paralyzed by his complicity.

---

54. For more information on Interface, Inc.'s environmental and social sustainability plan, see "Interface Sustainability." Ray Anderson and Interface, Inc., also started Mission Zero, a nonprofit network of persons, groups, and organizations committed to the goal of zero environmental impact. See "Mission Zero." Ray Anderson died in 2011.

55. Abbott and Achbar, *The Corporation*.

In a local meeting of the Presbytery of Greater Atlanta a couple of years ago, members deliberated a resolution that protested recent state legislation that forbade cities and towns from establishing living wage ordinances for contracts with private businesses. Much debate ensued, including expected objections to the resolution that the presbytery ought not direct the state on policy matters and that small businesses suffer as a result of living wage ordinances. The discussion took an interesting turn, however, when one elder took the floor in opposition to the resolution. He told the presbytery that he, himself, was not opposed to living wage ordinances. His objection rested in the fact that many congregations within the presbytery did not pay their own employees a living wage. Would it not be hypocrisy, then, to advocate *for* living wage ordinances in the public sphere? In response to this question, another member of the presbytery took the floor in response, saying that he hoped that the desire to avoid hypocrisy did not mean that Presbyterians could not speak out on issues like this. If it did, then the church would find it difficult to engage in social witness at all!

This example points to the complexity of sin, human complicity in these complex structures, and the relation of these to the practice of social witness. Both aspects of sin have bearing on social witness practice, and reflection upon them in the context of that practice might equip practitioners for more profound engagement. Complexity means that sin is deeper than, antecedent to, conditioning of, and more ambiguous than any single instantiation of actual sin. Complicity means that sin is not only pervasive "out there" in the social sphere, but also "in here," implicating each and all of us.

As is clear from the exposition above, the complexity resulting from the interrelational character of creation and the universal and social condition of sin creates a tangled mess in the social sphere. This tangled mess may sometimes seem an impossible one to unravel, even for Christians who engage in practices of activism. In the words of Fred Pratt Green's hymn, "How Clear is Our Vocation, Lord,"

> But if, forgetful, we should find
> your yoke is hard to bear;
> if worldly pressures fray the mind
> and love itself cannot unwind
> its tangled skein of care:
> our inward life repair.[56]

56. Green, "How Clear is Our Vocation, Lord."

What does this complexity mean in the context of social witness practice? To borrow Fred Pratt Green's language, when confronted with the complexity of suffering in the social sphere, activists may experience the mind as a "tangled skein of care." Which thread does the activist pull in this tangled mess? As noted above, we might name at least two contributions that acknowledgement of this complexity might make to the practice of social witness: increased attention to the wide-ranging condition of sin, in addition to more immediate emphases on actual sins; and a reminder that simplistic solutions rarely will heal complex systems of suffering. While these two themes may seem less like contributions and more like concessions, consciousness of them adds depth and integrity to the practice.

Reformed and process conceptions of interrelatedness offer practitioners a theological frame in which to reflect upon their contexts and develop complex systems of response. Take the case of Southside Presbyterian Church, for example. As noted in the last chapter, John Fife describes the congregation's decision to become a Sanctuary church as a movement from simplicity to complexity in their ministry on the border, beginning with a narrowly-defined practice—legal aid to asylum-seekers. As the members of the congregation were awakened to the complexities of the institutional, political, cultural, legal, and economic injustice in Central America, the suffering of the refugees compelled them to develop a more comprehensive practice of social action. The responsiveness of Southside members to the complexities of the situation positioned them to respond on a more foundational level, even to the point of challenging U.S. immigration policy. They continued to offer economic, medical, and legal aid to the refugees, but they also confronted the structures that perpetuated so much of the suffering. Each time participants in the Sanctuary movement assisted a refugee, they reported their actions to the border patrol, so that the U.S. government could not pretend to be ignorant of the vastness of the situation.

In this case, an awareness of the complexity of suffering helped the members of the congregation to adapt their practice to fit the context. While there is no evidence that individual members explicitly associated the complexity of suffering with the complexity of sin as they were making these decisions, the connections are ripe to be harvested. In addition to identifying and confronting the complex structures of sin, attending to the complexity of sin also creates a space in which activists might be honest about their frustrations, so that practitioners can engage in lament. When our practice of social witness does not have a measurable result, these theological resources provide a language by which we can recognize the tangled mess of social sin that relies on both multiple corporate agents and a universal condition of sin.

Alongside the lament, however, must also come confession. Reformed and process accounts of our complicity in social sin invite us to reflect upon ourselves not as righteous prophets, but as responsible participants. In other words, we do not stand outside this complexity, untouched by sin and suffering. We, too, are implicated in the tangled mess. We are complicit: not only does sin pervade all that is "out there," but sin also drenches us "in here," from the inside out. We might think of humanity as complicit in sin in two ways. First, each of us is bound by the condition of sin; thus, even if we are not culpable in a particular instance of sin, we recognize that if circumstances were different we might do the same.[57] Second, we all are implicated in systems of oppression and injustice, especially when we benefit from these structures. This type of complicity is particularly at issue in discussions of the meaning of the global economy. How do Americans benefit from discounted labor and products from the majority world? When John Fife was asked how the relationships between Southside Presbyterian and churches in Central America had affected the congregation, he replied: "The church in North America has been comfortable in its relationship with empire. We cannot continue to follow this path and remain the church. We need to understand that our conversion is going to require some blood, sweat, and tears."[58] To acknowledge ontological and practical complicity in the complexity of sin is not to refrain from action. Participants in social witness practice learn and exemplify humility when they acknowledge that they, too, are implicated in sin.

An historical example of the self-critical dimension of social witness practice comes to mind. In 1950, the drafters of the Stuttgart Confession of Guilt did not agree on how the document should be worded. Just the same, they developed a confession (some would say not confess-

57. Schleiermacher even made this argument about the Fall (the genetic and historical sense of which he rejected), that the situation of the "first pair" likewise "emerges in the case of every individual . . . so that in committing their first sin they were simply the first-born of sinfulness." Schleiermacher, *Christian Faith*, §72.4.

58. Yarger, "Holy Communion," 25.

ing enough) of the complicity of the Evangelical Church in Germany. It reads, "With great anguish, we say: Through us, infinite sorrow has been brought upon many peoples and countries. What we have often testified to our congregations we express now in the name of the entire church: To be sure, we have fought in the name of Jesus Christ through many long years against the spirit that found its terrible expression in the brutal government of the National Socialists; but we accuse ourselves that we did not confess more courageously, did not pray more faithfully, did not believe more joyously, and did not love more passionately."[59] The Stuttgart Confession illustrates the sort of self-reflection that, in the practice of social witness, might offer participants freedom and courage to pursue justice. Confession, of course, would be meaningless if it were not accompanied by an assurance that God's grace offers forgiveness. Serene Jones has said that this awareness of justification offers participants the freedom to "practice boldly."[60] This encouragement is important, countering temptations to shy away from the prophetic practice of social witness for fear that we are not worthy.

On Not Being the Frozen Chosen: Agency Despite Sin

The two aspects of sin discussed above—complexity and complicity— are understandably formidable obstacles to contemporary social witness practice. How can our small efforts have any positive impact in the face of this overwhelming and entangling sin and evil? What if we are discovered as the hypocrites that we are? One might be tempted to refrain from acting at all. What theological resources encourage us to act, despite sin?

First, as expounded above, honesty about sin has a freeing quality about it that equips us to practice without overestimating what we might actually accomplish. In the Reformed tradition, especially, sin always is accompanied by grace, to the point that we are not enamored of our own capabilities, but are freed to participate in God's work of grace in the world. Sometimes, however, Reformed theology has tended to play down humanity's participation in God's action for good, so that critics of the tradition hardly notice it: "The reason Barth asserts that we need an utterly transcendent God to save us is that we are completely powerless, not only to save ourselves, but even to affect the conditions in the world

59. Gerlach, *And the Witnesses Were Silent*, 226.

60. Jones, "Graced Practices," 65.

that perpetrate sin. The Augustinian-Calvinist doctrine of 'utter-depravity' has as its corollary a zero-sum notion of available power. . . . Even if we might be allowed some limited causal efficacy in our immediate environment, we are certainly bereft of true power: the power to determine one's own fate or to effect real good or progress in the world."[61] While Bowman's analysis of Barth's emphasis on God's transcendence is a fair one, total depravity does not exclude humans from working for good. Human beings, Calvin argued, *do* still have a "zeal for righteousness and goodness," and they still "yearn after the Kingdom of God."[62] Despite our miserable condition, we are rendered capable of good works by God's operating grace, by which we are able to will the good, and God's co-operating grace, by which we are helped to do it.[63]

In Reformed theology, we are reminded that because of sin, we *cannot* be agents for good on our own; however, because of grace, we are *reckoned* agents for good. In process theology, however, the story is a little different. The guilt that humans experience implies that we are free to transcend structures of ill-being and yet do not, Suchocki writes. While these structures are real and powerful, she argues, humans do (at some point and to some degree) have the capacity to transcend these structures of evil.[64] If appropriately harnessed, guilt can bring us to transformation: "The positive aspect of appropriate feelings of guilt is that they function much as pain does in signaling a dysfunction in the body. Feelings of guilt can be the catalyst toward transformation. . . . (T)he process of movement from naming complicity and guilt to discovering the positive power of transcendence is not automatic. It is possible to become stuck in guilt as if it were a stopping place rather than a transitional space."[65]

These disagreements about human moral freedom, particularly as it relates to sin and agency, are significant and ought not be ignored. At the same time, we find in both traditions an affirmation that human beings are forgiven by God and free(d) to do the good, whether by human power or by grace. In the end, however, the expectation that guilt would ultimately lead us to embrace human transcendence seems a bit

61. Bowman, "God for Us," 14.

62. Calvin, *Institutes*, II.I.3.

63. Calvin gets the language of "operating" and "co-operating" grace from Peter Lombard. Ibid., II.II.6.

64. Suchocki, *Fall to Violence*, 129.

65. Ibid., 142.

naïve, as if we might move beyond sin. In this case, Reformed theology better approximates the human experience. The transcendent character of human life never fully cancels out sin. In Reformed theology, we find an acknowledgement of this reality and an affirmation of the power and goodness of God's grace. Together, honesty about sin and trust in God's grace free us to work for the good in society via practices of social witness.

Jones makes precisely this point in her essay, "Graced Practices: Excellence and Freedom in the Christian Life." She describes her work with a strategic planning commission at her church, whose members felt discouraged by their inability to pursue all the good project ideas generated by the congregation. Upon an admission to such by one member, however, the group began to consider what it meant to consider the Christian life under the rubric of grace. As Jones puts it, a Reformed theology of grace frees us from the "burden of perfection."[66]

From Calvin to Suchocki, we find agreement on the basic assumption that we all remain bound by sin and that the process of sanctification—faith formation—is an ongoing process. When the burdens introduced by even the most inspiring practices of social witness are understood in this larger rhythm of Christian life, we might come to agree with Suchocki: "Yet sin is a salvific word, a word of grace."[67] We find, in this word of grace, cause for hope. That grace, ultimately, is what empowers social action despite sin.

66. Jones, "Graced Practices," 65.

67. Suchocki, *Fall to Violence*, 164.

5

With an Urgency Born of This Hope

Hope and Social Action

FOR THE SOUTHSIDE PRESBYTERIAN CHURCH OF TUCSON, ARIZONA, the sense of urgency was, and remains, palpable. Their proximity to the suffering and death occurring at the United States-Mexico border has made immigration a sphere of moral action and hospitality, rather than a distant political issue. According to an August 2006 report by the Government Accountability Office, deaths on the United States-Mexico border have doubled since 1995.[1] In such a life and death situation, the question of urgency is moot. The situation is urgent because, as every moment passes, more suffering and more deaths occur.

In situations of crisis, a sense of urgency arises not only because a situation is dire, but also because people recognize that some action is required of them. The Church, in particular, is challenged to assume special responsibility in the face of social crises. In 1985's *The Kairos Document: Challenge to the Church*, South African church leaders reflected on the urgency inherent in the Apartheid crisis. They wrote, "The time has come. The moment of truth has arrived. South Africa has been plunged into a crisis that is shaking the foundations and there is every indication that the crisis has only just begun and that it will deepen and become even more threatening in the months to come. It is the KAIROS or moment of truth not only for apartheid but also for the Church and all other faiths and religions."[2]

In a state of emergency in which the consequences of our decisions are a life-and-death matter, the call to responsibility and action is clear. At such times, inaction may exacerbate situations of social suffering

1. *Illegal Immigration: Border-Crossing Deaths.*
2. Brown, "Kairos," 26.

and evil. The signers of the Stuttgart Declaration of Guilt recognized this missed urgency in the context of Nazi Germany. Martin Niemöller, for example, despite founding the Pastors' Emergency League (and the subsequent Confessing Church, which issued the Barmen Declaration), lamented publicly his own failure to do enough to save the lives of Jews and other vulnerable peoples during the 1930s and 1940s in Germany.

Both the *kairos* theologians and the signers of the Stuttgart Declaration, however, understood urgency not only in terms of the dire need to confront suffering and evil, but also as opportunities for joy and grace. The *kairos* theologians, for example, identified in the *kairos* a "moment of grace and opportunity, the favourable time in which God issues a challenge to decisive action."[3] Similarly, in the Stuttgart Confession, we read this lamentation: "To be sure, we have fought in the name of Jesus Christ through many long years against the spirit that found its terrible expression in the brutal government of the National Socialists; but we accuse ourselves that we did not confess more courageously, did not pray more faithfully, did not believe more joyously, and did not love more passionately."[4] In other words, the situation in Nazi Germany was one of urgency not only because it demanded a response to a "regime of violence," but also because it issued a call to courage, faith, passion, and—yes—*joy*. Dire situations give rise to a sense of urgency, but many theological voices would hasten to add that urgency finds its deepest roots in hope.

The crafters of the Presbyterian Church (U.S.A.)'s Confession of 1967, for example, explicitly named hope as the source for urgency in social action. The confession reads: "Already God's reign is present as a ferment in the world, stirring hope in men and preparing the world to receive its ultimate judgment and redemption . . . With an urgency born of this hope the church applies itself to present tasks and strives for a better world. It does not identify limited progress with the kingdom of God on earth, nor does it despair in the face of disappointment and defeat. In steadfast hope the church looks beyond all partial achievement to the final triumph of God."[5] Hope is born of God's reign, already present as a ferment in the world. Hope is the theological frame in which Christians imagine a context of flourishing and are stirred to act in the interest of

3. Ibid.

4. Gerlach, *And the Witnesses Were Silent*, 226.

5. Presbyterian Church (U.S.A.), "Confession of 1967," 9.55.

this vision. Hope is the means by which Christians look beyond present, concrete experience toward something deeper, fuller, and more constitutive of the good. The disposition of hope, which seeks expression in joy, love, and faith, provides a framework for action in a context of complex and pervasive sin. Hope has an *object*, or telos,[6] toward which we are moving; a *foundation*, or source, the remembrance of which inspires trust; and a *function* that enriches and supports our action in the public sphere.

In what follows, I first examine how the disposition of hope operates in the context of sin, and develop a provisional definition of hope. After these introductory comments, I explore the dynamic disposition of Christian hope, exploring its object, its foundation, and its function in social witness. This chapter concludes with some proposals for the practicing of hope in the midst of social witness.[7] Throughout this chapter, I engage root concepts in eschatology suggested by Jürgen Moltmann, and the development of these concepts in some of Moltmann's contemporary conversation partners from the feminist, womanist, and process perspectives. These conversation partners, in particular, retain, broaden, and strengthen the important and pertinent political and social themes in Moltmann's eschatology.

Sin and Hope Together

In the previous chapter, I established that sin, as those aspects of the web of interdependence that cause harm, is what creates the systems of injustice and suffering that activists seek to change. Sin is the theological frame in which Christians can identify the sources and consequences of

---

6. It is important to note that I mean "object" in the broadest possible sense, in that there is a thing(s) hoped for. As will be evident in what follows, we must be very careful not to confuse limited and provisional objects of hope with the end goal or telos of hope, which is in the mind of God and discerned in bits and pieces via theological imagination. To say that hope has an object is to say that when we hope, we orient ourselves toward something beyond all present historical possibility. I also use the word telos to describe that for which we hope. See Marshall, *Though the Fig Tree Does Not Blossom*, 68, 70.

7. As it was originally written before the publication of Ellen Ott Marshall's *Though the Fig Tree Does Not Blossom*, this chapter shares many important themes with that text, and now benefits from some of Marshall's language. Marshall also uses the rubric of hope's object, source (foundation), and practice. There also are some key distinctions between Marshall's perspective and what I present here, and I will note those where appropriate. Marshall, *Though the Fig Tree Does Not Blossom*.

injustice. The reality of sin accounts for the paralysis of activists, binding them by their complicity in systemic structures. In my description of sin as it relates to social witness, I argued that to violate the well-being of another person, community, or the earth is to violate the aims of God. To develop this argument fully, however, we must take up the theological alternative with which to compare the current situation: a theology of hope. Without a theology of hope, we may all agree that things may be *going wrong* and that we are responsible for action. But hope gives Christian activists a frame by which they discern what constitutes *the good*. Further, without hope, our entanglement in sin is not countered by God's stronger force for good in the world.

A complementary consciousness of hope and sin is necessary to the flourishing of social witness practice for two reasons. First, sin and hope provide an honest account of the paradox of Christian life. We are both discouraged and inspired, both numbed and stirred, both broken and healed. Reinhold Niebuhr famously describes this paradox as the human condition of being both finite and free, that our nature is bound; but at the same time, humans are meant for transcendence.[8] An honest account of sin helps activists to accept the limitations of their efforts in light of the complex character of social sin. The sources and manifestations of sin are too numerous, too ambiguous to be changed by simplistic efforts. Likewise, the condition of sin that binds us all makes it impossible for us to see rightly and do the good.

And yet, mere acknowledgement of these realities is not enough to nurture and compel us to engage in practices of social witness. While such acknowledgement offers us comfort when our efforts are met with resistance, inertia, or failure, it does not offer us inspiration to try again. In fact, a deep awareness of sin might, on its own, lead us to despair instead of action. Without a contrasting reality, sin is deadly. When the language of sin is framed in relationship to the possibility of goodness, however, *then* we are able to accept our failures *and* persevere. About this contrast, Marjorie Suchocki writes, "Yet sin is a salvific word, a word of grace. Sin can only be named as such when there is the possibility not simply of judgment, but of forgiveness and transformation. The naming of sin bespeaks a vision where violence is not the norm; it bespeaks

---

8. Niebuhr, *Nature and Destiny*.

transcendence through imagination of a new and different future. Such a vision measures sin."[9]

To encourage perseverance and discourage despair, an honest accounting of sin must be balanced by hope. Hope is the knowledge that the present failures, the pervasiveness of suffering, and the seemingly insurmountable condition of sin binding us do not have the last word. As Paul wrote to the church in Rome, "And not only that, but we also boast in our sufferings, knowing that suffering produces endurance, and endurance produces character, and character produces hope, and hope does not disappoint us, because God's love has been poured into our hearts through the Holy Spirit that has been given to us."[10] Even in the midst of suffering, hope is born in us. In this way, hope is a living thing, beyond cognitive knowledge or awareness: hope is the disposition by which we commune with something deeper, broader, and a closer approximation of the good than our human experience otherwise affords us. This communion comes from God, by whose love, poured into our hearts, we are able to pursue the good.

The complementary consciousness of sin and hope is also necessary to the practice of social witness in another way. The theological orientation of hope, in light of sin, invites a peculiar sort of freedom in religious practice. This freedom is rooted in the knowledge that, given the pervasive and binding character of sin, we seek and attain the good only in so far as we participate in God's activity in the world. The accomplishment of a just world is not, finally, up to us; if it were, we would be lost. Instead, we rely on God's grace and allow ourselves to be nurtured and challenged by it. Here is a place where Reformed theology might offer a real gift of freedom to practitioners of social witness.[11] By God's grace, we are invited, compelled, inspired, and equipped to work with God toward the coming of a new heaven and new earth. Especially in the Reformed tradition, we find that when it comes to the advent of the kingdom of God, God does it. We work with God, collaborating, contributing and participating in God's work toward a new world.

9. Suchocki, *Fall to Violence*, 164.

10. Rom 5:3–5.

11. This is a key point of divergence between what I argue here and what Ellen Ott Marshall says about hope and divine immanence and transcendence. I discuss this difference and my own interpretation of divine transcendence and eschatology below, in my discussion of hope's foundation. See Marshall, *Though the Fig Tree Does Not Blossom*.

In Serene Jones' story of the long-range planning committee meeting, described at the end of chapter 4, we see how easily despair can creep into our discernment process.[12] Upon acknowledging the fatigue and guilt that plagued them, the group entered a period of discernment about what it means to view Christian life and practice under the rubric of grace. In relation to Christian practices, the group discussed how they might both embrace the freedom offered by God's grace and strive for the excellence inspired by God's grace. Jones writes, "To see the church in this manner is to imagine it as a community in which there is both constant striving for excellence of form and continued realization that grace cannot be earned, only received as a gift. In this sense, the church is a community of the beautiful in which the patterns of Christian living—the many practices we do and are—both matter not and matter enormously."[13] As Jones describes it, a Reformed theology of grace frees people from the "burden of perfection," so that we might take greater risks in practice, engaging our imagination and creativity.[14] Ellen Ott Marshall makes a similar argument against "perfectionist cynicism," whereby we risk missing beauty and joy in the midst of our striving against suffering and injustice.[15] The "community of the beautiful,"[16] to borrow Jones' evocative phrase, is able to release these simplistic and idealistic expectations of perfection, engaging both sin and hope in a dialectical playfulness.[17]

In this dialectical and artistic playfulness, social witness might be practiced with "both strenuous seriousness and relaxed joy."[18] In its most

12. Jones, "Graced Practices," 65.

13. Ibid., 70.

14. Ibid., 65.

15. Marshall, *Though the Fig Tree Does Not Blossom*, 105.

16. It is important to note that although Jones does not engage his contemporaneous text, Alex García-Rivera develops the category of the "Community of the Beautiful" more fully in relationship to social justice and in a slightly different trajectory (theological aesthetics): "'(L)ifting up the lowly' reveals God's gracious glory shining forth into the darkness of the fallen human spirit only to lift up the human heart back towards itself creating the Community of the Beautiful so that songs of praise may be heard once again, even, amidst the tombstones." García-Rivera, *Community of the Beautiful*, 38.

17. Of course, one ought not conflate the justification/sanctification dialectic with the sin/hope dialectic. At the same time, the dispositions of freedom and striving, as described by Jones, are at the heart of my use of sin and hope as they relate to social witness practice.

18. Jones, "Graced Practices," 70.

excellent form, social witness is practiced with seriousness in that activists both seek to do their very best and with joyful freedom in that they do not despair when met with obstacles. Hope compels practitioners of social witness to strive for excellence, seeking political and social expertise, theological integrity, and real change. At the same time, practitioners can relax in their practice, aware that we persevere by God's grace and cooperate with God in the seeking and establishing of the good.

An Alternative Future: Hope Defined

We have examined hope's salutariness as a dialectical partner to doctrinal formulations of sin, and begun to unpack its meaning as a theological disposition. It is to the latter that we now turn with more precision: what constitutes hope? To what do we refer when we affirm, with the prophet Jeremiah, God's plans for a "future with hope"?[19]

First we must acknowledge that hope is not easily or succinctly defined, precisely because its future and imaginative character mean that we do not yet know that for which we hope. It is constituted by newness, change, and promise. Hope is defined, in part, by what it is not.[20] Furthermore, the structures of sin that bind us are powerful because they blind us to hope and lead us to despair. Walter Brueggemann describes how hope is sometimes difficult to bring to light, even within the community of faith:

> The task of prophetic imagination and ministry is to *bring to public expression those very hopes and yearnings* that have been denied so long and suppressed so deeply that we no longer know they are there. Hope, on the one hand, is an absurdity too embarrassing to speak about, for it flies in the face of all those claims we have been told are facts . . . On the other hand, hope is subversive, for it limits the grandiose pretension of the present, daring to announce that the present to which we have all made commitments is now called into question.[21]

---

19. Jeremiah 29:11.

20. For example, Jürgen Moltmann argues in *Hope for the Church* that the kingdom of God, that toward which our hope is oriented, cannot be wholly identified with the success of purely human works. He also warns against identifying the kingdom of God with a completely otherworldly escape from life on earth. See Moltmann, "Diaconal Church."

21. Brueggemann, *Prophetic Imagination*, 65. Emphasis in original.

In these words, Brueggemann argues persuasively that hope is not easily expressed. To the ear of the oppressed, it sounds foolish, fantastic, and impossible. To the ear of the powerful, it sounds revealing and threatening. At its core, hope is the conviction that the way things are is not all that there is, and will not remain forever. Elaine Crawford defines hope as, simply, the "passion for the possible."[22] In other words, despite the suffering and evil we encounter in the world, hope believes that another world—God's reign of peace and justice—is possible. In hope, furthermore, we find passion to anticipate and work toward that other world. Hope also points to a reality beyond and beneath the flawed and sinful historical context of human experience. Hope recalls a sacred reality deep within human experience and the life of the world, and it anticipates the coming of a new depth of this sacred reality.

Hope is the deep trust that God's intention is for the good, the unbounded flourishing of all of life, and that God is active (with human participation) in bringing about the good, both in present realities and in a yet-to-be-imagined future. Implicit in this definition are the two orienting realities in which hope finds its meaning: God's promise of a good future, and God's activity for good in present and past history. Jürgen Moltmann writes, "biblical thought always understands hope as the expectation of a good future which rests on God's promise."[23] Trust in God's promises of a good future furthermore requires knowledge (and thus memory) of the one who makes *and keeps* promises.[24]

In a collection of essays written in honor of Letty Russell, Rosemary Radford Ruether describes the paradoxical character of Russell's eschatology, which urges us to address all of our theological questions from the perspective of the "New Creation":

> This does not mean that there are not reference points for Christian theology in paradigmatic memories of the past, . . . (b)ut all these past moments are to be understood as "memories of the future." . . . Ultimately, our liberating memories of the future are rooted in God working in history, seeking to make us God's partners in redeeming creation. It is we, all humans, all creation, who are "God's utopia," God's future. Our memories of the many ways in which we have experienced redemption are

22. Crawford, *Hope in the Holler*, xii.

23. Moltmann, "Hope," 271.

24. Moltmann, *Theology of Hope*, 104, 106.

finally memories of our response to and partnership with God
when we acted for transformation and justice, when we celebrated its signs of presence in our midst.[25]

The New Creation, then, is the true reference point and object of hope.
Even our memories of God's activity for good in the world are understood through the lens of the object of Christian hope, the advent of
God's New Creation. All of our work for liberation, peace, and the care of
creation in history are given meaning and purpose by God's alternative
future in which the whole creation is redeemed.

Hope is trust in the truthfulness of this claim, that God is working
in and beyond history to redeem the whole creation.

In the remaining pages of this chapter, we will explore the relationship of hope to social witness through three questions: what is hope's
object, and how does it inform political and religious practice in the
present? In what do we find hope's source and foundation? And, in the
present social and political situation, what does the disposition of hope
do: how does it shape and inform our work in the public sphere as we
seek to be faithful disciples in our context? In conclusion, I will pursue
a fourth question: what are some grounded practices that can cultivate
and strengthen hope?

"Assurance of Things Hoped For": Hope's Object

As noted above, hope always is oriented by its object, a "thing hoped
for," as we read in the eleventh chapter of Hebrews. The writer of the
epistle adds, "the conviction of things not seen."[26] That hope is, in part,
constituted by that which we have yet to imagine, reminds us that there
is much yet to be seen about hope. Thus, hope has about it a palpable
expectancy, the perception of which requires our imagination.

Just the same, we find ample images, metaphors, and affirmations
of "the things hoped for" throughout the biblical witness and woven
through the work of theologians and ethicists. The writer of Second
Isaiah, for example, presents an image of new life to the Judeans who are
displaced as a result of the Babylonian exile:

> I am about to do a new thing;
> now it springs forth, do you not perceive it?

25. Ruether, "Theological Vision of Letty M. Russell," 20–21, 22.

26. Hebrews 11:1.

I will make a way in the wilderness
and rivers in the desert.[27]

In this text, God promises a "new thing" and, in the same breath, asks the exiles whether or not they perceive it. In the text, God's new thing is described as imminent, but God's promises of protection and sustenance must have seemed far off and not trustworthy for those in exile. In response to God's question of them, their answer likely would have been, "No, we do not perceive this new thing springing forth."

Such is the difficulty with perceiving and expecting a new future. On the one hand, we are meant to know and trust God's work among us to bring about a new thing; on the other, this same new thing rests just beyond our grasp and comprehension. Certainly, throughout biblical literature, we find many examples of how hope points us to a future that is new and, to a large degree, unknown. This future is peculiar because, while its particulars remain unknown to us, its reality *is* known at the very depths of human experience. It is so deep, however, that we sometimes are unable even to perceive it.

Richard Bauckham and Trevor Hart write about how we grapple with the character of God's future as known, yet profoundly unknown. They describe it as *essentially new*: "God's promised future both is and is not like the present, continuous and discontinuous with it; such is the radical nature of its essential newness."[28] Perceiving the future is something like standing at the shore of the ocean. Most of the time, we notice the sand and the water. We notice the smell of sunscreen and the squeals of children. Every once in a while, all of these particulars weave themselves together in such a way that we are palpably conscious of our connectedness with the earth and of the connectedness of all of creation. As the sun warms our skin and the cool water bites at our toes, we *feel* the web of interdependence as well as our connectedness to it.[29] Just as soon as we have recognized this connectedness, however, our fragile grasp of its depth and vastness slips away. This moment will not be the only time that this awareness springs up. God will, again and again, show us a "new thing."

27. Isaiah 43:19.

28. Bauckham and Hart, *Hope Against Hope*, 96.

29. Gerald May famously described this sense of connectedness as the "unitive experience." See May, *Will and Spirit*, 53.

This analogy is particularly apt because it reminds us, as above, that the task of grasping hope's "essential newness" requires an extension of our knowing beyond intellectual assent; it incorporates our physical, emotional, and creative selves, as well. To describe hope as a *disposition* brings to mind holistic positionality and tendency toward a yet-to-be-known object: God's promised good future. To hope is to lean into God's alternative future, and to allow that reality to shape our life and work in history. To cultivate and nurture the theological disposition of hope, we place our whole selves in service of that good future.

Hope's Object: Two Images of God's Good Future

Particularly for social witness practitioners, imagining the alternative future as the reality in which God's governance overturns unjust structures of power and domination provides a powerful and salient orienting image. Moltmann argues that Christian hope expects that real life, "what it was truly meant to be," will accompany the advent of the kingdom of God.[30]

What is the shape of God's promised future, of "what is truly meant to be"? Two biblical and theological themes that help us imagine hope's object are *basileia tou theou*, often translated as kingdom of God, and *eudaimonia*, often translated as human flourishing. These two themes are interwoven, and many writers consider *eudaimonia* to be a central component to the realization of "*basileia* vision."

Based on Jesus' teachings about the kingdom of God, prophetic literature, and the visions described in Revelation, we find ample theological resources by which we might more deeply understand the aspect of well-being associated with God's alternative future. Marjorie Suchocki describes it as the vision of the "community of God":[31]

> There is a vision that informs us. The vision is drawn from the whole universe of relations, and it bespeaks the beauty of recipro-

---

30. Moltmann, *Theology of Hope*, 216.

31. Suchocki, like other feminist and process scholars, rejects the language of "kingdom of God," on the grounds of its hierarchical and androcentric implications. While her point is well taken, I have chosen to use the more traditional phrase "kingdom of God" for clarity's sake. In addition, given the very alternative-ness of God's future, we might be well to question our assumptions about the essential character of "kingship." In either case, however—community or kingdom—both phrases point to the *social* aspect of God's future.

cal well-being, of justice, of love without boundaries. It bespeaks a vision of no less than the community of God. This vision calls us to recognize who we are individually and communally, and to live toward the hope of transformation. This hope is itself mediated through the peculiar togetherness of memory, empathy, and imagination. It brings intuitions of the well-being of the earth and its inhabitants, luring us away from violence and toward transformation.[32]

The vision, as Suchocki so eloquently describes it, carries us back to the web of interdependence: hope is located in the "universe of relations" and points us toward "reciprocal well-being." As a vision that informs us, it serves as an orientation or goal by which we measure our lives. Ellen Ott Marshall describes the *basileia* vision as the highest good in the Christian tradition.[33]

The vision calls us to live *toward* it, acknowledging that it is not present or perhaps even possible in current realities. But it does bear enough power within it to lure us to approximate it as best we can. Such is the practice of Christian faith on the whole. Caroline Kelly is a local pastor who regularly works with congregation and presbytery members who practice various forms of social witness. Echoing Mother Teresa, Kelly laments, "I wish we could move away from the 'success' language. That's one frustration I have. It's not being successful that we're about, but being faithful."[34] If we can reorient our perspective with regards to the *basileia tou theou*, then our question moves beyond, "Will action X bring about result Y?," to, "Will action X most closely approximate what we understand to be what life is 'truly meant to be'?"[35] While the former question is not unimportant, the latter points us to questions of identity and orientation toward hope's object. Hope's object becomes, then, something beyond a concrete goal to be reached with prescribed strategies and tactics.

As hope's object, *basileia* is a "tensive symbol," set in opposition to structures of domination, oppression, and victimization. In the life and

32. Suchocki, *Fall to Violence*, 160.

33. Marshall, *Though the Fig Tree Does Not Blossom*, 6.

34. Mother Teresa is known to have drawn the distinction between success and faithfulness in a number of contexts, including in conversation with her biographer, Navin Chawla: "We are called upon not to be successful, but to be faithful." See Chawla, *Mother Theresa*, xxiv.

35. Moltmann, *Theology of Hope*, 216.

ministry of Jesus, we see the values and social arrangements of the kingdom of God. Elisabeth Schüssler Fiorenza describes the characteristics
of the *basileia* vision: "It envisions an alternative world free of hunger,
poverty, and domination. This 'envisioned' world is already anticipated
in the inclusive table community, in the healing and liberating practices,
as well as the domination-free kinship community of the Jesus movement, which found many followers among the poor, the despised, the ill
and possessed, the outcasts, prostitutes and sinners."[36] Fiorenza describes
well the orienting power of the *basileia* image for the earliest Christian
communities, and for contemporary Christian communities, as well. For
feminist and womanist scholars, in particular, the values of well-being
and agential freedom are central to the image of *basileia*. (In fact, well-
being includes, for many feminists, the power and capacity to exercise
moral agency.) Our identity as Christians—and more precisely, feminist
Christians—is grounded in this image, and it orients our activity in the
world: "In sum, a feminist Christian identity is to be articulated again
and again in the emancipatory struggles for the vision of G*d's *basileia*,
which spells well-being and freedom for all in the global village."[37]

Thus, the *basileia* vision incorporates flourishing. Ellen Ott
Marshall defines the *basileia* vision (our highest good and end) in terms
of God's active presence toward *eudaimonia*: "The *telos* is a flourishing
whole, a system in which all creatures realize their potential. This is the
suitable end for human beings in an interdependent system ... God's
movement in the world entails creating, sustaining, and transforming
conditions such that life can flourish."[38] In attempting to live into the
vision of individual and communal well-being, we begin to discover,
perhaps paradoxically, what it means to be a flourishing human being.
In the introduction, I quoted South African scholar John de Gruchy,
who includes among the markers of well-being the human capacities
for action and relationship.[39] Inherent in de Gruchy's description is the
assumption that, in pursuing the well-being of other persons and the
earth, we discover our own well-being. Well-being, de Gruchy argues,
includes the very same capacities that we recruit in order to seek well-
being for others: the capacity to love, to imagine, to sense injustice, to

36. Schüssler Fiorenza, "To Follow the Vision," 135.

37. Ibid., 137.

38. Marshall, *Though the Fig Tree Does Not Blossom*, 70.

39. de Gruchy, *Confessions of a Christian Humanist*, 50–51.

live responsibly, to be angry when it is just. In social witness, the most pressing issues usually are those that make up what Suchocki describes as a minimal level of well-being, such as nourishment and shelter.[40] But, if we take into consideration the nurture of moral agency, the goodness of reciprocal relationships, and the communal implications of even individual flourishing, we begin to imagine well-being not as that which we seek *for* the *other*, but that which we embody as we build new forms of social relationships. We also begin to recast *eudaimonia* through a social lens, whereby one flourishes precisely in her working for justice and equality for another.[41]

Finally, we do well to remember that hope's object—*basileia tou theou*, characterized by a broad and multivalent *eudaimonia*—serves a distinct purpose in pricking our conscience and encouraging us in our work in the political and social sphere. It orients us toward God, toward the world, toward the "not yet," and to the already realized. Ellen Ott Marshall recounts all of the ways, through social witness, we glimpse "God's project" in the here and now:

> God is One who creates, sustains, and renews life continually. Through the lens of this faith claim, then, I interpret efforts to dismantle debilitating conditions as efforts that are consonant with, if not responding to, the spirit of God in the world. Similarly, I perceive certain moments to be glimpses of God's project, that flourishing creation. A successful small business breathes some life into an economically depressed neighborhood. A major pharmaceutical company donates research and drugs to treat parasitic infections in developing countries. Representatives from different religious and ethnic groups forge a more integrated political system. Uprooted persons return voluntarily and peacefully to their homes. Middle school students resolve a conflict through peer mediation. Survivors of domestic violence rebuild their lives. A green sprig takes hold in a blighted landscape. These are occurrences in which life asserts itself. And through the lens of this faith claim, such occurrences suggest something about the movement of God and the approximation of God's project.[42]

---

40. Suchocki, *Fall to Violence*, 67.

41. Recall also Rebecca Todd Peters' description of well-being, which informs the discussion of *eudaimonia* here in and in chapter 1. See Peters, *In Search of the Good Life*, 28–31.

42. Marshall, *Though the Fig Tree Does Not Blossom*, 75.

Even as we lean into a future that is yet-to-be-known (or, as Bauckham and Hart describe it, "essentially new"), we approximate the vision of the *basileia tou theou*. As the writers of the Confession of 1967 poignantly described: "Already God's reign is present as a ferment in the world, stirring hope in men and preparing the world to receive its ultimate judgment and redemption."[43] This ferment stirs the human theological capacities of imagination and creativity.

Grasping "Essential Newness": The Role of Imagination and Creativity

How do we cultivate our disposition toward these two core images? The cultivation of hope, as a disposition toward that which is not yet realized, requires us to develop the theological capacities of imagination and creativity. Hope is not hope unless it pricks and relies upon human imagination. That is, when people within the community of faith engage in hope, they are placing their most creative selves in service of God's intentions for the world. Because the future cannot be fully identified with current social and political realities, hope requires us to envision new ways of living that approximate the *basileia tou theou*, in which God's intention of *eudaimonia* is sought and provisionally realized. Without imagination, all we have is an outcome resulting from the trajectory of current circumstances. Even for Christian activists who are optimistic about their influence, this prospect is limited at best. Can we imagine something different and better than our own best hopes for political change?

Imagination is the theological capacity by which we grasp, even provisionally, the "essential newness" that is the object of Christian hope. Baukham and Hart write, "In faith, we shall see duly, our imagination is engaged, stretched, and enabled to accommodate a vision of a meaningful and hopeful future for the world, a meaning which could never be had by extrapolating the circumstances of the tragic drama of history itself."[44]

To do this, there must be an alternative or even "oppositional" quality about eschatological imagination. Evelyn Parker argues that oppositional imagination, as a way of relating to the *basileia* vision, is necessary in order to resist present circumstances, and to envision alternatives.[45]

---

43. Presbyterian Church (U.S.A.), "Confession of 1967," 9.55.

44. Bauckham and Hart, *Hope Against Hope*, 51.

45. This is particularly true in the context of the "hegemonic relations of race, class,

As a theological capacity necessary for emancipatory hope, oppositional imagination contributes to *eudaimonia*, or the freedom to live into the fullness of humanity's God-given potential.[46] Another womanist scholar, Joan Martin, describes the paradox of living in, and in critical relationship to, the present: "Yet I still congregationally sing such spirituals as 'My Lord, What a Mornin'' and attempt to live within the reign of God. Further, I dare to learn about and teach Christian moral agency as a spiritual practice and as a web of social relations."[47] In the work of Parker, Martin, Elaine Crawford, Emilie Townes, and others, one can see the centrality of creativity and imagination in the work of living in dynamic relationship to the present. As a means to engage these theological themes, womanists draw on (and create) spirituals and songs, literature, poetry, and narratives. Through the arts, they find and demonstrate the capacity to imagine another, essentially new, way.

Theological imagination is crucial to the practice of social witness, more generally, as well. To many activists, even the most destructive historical circumstances seem loath to change, fitting Nelson Tharp's vivid description of a glacier. Given that the practice of social witness encounters such mighty structural resistance and bears few measurable fruits, religious activists are vulnerable to fatigue and burnout. According to Brueggemann, however, imagination "touches the hopeless person."[48] Hope calls us to open ourselves to be touched and stretched in creative relationship with God and the world around us. In imagining, we not only look toward what will be but, in the very process of imagination, we allow our apprehension of the "new thing" to generate a creative tension with the present. We are reminded that the *basileia* vision is a "tensive" symbol.[49] It is in creative tension that new, present possibilities emerge. Martin Luther King, Jr. described the creative tension faced by activists in the Civil Rights movement. In his letter to white clergy from the Birmingham City Jail, he wrote: "I must confess that I am not afraid of the word, tension. I have earnestly worked and preached against violent

---

and gender" that shapes the experience of many African American adolescents, the community with which Parker is particularly concerned in her study. Parker, *Trouble Don't Last Always*, 48.

46. Ibid., viii.

47. Martin, "Sacred Hope and Social Goal," 211–12.

48. Brueggemann, *Prophetic Imagination*, 65.

49. Schüssler Fiorenza, "To Follow the Vision," 135.

tension, but there is a type of constructive tension that is necessary for growth . . ."[50] This tension is not always comfortable, however; it produces an aching when people are confronted with current realities.

In a peculiar way, hope seemingly exacerbates suffering for those who seek to engage, reform, and transform social systems. As practitioners of social witness work earnestly toward the realization of *basileia tou theou* in history, they are repeatedly confronted with the limitations of the present: "Hope transcends the present precisely by enabling us to transcend it imaginatively and, upon our return, to perceive all too clearly its lacks and needs. . . . to imagine is, for all practical purposes, already to have had, to have tasted the fruit which lies beyond, to have one's appetite for the possible thoroughly whetted so that the actual begins to taste sour by comparison."[51] When we imagine the "fruit which lies beyond," we see clearly the inadequacies of the present, to the degree that we might be moved to despair. We might fight an understandable urge to withdraw, to focus solely on the coming of the possible. In particular historical circumstances, this sort of otherworldly perspective has often equipped those suffering violence and oppression to persevere. In some contexts, emotional and mental withdrawal from the present makes survival possible.

For practitioners of social witness, however, withdrawal is not an option. Imagination cannot be limited to escapism, but must serve as a catalyst and source of demands for change within the present. This is how practitioners work *with* God in imagining and working toward an alternative future, the new heaven and new earth. In the process, the "lacks and needs" of the present are laid bare, and the truth-telling component of social witness is called into action. Not only is it called into action, demanding something of us, but it is grounded in an "expectation of a good future which rests on God's promise," to use Moltmann's language.[52]

In imagination, we live into what often is described as the "already" and "not-yet" aspects of Christian hope. The alternative future is already breaking through into the present, but not fully realized. As Moltmann so compellingly puts it, "The Kingdom is breaking in where we least ex-

---

50. King, "Letter," 291.

51. Bauckham and Hart, *Hope Against Hope*, 56.

52. Moltmann, "Hope," 271.

pect it."[53] The creative tension borne out of the already/not-yet character of hope is one of the great strengths of Christian social witness. Activists are not bound by the realities of the present to imagine an alternative future, but draw much of the content of imagination from images and the lyrical language of Christian faith. Hope sustains trust in God's alternative future of flourishing, a trust that places Christian activists in a tense relationship with current reality.

As such, hope demands not only imagination and creativity, which lean toward God's promises for the future, but also memory and trust, which lean towards God's capacity to fulfill these promises. Despite its essential newness, hope's object is made intelligible by hope's foundation. In imagining the advent of the kingdom of God—in which all creation flourishes physically, emotionally, vocationally, socially, culturally, and ethically—we do not play in the realm of mere speculation. We draw our images of the alternative future of human and environmental flourishing from multiple sources within the tradition, like the text from Revelation, above, and from our own experience of God's will for good in the world. Together, these sources of knowledge about God's intention for life point to God's promise of direction and care for creation.

Memories of the Future: Hope's Foundation

God's promise of a "future with hope" is grounded and legitimated in God's sustaining and redeeming activity in history. We make many promises in life: we enter into covenants with other persons, we make vows of commitment to vocational callings and to communities, and we promise to ourselves that we will pursue new and healthy practices. These promises are important, and tell us *something* about God's commitment to us. But these promises are insufficient to tell us *everything* about God's commitment to us. We inevitably disappoint those to whom we make promises. God will not disappoint. We will not be able to maintain the trust of those whom we love. God can be trusted. Commitment, promise, and trust are all relational words. A promise implies a future in which something will happen. A promise does not make sense, however, outside of the context of how the relationship has unfolded in the past.

Particularly in reference to God's promised future, we look with particular interest to God's history of faithfulness to creation. As Brueggemann describes it, "It will finally be about God and us, about

---

53. Moltmann, "Diaconal Church," 36.

his faithfulness that vetoes our faithlessness."[54] Happily, God's alternative future also is beyond our imagining and does not depend solely on humanity's capabilities to live into that vision. This is, indeed, very good news, since we sometimes are not only unsuccessful, but also unfaithful! God remains faithful to God's promise. As the Brief Statement of Faith, partially quoted at the beginning of Part II, so compellingly affirms: "Like a mother who will not forsake her nursing child, like a father who runs to welcome the prodigal home, God is faithful still."[55]

God's promises are at the heart of Moltmann's theology of hope. Moltmann describes the promise as "a declaration which announces the coming of a reality that does not yet exist . . . (which) binds man to the future and gives him a sense for history."[56] In other words, the promise whose content is the future also serves to make sense of history.[57] Moltmann supports this claim with two rationales. First, a history related to a promise is teleological. It always is determined by promise, and its meaning is revealed in the promise.[58] Second, the promise cannot be understood apart from knowledge of the one making the promise. If we always consider the promise to be related to a God who makes and keeps promises, then abstract calculations or predictions of the future become far less compelling.[59]

This God—who promises a future in which suffering ends, in which we all feast together, in which our connectedness with all creation is realized—this God is the very same God who creates and sustains life, whose compassion led to God's own presence among us as a living and dying human being, whose life power exceeds the power of death in the resurrection. It is this God whom we find trustworthy, in whose promises we believe.

---

54. Brueggemann, *Prophetic Imagination*, 65.

55. Presbyterian Church (U.S.A.), "Brief Statement of Faith," 10.3.

56. Moltmann, *Theology of Hope*, 103.

57. Theologians in the postmodern school critique this idea of a "meta-narrative"—the totalizing story that makes sense of everything. Such critiques are rightly grounded on the affirmation of multiple narratives, which are culturally, psychologically, socially, and economically determined. Even within an open-ended system such as process theology, however, we find core "intentions," in which God is attributed with desire for well-being.

58. Moltmann, *Theology of Hope*, 103.

59. Ibid., 104, 106.

This trust in God's beneficence is central to the Reformed tradition. John Calvin described this as *pietas*: "I call 'piety' that reverence joined with love of God which the knowledge of his benefits induces."[60] Piety says something about what it means to be a human in faithful relationship to God, but it also, and perhaps more importantly, tells us something about God and God's relationship of faithfulness to humanity and creation. Kathryn Tanner continues the Reformed understanding of human relationship with God, arguing that in benevolent faithfulness, God is the giver of all good gifts.[61]

Hope rests in a *relationship* to God. As such, hope is dynamic and relational, resisting neat strategic plans for achieving hope's object. Brueggemann argues that to limit talk about hope to these terms is to miss its true power: "I am not talking about optimism or development or evolutionary advances but rather about promises made by one who stands distant from us and over against us but remarkably *for* us."[62] This description of hope makes clear its relational dimension, affirming that it can only be understood in relation to the promises made by a God who is "remarkably for us." The God who makes promises is the same God whom we know to be a beneficent source of good gifts. This God is both deeply known to us and ultimately mysterious to us.

On Newness and Yet Knowing: Trust and Memory in Relationship to an Immanent and Transcendent God

When we remember God's immanence *and* transcendence, we are reminded of hope's deep familiarity and essential newness. Keeping this balance between the "already" and "not yet" of eschatology demands much of us. Ellen Ott Marshall resists an unbalanced emphasis on God's transcendence, particularly as it relates to eschatology. She argues that the *basileia* vision should not become too otherworldly to us: "The *basileia* vision is an image of our realized potential, and it is something to which we must give expression rather than a transcendent ideal that we approximate or a historical end point toward which we progress."[63] Marshall also takes issue with some Reformed readings of divine transcendence and sovereignty, in contrast with human capacities for the

60. Calvin, *Institutes*, I.II.1.

61. Tanner, *Jesus, Humanity and the Trinity*, 2.

62. Brueggemann, *Prophetic Imagination*, 65.

63. Marshall, *Though the Fig Tree Does Not Blossom*, 38.

good. She argues, with Sharon Welch, that the theological tendency to "deify" God's sovereignty potentially "legitimates imperialistic behavior on the part of human beings, as well."[64] In addition to legitimating harmful behavior, Marshall argues, an overzealous insistence on divine sovereignty and transcendence undervalues the goodness in human efforts of the sort evidenced by those who practice resistance, compassion, and love in the face of violence: "(W)e need a theological anthropology that celebrates these figures as individuals who chose to collaborate with God on behalf of the flourishing whole rather than questionable creatures whom God managed to utilize in spite of themselves."[65]

Marshall's cautions are good ones, and reveal a point of tension in the Reformed tradition, itself. The temptation to "overcorrect," however, is very strong: we may find ourselves, in an effort to address imbalances in Reformed understandings of eschatology, tempted to argue that God's immanence, *rather than* God's transcendence, is the source of our hope. The mystery of hope, on the contrary, demands that we hold these sensibilities in tension. Amy Plantinga Pauw writes, "The fact that 'God is not through' means there are still many surprises in store; but our eschatological convictions are shaped by the trust that what lies ahead will not contradict the creative, redemptive, and transformative grace already revealed by the triune God."[66]

"God is not through." Such a deceptively simple phrase! Pauw takes this simple theme from Emilie Townes, who writes: "Hope, that which scares us and yet prepares us, gives us the wisdom to know that God is not through. Our task is to take the challenge that hope gives us—the joy along with the disappointment—and to work *with* God until our lives begin to pulse with something vaster and greater than anything we have known before.[67]" Hope, then, assumes that the God *whom we know and trust* has yet many things in store. Hope assumes that God's work in the world is oriented toward the good, that we are able to connect with God's work in the world, and that God's work in the world also will *always* transcend even our best efforts. This is, in part, what Rosemary Radford Ruether suggests when she recasts eschatology as "memories of

---

64. Ibid., 79.
65. Ibid., 86.
66. Pauw, "Some Last Words About Eschatology," 222.
67. Townes, "'Doctor Ain't Taking No Sticks,'" 192. Emphasis in original.

the future."[68] Paradoxically, that which we remember, when we seek to be God's partners in redeeming creation, is a vision that has not existed in history. It is both deeply known (and thus remembered) and essentially new (and thus unknown).

For the affirmation that "God is not through" to be good news and cause for hope, requires that the story of God's activity in the world, the part that has already happened in history, is of sufficient goodness that the idea that this story is not yet finished evokes hopeful anticipation rather than indifference or fear. It also requires that the unfinished story be shaped by a degree of essential newness and difference, such that we do not affirm only that *we* are not through, but that "*God* is not through." This affirmation means that our disappointment and disillusion vis-à-vis our own efforts toward creating a just society are not all that we have. God will yet do a new thing! Do we not perceive it?

The theological capacities of imagination and creativity, which supply Christian hope with a means to grasp essential newness, are complemented by the theological capacities of piety and memory, which supply Christian hope with a means to grasp God's action in history. By cultivating piety (Calvin's reverence and love) and memory, we find means to trust in God's promised future. We remember God's fulfillment of promises and God's faithfulness through the biblical narratives and through our own experiences in the community of faith. With these two types of theological capacities—imagination and creativity leaning toward hope's object, and piety and memory leaning upon hope's foundation—we are prepared to engage the world with hope. In other words, the theological orientation of hope serves a particular function in the practice of social witness.

"A Ferment in the World": Hope's Function in Social Witness

Oriented by hope's object (*basileia tou theou*, characterized by a broad and multivalent *eudaimonia*), and grounded by trust in God's effective activity in history, practitioners of social witness are buoyed by hope's capacity to cultivate expectation, encouragement, emancipation, and energy. Without resorting to unduly functionalist interpretations of hope, it does behoove us to consider how hope orients, grounds, and

68. Ruether, "Theological Vision of Letty M. Russell," 21.

supports social witness practice; and further, how it shapes the identity of practitioners.

Expectation

Growing up in southern Mississippi during the Civil Rights movement, Evelyn Parker describes her Christian Methodist Episcopal (CME) congregation's spiritual identity as deeply shaped by the social justice tradition. From that tradition, she remembers, the youth were "bathed . . . in social theology of involvement and confident expectation":[69] "The youth group that nurtured me was an island of hope in the middle of a sea of racist, political, and economic despair. My congregation, neighbors, teachers, and church family encouraged me, sometimes demanding that I move beyond my circumstance of hopelessness with the confidence and power to change the world. My fledging spirituality was rooted in the belief that with God all things are possible."[70] Parker describes a not-naïve, but confident sense of expectation that, through the Church, God is working to transform and upend hegemonic relations and structures of injustice. This expectation was founded in what Parker describes as "emancipatory hope," by which we "expect transformation of hegemonic relations of race, class, class, and gender and to act as God's agent ushering in God's vision of human equality."[71]

The kind of hope described in these pages cultivates within and among us an expectation of God's transformation and redemption of the world, which is also deeply cognizant of the vulnerability of life. It demands that, although we anticipate the realization of God's vision, we remain responsible and accountable to the suffering in this world. It is this dance between expectation and vulnerability that Jürgen Moltmann describes as the "unquiet heart": "In this hope the soul does not soar above our vale of tears to some imagined heavenly bliss, nor does it sever itself from the earth . . . It does not calm the unquiet heart, but is itself this unquiet heart in man. Those who hope in Christ can no longer put up with reality as it is, but begin to suffer under it, to contradict it."[72]

69. Parker, *Trouble Don't Last Always*, 3.

70. Ibid., 5.

71. Ibid., 6. The function of hope in cultivating an emancipatory imagination is further explicated below.

72. Moltmann, *Theology of Hope*, 21.

In other words, those who hope are not shielded from suffering in the world. In fact, because they expect the transformation of it, they find their consciousness pricked by the vulnerabilities they encounter in the world. The contradiction between expectation and current circumstances is part and parcel of the life of Christian discipleship. As Ellen Ott Marshall puts it, we seek to "cultivate a sense of possibility without glossing over the real losses and limits of life."[73] In her own practice of hope, in the public sphere and in her personal life, Marshall reminds herself (and the reader) that, "if my hope is to be a responsible one, I still have work to do. I must engage practices that keep me accountable to life's vulnerability so that my hope does not slip into optimism."[74] Accountability to life's vulnerability, even as we expect God's effective activity in history, cultivates an uncomfortable, yet creative, context in which to practice social witness.

Emilie Townes concludes her sobering essay on race and medicine with an extended reflection on the centrality of hope in response to, and despite, the inequitable health care system in the United States. While, as noted above, Townes affirms that "God is not through,"[75] she also paints a realistic portrait of the precariousness that hope's expectation introduces into our lives: "It *is* frightening, this hope, because we know that Jesus interrupts the mundane and comfortable in us and calls us to move beyond ourselves and to accept a new agenda for living. We are led into a life of risk . . . When we truly believe in this hope, it will order and shape our lives in ways that are not always predictable, not always safe, and rarely conventional."[76] This life of risk is resonant with Moltmann's "unquiet heart." Expectation brings with it yearning and discontent. We may expect God to act in history, expect God's transformation of hegemonic relationships, even expect God to bring history and its earthly structures to an end. In the midst of these forms of holy expectation, we may also remain accountable to suffering, injustice, and vulnerability in this world. Hope cultivates among us both expectation and accountability.

Hope does more than this, however. Hope also encourages us in our efforts to participate in God's transformation of social structures.

---

73. Marshall, *Though the Fig Tree Does Not Blossom*, xv.

74. Ibid., xvii.

75. Townes, "'Doctor Ain't Taking No Sticks,'" 192. Emphasis in original.

76. Ibid., 191.

Somewhere in between our realistic appraisal of what is before us, and our expectation that God will do something different, we must find the places where we are encouraged to cooperate *with* God's transformation of the world, even now.

Encouragement

Adding encouragement to expectation adds an ethical dimension to hope. It is the aspect of hope that keeps us engaged in the present, without cynicism or undue otherworldly longing. When encouragement is cultivated in the practice of hope, practitioners of social witness find meaning in their work, even when systems of suffering and injustice are slow to change. Hope's encouragement is about the goodness in cooperating with God in the pursuit of the *basileia tou theou*. It is about the courage to press on, in the face of persistent social problems. Ellen Ott Marshall writes: "If hope is to generate and sustain moral action, it must be accountable to the tragic, and it must grapple honestly with the elemental questions that radical suffering unleashes. But it must also soar at times . . . (T)he prophetic imagination (is) that capacity we all have to envision something other than what is before us."[77] Hope must soar. It must soar, not to take us away from the work of accountability and grappling, but to push us onward, to keep us company, and to expand our hearts and minds in imagining a different reality.

Encouragement is cultivated in daily engagement with the world, in service of God's alternative future. As Emile Townes put it, through this engagement, we "work *with* God until our lives begin to pulse with something vaster and greater than anything we have known before."[78] Moment by moment, we are confronted with beauty and meaning that give us a glimpse of what *eudaimonia* looks like. When our work in the world is oriented by hope, we do encounter God there, and God infuses our efforts with goodness, courage, and even joy. Recall that the writers of the Stuttgart Confession of Guilt lamented their own failure to believe "more joyously."[79]

When we cultivate encouragement in social witness, we actively seek joy in the practice. Joy may be discerned in a small political victory,

77. Marshall, *Though the Fig Tree Does Not Blossom*, 64.

78. Townes, "'Doctor Ain't Taking No Sticks,'" 192. Emphasis in original.

79. Gerlach, *And the Witnesses Were Silent*, 226.

in a new friendship born, in shared laughter, or in voices joined in song. When asked what sustained the congregation of Southside Presbyterian Church during their work in the Sanctuary Movement and beyond, John Fife describes the deeply symbiotic relationship between worship, justice, and other ministries of the church: "Well, I think the art form is to make some sort of coherent whole out of the whole ministry and mission of the church. So it's got to be connected with worship, it's got to be connected with education, it's got to be connected with the kind of . . . what Jack (Haberer) described as the altruistic ministries of the church. And then the justice stuff has got to be integral to that, too. The art form, . . . I've always assumed, was to make the worship experience connected with the mission of the church."[80]

As he describes the weaving together the worship and mission of the church, Fife argues that this is how the congregation is sustained in social witness: "Oh, it's definitely the worship." In worship, we encounter hope in many tactile and aesthetic forms: water, table, song, poetry, and story. In these moments, we remember and encounter hope, as it encourages us and instills in us an expectation that God is doing something new among us. As we join together in God's project, even as we are bound by complicated and unjust social relationships, we find freedom and flourishing. Hope cultivates emancipatory imagination.

Emancipation

With regard to eschatology, the kind of freedom and flourishing described by feminist and womanist scholars depends on the restoration of human agency in service of the good. Elisabeth Schüssler Fiorenza, for example, argues that the image of *basileia tou theou* "spells freedom from domination."[81] Fiorenza writes that the Jesus movement, as an emancipatory movement, demonstrates women's centrality as historical and theological agents (rather than as non-agential victims of patriarchal marginalization).[82] In the Jesus movement, women engaged in practices like prophetic pronouncements and theological argumentation, prefiguring God's "alternative world of justice and salvation."[83]

---

80. Fife names worship as a central element in social witness on several occasions. Here, he makes reference to Jack Haberer's book, *GodViews*. See Haberer, *GodViews*.

81. Schüssler Fiorenza, "To Follow the Vision," 134.

82. Ibid., 131.

83. Ibid., 137.

In other words, hope evokes agential participation in the world. It would be naïve, at best, to assume that full human emancipation is realized in our present context, with all of its structural and social injustice. Paired with an honest appraisal of the realities of sin in the world, however, hope *does* have the capacity to free us to imagine and act toward a different future. Evelyn Parker argues that Christian hope is necessarily emancipatory in that it responds to the context of oppression and marginalization. She writes that Christian hope is both "liberative and efficacious,"[84] and that it "pursues personal and communal freedom and agency in transforming economic, political, and racial oppression in the global society."[85]

If hope is both liberative and efficacious, it has a freeing quality about it even as it sets out to infuse social structures with freedom. It does not merely free the mind without also working on restrictive and oppressive structures. Because hope is built upon the core assumption that "God is not through," we work for social change with the trust that God is consistently and effectively bringing about the good future, in which our structures of interdependence will become sources for mutual flourishing. Along the way, human imagination is engaged and freed, so that practitioners of social witness may become partners in God's project of transformation. Hope works to scrape away the limitations, oppression, and harmful structures that work together to suppress and deny human imagination, unearthing new longings and energizing practitioners of social witness to work toward the *basileia* vision.

Energy

Finally, hope energizes persons and communities to continue striving for the realization of God's good future. Above, I noted that consciousness of sin may comfort us when our efforts are not politically successful. Alone, however, consciousness of sin does not inspire us to try again. What gives activists the energy to persevere in the absence of measurable social change? Such is the role of hope in social witness practice.

As Brueggemann writes, the kind of alternative consciousness that criticizes dominant structures (grieving that "things are not right") must also energize persons and communities with the promise of new life: "The royal consciousness leads people to despair about the power to

84. Parker, *Trouble Don't Last Always*, 11.
85. Ibid., 17.

move toward new life. It is the task of prophetic imagination and ministry to bring people to engage the promise of newness that is at work in our history with God. . . Numb people do not discern or fear death. Conversely, despairing people do not anticipate or receive newness."[86] Brueggemann critiques the more liberal theological perspectives for fixating on the critical work of prophetic ministry, with little attention to the energizing work of prophetic ministry. Where is the life of the new community?

This challenge rings particularly true for mainline and progressive practitioners of social witness, who sometimes seem loathe to embrace eschatology, perhaps because they confuse it with "wishful thinking." As Evelyn Parker reminds us, however, "Wishful thinking is far from the hope that I propose . . . Emancipatory hope offers personal agency in partnership with God and the conviction that God will end unjust powers of domination."[87]

Agency. Partnership. Conviction. All of these are realms of human action that imply deep sources of energy. To those of us who have been inspired by lifelong practitioners of social witness, their unflagging energy dedicated to the pursuit of justice and flourishing is apparent. The question then becomes, how do activists access these sources of energy that inspire, sustain, and fund them?

This question can be asked about all four of the dynamics cultivated by hope in social witness. How can practitioners of social witness prepare the soil in which hope can cultivate expectation, encouragement, emancipation and energy? What is required to evoke Elaine Crawford's "passion for the possible?"[88] In closing, let us name just two means by which we might actively nurture the disposition of hope in the practice of social witness: gratitude and aesthetics.

Practicing Hope in Our Social Contexts

As noted above, practitioners of social witness frequently exhibit a degree of hesitancy when it comes to eschatology and the four dynamics of hope, a hesitancy that ranges from healthy suspicion to outright cynicism. Ellen Ott Marshall rightly identifies the problem for many

86. Brueggemann, *Prophetic Imagination*, 59–60.

87. Parker, *Trouble Don't Last Always*, 26.

88. Crawford, *Hope in the Holler*, xii.

socially-conscious Christians: how can we faithfully "cultivate a sense of possibility without glossing over the real losses and limits of life"?[89] This hesitancy can be attributed to both an imbalanced emphasis on the criticizing component of prophetic imagination, and an overly-cognitive approach to theology and practice. As antidotes to these two tendencies, practitioners benefit from the cultivation of joyful gratitude and aesthetic creativity within social witness.

Joyful Gratitude, Or Resisting Perfectionist Cynicism

John Fife has been working in behalf of vulnerable migrants for more than thirty years. While he and others in the movement have seen some political change, one might argue that the legal and political context in which the immigration conversation is taking place is getting more polarized and toxic, not less so. Alongside his sober analysis of the situation, Fife holds on to a sense of gratitude and enthusiasm regarding the transformation of the Southside congregation in the interest of compassion and justice. When describing how the congregation became a "Sanctuary" church, Fife smiles widely and speaks with reverence about the project, saying that the presence in their midst of the migrants that the congregation assisted in applying for political asylum compelled the congregation. Their stories, their narratives were compelling: "And so, when the question of Sanctuary came up, we took a vote. We did a secret ballot, so nobody felt coerced. And people had to vote, really, what their faith indicated to them. And there were only two negative votes in the whole congregation . . . It blew my socks off." Clearly, for those who have worked for a just immigration system, there is much to lament in the current system. Despite the persistence of injustice, however, Fife manages to find himself surprised and energized by small victories in the movement.

There is *always* more work to do. The "not yet" of eschatological hopes are very real and present in the lives of religious activists committed to social change. The practitioner of social witness, committed to the hard work of critical analysis, may find herself, even while acknowledging progress, lamenting all that is left undone. Ellen Ott Marshall calls this tendency "perfectionist cynicism," drawing on Sharon Welch's category of "cultured despair," and identifies it as something that we must resist

---

89. Marshall, *Though the Fig Tree Does Not Blossom*, xv.

if we are to cultivate the disposition of hope. She writes, "Sometimes we practice hope by doing everything we can to unearth a moment of beauty and then to defend it vigorously from all that threatens to push it back underground. If that moment of beauty is an act of unexpected generosity, we fight off the voices of perfectionist cynicism that remind us how far it falls from addressing structural injustice. Yes, we must address structural injustice, but we can also celebrate an act of generosity."[90]

To cultivate hope, it is important that we unearth, defend, and celebrate small moments of beauty, even as we remain committed to the hard labor of criticizing social injustice and doggedly pursuing social change. This is, perhaps, how Fife recalls the vote to become a sanctuary congregation—as a moment of beauty, worthy to be unearthed, defended, and celebrated. These postures, together, comprise a kind of gratitude for small movements—chinks in the glacier—that do not mean that the movement for social change is complete or fulfilled, but that there are, everywhere, tiny signs of the inbreaking of the *basileia tou theou*. There is always more to do, but there *also* is always something for which to be grateful.

Activists may be helped in resisting "perfectionist cynicism" by rituals that invite reflection upon and gratitude for these tiny moments of beauty in the midst of practice. It may be a brief time at the beginning of a gathering for practitioners to name moments of beauty they've witnessed in their work together. Or, perhaps, one member of a group may be designated to watch for moments of beauty in the midst of the practice: a sentinel, of sorts. Strategies like these for practicing watchfulness and remembering, *even in the midst of practices of social witness,* contribute much to the cultivation of hope in social witness.

Aesthetic Creativity, Or Getting Out of Our Heads

Alongside postures of gratitude and joy for moments of beauty, practitioners of social witness must also exercise their own capacities for aesthetic creativity. Noticing beauty is important, but we do well to remember that social movements also *create* beauty. Recall the conclusions drawn by social movement theorist James Jasper, who celebrates the poetic contributions of activists, arguing that their "(e)ntire lives can

---

90. Ibid., 105.

be artful creations."[91] He describes, at length, the creative contributions of social movements, writing, "For many, the creativity of protest provides the experience of sheer joy, the play of a utopian vision . . . Like artists and intellectuals, protestors are key articulators of (diverse and meaningful) alternatives . . . They are offering us visions to 'try on' so we can see what fits."[92]

Christians committed to social change may, from time to time, exhibit impatience with regard to the creative, poetic, and aesthetic dimensions of social witness practice. If we take the analysis of sociologists like Jasper seriously, however, we are challenged to move beyond rationalistic interpretations of what is happening in social witness, and to embrace the multivalent creativity expressed and formed within the practice. If social witness is to be oriented by a disposition of hope, we must attend to the creative and aesthetic aspects of the practice. After all, as Brueggemann writes, "Speech about hope cannot be explanatory and scientifically argumentative; rather, it must be lyrical in the sense that it touches the hopeless person at many different points."[93]

Much of our language about hope finally reaches a limit, a horizon, over which rationality alone is not capable of carrying us. To cultivate hope in social witness, we need the aesthetic and the poetic to breathe life into the practice. Only with deep and holy attention to the aesthetic and affective dimensions of social witness are we able access the theological capacities of imagination and creativity required to grasp the "essential newness" that is at the heart of Christian hope. Brueggemann describes this as the doxological character of prophetic ministry:

> The hope-filled language of prophecy, in cutting through the royal despair and hopelessness, is the language of amazement. It is a language that engages the community in new discernments and celebrations just when it had nearly given up and had nothing to celebrate. The language of amazement is against the despair just as the language of grief is against the numbness. I believe that, rightly embraced, no more subversive or prophetic idiom can be uttered than the practice of doxology, which sets us right before the reality of God, of God right at the center of a scene from which we presumed he had fled.[94]

91. Jasper, *Art of Moral Protest*, 340.

92. Ibid., 367, 370.

93. Brueggemann, *Prophetic Imagination*, 65.

94. Ibid., 67–68.

As an example of the language of amazement, Brueggemann points to the poetics of Second Isaiah, in which these energizing images might serve as the "staging ground" for real, material inversions of social and political relations in history.[95]

Even in its earnest attempts to change unjust social structures, to redress wrongs, to seek an alternative vision of human and earth flourishing, the practice of social witness is, itself, an alternative way of being. Brueggemann urges us to re-invigorate this aspect of the prophetic imagination: to receive and become God's alternative community. With deepened attention to poetics, social witness is revived as a practice deeply oriented toward hope, and sings doxologies to the God who is bringing about this alternative way of being.[96] It is a practice in which we play—seriously play—at being an alternative kind of society in which all kinds of flourishing happen. This sort of play requires art and beauty. The movement for just immigration policy is deepened by Sebastião Salgado's heart-pricking photographic essay, *Migrations*.[97] The movement for racial justice is fortified by the heart-expanding tunes and lyrics of "Lift Every Voice and Sing."[98] The movement for ecological sustainability is spurred on by the plaintive lyrics of The Avett Brothers and the animated paintings of Jason Ryan Mitchum in "Head Full of Doubt/ Road Full of Promise."[99]

The arts have a capacity to communicate something about eschatology that is beyond rationality. Practitioners of social witness can cultivate hope in the practice by protecting these aesthetic aspects of the practice; making time for song, poetry, visual arts, and dance; and celebrating these gifts. Along the way, they may very well discover "lives worth living."[100]

95. Ibid., 74.

96. Brueggemann acknowledges the difficulty of doing this, particularly for middle-class Christians: "In a society strong on self-congratulation, the capacity to receive in doxology the new world being given is nearly lost. Grief and praise are ways of prophetic criticism and energy, which can be more intentional even in our age." Ibid., 117.

97. Salgado, *Migrations*.

98. Johnson and Johnson, "Lift Every Voice and Sing."

99. Hilton, "Exclusive Premiere: New Avett Brothers Video."

100. Jasper, *The Art of Moral Protest*, 337.

PART THREE

Toward the Nourishment
of Social Witness Practice

6

Thinking and Expressing

Theological Reflection in Social Witness Practice

AFTER TWO HOURS OF LIVELY DISCUSSION WITH SEVERAL OF THE AC-
TIVISTS from Baltimore Presbytery, the four of us sat quietly in the formal
living room of Nelson and Ellen Tharp's retirement-village apartment.
We had shared a lunch together in one of the facility's many cafeterias,
and had then retired to the Tharp's apartment to continue our conversation. Thurston Griggs looked at his hands, folded in his lap. Quietly, he
said, "I feel we should thank you for letting us think about these things
and express ourselves." Was this expression of gratitude due to the rivet-
ing questions posed over lunch in the cafeteria? I am doubtful that this is
so. The gratitude does, however, point to a seldom-expressed desire for
opportunities to dig more deeply into the practice of social witness and
reflect upon its meaning and function. At the same time, these opportunities must be approached subtly in order to persuade activists, who
might otherwise be loath to interrupt their work for justice.

In this concluding chapter, I make an argument and constructive
proposals for the revitalization of social witness through the strengthening of theological reflection within it. In theological reflection, practitioners remember their experience in practice; identify the connections
with and challenges to theological knowledge in that experience; and
imagine new ways to engage in practice. As I have noted in the chapters
on sin and hope, we find very little by way of *explicit* theological reflection occurring in the context of social witness as it is practiced among
some progressive mainline Protestants. One cannot say that theologizing
is absent from the practice, but theological reflection is rarely identifiable
as a distinct component of social witness. How might we engage in theological reflection so that it honors and sustains the already strong commitments of Christian social activists? How might a committed activist,

161

like Nelson Tharp, be more deeply nourished in social witness and not merely persevere? This chapter makes proposals in response to questions like these. I focus specifically on theological reflection as the means to nourish social witness because the models that I propose respond to the diverse challenges generated by this particular practice.

Of course, one *could* make proposals with regard to the role and function of theology within social witness without having engaged in an interdisciplinary and mutually critical conversation. That strategy, however, would reflect a practical theological method different from the one proposed in the introduction to this book. To do so would assume that theology speaks constructively to experience, but not vice versa. It would place the theological tradition in the position of "answering" the questions posed by practice. Instead, I have created a larger conversation, engaging with practice and social movement theories, theologies of sin and hope, and concrete examples of practice, allowing each component to be probed and challenged by the others. The proposals I make in this chapter about theological reflection in the practice of social witness are responsive to the insights gathered in that conversation.

First, I offer a brief review of the discoveries from the preceding chapters, identifying places for further development. I then consider how theological reflection fits into social witness practice, with particular attention to the questions raised in the review of earlier chapters. Having determined the possibilities for theological reflection in social witness, I elaborate on the purpose and place of theological reflection therein, consulting several contemporary scholars who are doing work in just this area. Finally, I propose a concrete method of theological reflection by which practitioners of social witness might reflect theologically upon their commitments, actions, and identities. This chapter serves as an invitation to theological reflection for activists, pastors, and scholars, and to further conversation within the Church and academy.

Social Witness: Current Practice and Future Possibilities

In the preceding pages, I have explored the practice of social witness in light of its shape as a Christian *practice*, its impact upon participants' *identity*, and its connections with theologies of *sin* and *hope*. Taken together, these particular lenses on social witness lend themselves to a

Reformed and feminist interpretation of the practice in the context of the Christian life. A Reformed understanding of social witness is marked by a deep consciousness of both human sin and trust in God's promise of an alternative future. More specifically, however, a *feminist* Reformed reading of social witness also pays particular attention to the agency of activists, the sin inherent in social structures, and God's intention of well-being for creation. A feminist and Reformed reading of social witness requires that we remain cognizant of how we, in practice, relate to theological traditions.

My feminist and Reformed interpretation leads to a particular way of doing theological reflection within social witness that draws on all facets of the practice: experience, theological tradition, and social and political theory. This way of doing theological reflection seeks to do more than justify or evaluate practice, although these are important components of reflection. For one thing, theological traditions also are challenged by the practice. Perhaps more importantly, however, in a Reformed and feminist understanding of social witness, the experience and formation of practitioners must be taken into account by theological reflection, so that the practice is integrated into the whole of Christian life. In other words, theological reflection happens not only before and after, but also within an instance of social witness and within the larger practice. Before we turn to the nuts and bolts of theological reflection, let us name some of the implications for the integration of theological reflection within the practice of social witness. To do this, I will name some of the trajectories introduced in earlier chapters.

Social Witness as a Practice

The argument I have been building in this book responds to several critical questions regarding social witness. First, it examines social witness as a practice. In so doing, this work proposes new trajectories for further exploration, particularly in pursuing how theological reflection can nourish the overall practice of social witness. In the first pages of this book, I described social witness as a religious practice in the following way:

> Christian social witness practice is a complex and interrelated set of theologically, politically and structurally-oriented activities, with standards of excellence that vary according to the prioritizing of these orientations, and with the capacity to generate

among participants internal goods related to their identity and faith formation. This set of activities is embedded and given life in the lived social patterns, historical experience and traditions of a particular religious institution.

In this theoretical definition, I drew upon and challenged Alasdair MacIntyre's categories of analysis in order to account for the multiple dimensions of social witness. The complexity and interrelatedness of the components of social witness practice, which complicate any simplistic identification of the practice with a singular activity like protests or letter writing, are precisely what open up so many questions for further reflection. I will name three generative areas that seem particularly ripe for further development: the identification and use of standards of excellence, the discernment and nourishing of internal goods, and the relationship between social witness practice and the institutions and traditions from which it is born and to which it gives rise.

STANDARDS OF EXCELLENCE

Sometimes, a practice that seems a colossal failure might, if examined under varying standards of excellence, look quite different. As I noted above, Presbyterian minister Caroline Kelly lamented the emphasis on political success among Christian activists. As she says, "I wish we could get away from 'success language.' What we are called to be is 'faithful.'" What Kelly describes could be interpreted as a commentary on the difficulties of negotiating what sometimes seem to be competing standards of excellence (explicated in chapter 2). The value of social witness might be discerned along a number of trajectories—its political efficacy, its structural influence, or its theological integrity. Part of the challenge of the practice of social witness is coming to agreement about its guiding principles. Inherent in that challenge, however, is opportunity. In the process of negotiating what makes for good practice, participants in social witness stand in the nexus of theory and practice. In this liminal space, practitioners can consider questions that are foundational to a practice and, at the same time, call upon a peculiar kind of wisdom. *Phronesis*, sometimes reductively translated as "practical wisdom," demands that practitioners examine their actions, their values, their relationships, their traditions, and all facets of a practice, in order to imagine the meaning of it for Christian life and God's creation. In this mode, practitioners might generate a more integrative standard of excellence. Drawing on Bernard

Lee's phrasing, practitioners might ask themselves, "Is this of a piece with the kind of world (or church, or city, or corporation) we would want to call to life?"[1]

Internal Goods

One of the means by which social witness might be judged excellent is the degree to which practitioners acquire intangible benefits via their participation in the practice. The word "benefits" may conjure images of rewards or perks, but the benefits gained in the participation in social witness practice are much deeper and formative than the limited meaning that we might associate with that word. The benefit is the formation of virtue, which in turn the practitioner reintegrates into the practice. This continual process of formation in practice has broad implications for the larger life of discipleship, both for the individual practitioner and the whole relevant community. In other words, as practitioners of social witness are shaped by their practice, their participation in the whole constellation of practices that makes up the Christian life will be strengthened.

As many activists will attest, social witness influences not only the social and political spheres in which it is practiced, but also the practitioners themselves. They derive meaning and significance from their participation, despite meeting failure in the pursuit of their goals. Practices of social witness, like other kinds of practices, are sustainable even despite seeming failure because, as Craig Dykstra writes, they have "effects on their minds, imaginations, and spirits."[2] Within the minds and hearts of social activists, something is ignited in the practice of social witness. They discover new self-understandings that are ripe to be harvested for their significance in Christian life. Furthermore, these goods that are internal to social witness are more than mere rewards of pleasure for an individual's good behavior. The real goods, MacIntyre and Dykstra would suggest, are the development of the moral life, both for the practitioners and within the larger community of faith. More attention to these less defined positive outcomes of a practice may actually yield new standards of excellence. We would then use different standards (or perhaps order our standards differently) to measure the value of a seemingly

---

1. Lee, "Practical Theology as Phronetic," 14.
2. Dykstra, "Reconceiving Practice," 45.

failed practice. When Christians in Georgia protest an anti-immigration bill that still ultimately becomes law, their practice is not necessarily a "failed" one, because that particular instance of social witness *also* generates among the practitioners new ethical understandings of welcoming the stranger, caring for the sick, and the intricacies of race in the United States.

TRADITION AND INSTITUTIONS

Finally, I have argued that a full analysis of the practice of social witness must take into account the ways in which participants relate to their theological traditions, their congregational and denominational institutions, and the myriad community groups with whom they partner in activism (chapter 2). For some, the relationship between their religious tradition and the practice of social action has always been quite clear. For others, a more recent epiphanal moment has compelled them to reconsider the resources for social action within their traditions, looking for elements that might be retrieved, reconstructed, or perhaps rejected. In relation to institutions, some practitioners of social witness, like Thurston Griggs, may feel alone in their congregations. Others, like Nelson and Ellen Tharp, describe themselves as the "lovable kooks" within their congregations. While they feel welcomed within their congregation, they suspect that many members discount their activism. Still other congregations may embrace their identities as "peace and justice" churches, either generally or in response to a particular issue, such as Southside Presbyterian's identification as a sanctuary church. In community cooperative action, Christian activists may wonder how their religious affiliation will affect their relationships with persons from other traditions, religions, or who claim no religious tradition at all. In some cases, these diverse understandings of what it means to be attached to a tradition or to be a member of an institution provide fuel for arguments. If practical theology offers structures that invite and provide space for these arguments about what is most important to us, it engages tradition in its best sense.

In the religious institutions that are home for many practitioners of social witness, an intentional effort to understand and reflect upon all of the intricacies that shape activists' relationships with traditions and institutions will nourish social witness. For some activists, this may mean learning how to be a minority political and theological voice in their congregations. For others, it means reflecting together, as a faith community, upon the vocation and social mission of the entire congregation. For many, this intentional effort must include opportunities to reflect upon the meaning of Christian faith itself, as well as the social role of Christians in pluralistic contexts.

Social Movement Theory and the Construction of Identity

In chapter 3, I framed identity as a good realized by participants as they engage in a practice and that, subsequently, practitioners become different kinds of people via social witness. In social witness, persons and groups discover the good of a certain kind of life, as MacIntyre puts it. Drawing on MacIntyre, James Jasper writes about protestors: "They epitomize Socrates' call for 'the examined life.' Protestors often find new ways of living, new modes of applying moral visions in everyday life. . . . Protest offers many virtues to its practitioners, giving meaning to their lives."[3] In one of the concluding chapters of *The Art of Moral Protest*, Jasper describes the goods derived via protest collectively as "lives worth living."[4]

Of course, Jasper is not particularly interested in religious identity, but his observations can be applied to the Christian activists. When asking questions about identity, we can ask, "How does social witness influence Christian activists *qua* Christians, both personally and collectively?" If we connect this question with the thesis of this book, we can also ask a more specific question: "How does theological reflection within the practice equip participants to participate in it with more theological depth and consciousness?"

The above questions should not be taken as an argument for more explicitly "Christian" social witness in the evangelical sense. Between the Christian Right and the progressive evangelical movement, represented by leaders like Jim Wallis, explicitly evangelical social activism is in no short supply. While their presence in public discourse is important and fitting in the context of politics in the United States, not every practice of social witness can or even should have the same degree of explicit theological certainty and commitment to evangelical principles.

---

3. Jasper, *Art of Moral Protest*, 340.
4. Ibid., 337–43.

The questions above, rather, dig into the conversations and elements of the practice that happen "behind the wall," when Christian activists gather among themselves to discern how their practice best connects them with Christian faith. Walter Brueggemann has proposed the descriptor "behind the wall" to differentiate the language Christians use when among themselves from the language they use in conversation and negotiation with non-Christians.[5] Language behind the wall is not evangelical language (necessarily), but it employs a community of faith's shared histories, practices, narratives, and values, thus influencing their collective and personal identity. It is the place where Christians can engage in self-criticism *and* theological imagination. The identity thus discerned operates as both an outcome of social witness and a resource for the continued practice.

In the process of discerning identity, we also might ask questions about the unity of moral life. Jasper uses MacIntyre's category of goods internal to a practice, suggesting that part of what makes activists' lives "worth living" is the process of discerning *both* the good as it is experienced personally as well as the good for humankind. For Christian activists, this is a theological question that requires the presence of imagination in identity formation. What is the best that we can imagine that God wants for the world?

Theologies of Sin and Hope

In chapters 4 and 5, I outlined how a consciousness of the condition of sin and the elusive yet present character of God's alternative future illumine and sustain the practice of social witness. The structures of interrelatedness that define our common life are evidence of God's *basileia* vision of creation's mutual *eudaimonia* and also give rise to sin that perpetuates harm and injustice. We participate in structures that perpetuate harm and injustice both consciously and unconsciously, both with and without malice. We sometimes see the good and cannot do it, and we sometimes cannot see the good at all. In this way, we can understand sin as being "entangled in the curse," to use Calvin's language.[6]

Just the same, we are always conscious of some deeper reality of good, even when we are unable to name or grasp it. Furthermore, so-

---

5. Brueggemann, "Legitimacy of a Sectarian Hermeneutic," 47–48.

6. Calvin, *Institutes*, II.I.8.

cial witness is nourished by the knowledge that God gathers up even our failures into the advent of God's alternative future of peace, justice, and flourishing. Knowing that we are meant to flourish collectively makes us painfully aware of the means by which we fall short of God's intent. Despite an overwhelming sense of sin's complexity and complicity, Christians continue to "yearn after the Kingdom of God."[7] For Presbyterians, in particular, the work God is doing in the world is the source of human work for good in the world. We are freed to pursue that good by the knowledge that it is not left only to our limited human effort: "With an urgency born of this hope the church applies itself to present tasks and strives for a better world. It does not identify limited progress with the kingdom of God on earth, nor does it despair in the face of disappointment and defeat. In steadfast hope the church looks beyond all partial achievement to the final triumph of God."[8] While the activists I interviewed did not seem despairing, they *did* describe some frustration and restlessness. Might a more robust eschatology remove some of the pressure shouldered by activists and offer a theological account for the meaning of human restlessness in the face of social harm? The consciousness of God's alternative future serves as a reminder that we are not solely responsible for the coming of this alternative community. Even more importantly, hope is the trust that God has better intentions for the world.

My proposal for greater attentiveness to sin and hope in social witness is not, again, an evangelical argument. For some liberal mainline social activists, the idea of using language like "sin" or "God's kingdom" in the public sphere is particularly distasteful, insofar as it is reminiscent of the heavy-handed moralistic language of the Christian Right. They also are concerned that the use of such language will "turn people off," as elder Nelson Tharp put it. Is there a means by which Christian activists might be nourished by reflection upon these theological questions, without using theological language strategically in the more public aspects of social witness?

---

7. Ibid., II.I.3.

8. Presbyterian Church (U.S.A.), "Confession of 1967," 9.55.

Theological Reflection in Social Witness: Opportunities and Challenges

Given the discoveries outlined above, I now turn to theological reflection and identify the ways in which this particular genre responds to the challenges and opportunities generated within social witness. In this section, I first address the challenges of proposing theological reflection at all, given many progressive mainliners' suspicion of the use of Christian theology in the public sphere. I then argue that theological reflection is not only an important piece of social witness, but is necessarily evoked by the ambiguities of the practice.

As admitted in the opening pages of this chapter, activists sometimes express resistance to the suggestion that they should pause to reflect upon their practice. As one veteran Presbyterian activist put it: "We probably spend three-quarters or nine-tenths of our time preaching to the choir. And it's good, in the sense that it re-inspires you to get out there and work. But it bothers me that we spend so much time talking to people who are already convinced. . . . We do a good job of preaching to ourselves. I think that's one of our biggest failings." This point is well taken, but can we draw a distinction between engaging in theological reflection and "preaching to ourselves"? Is there something more to theological reflection than a wholly inward, self-satisfying rationalization? Surely, if practitioners engage in theological reflection with depth, integrity, and openness, it would serve to do more than feed attitudes of self-satisfaction among participants. The most significant aspect of theological reflection that I propose below is that it always requires practitioners to be open to the workings of God within their experience of the practice, within their own hearts and minds as practitioners, and within the tradition as they receive it. Particularly within the broader Reformed tradition, practitioners of social witness, as they enter into the reflective mode of the practice, place themselves before God. They lay bare their goals, strategies, failings, and joys, and they seek to discern God within them. In theological reflection, practitioners of social witness examine how they have engaged in the practice *coram Deo*, before God.[9]

For some activists, the component of theological reflection may seem an extraneous, albeit nice and pious, addendum to social witness practice. I propose, however, that it is an essential component of

---

9. Stroup, *Before God.*

Christian social witness. Its omission results in the fatigue and frustration of activists, as well as the strained connection between the practice of social witness and the larger shape of Christian life. Furthermore, in the experience and narratives of activists and in the stories of entire communities of faith dedicated to social witness, we can recognize the seedlings of theological reflection bubbling up within social witness practice. Kathryn Tanner writes that theological reflection is an integral part of Christian practice:

> To see the importance of theology for everyday Christian life, one must understand how theological inquiry is forced by the vagaries of Christian practices themselves and is, consequently, a necessary part of their ordinary functioning. Theological reflection does not merely come to Christian practices from the outside—either before the fact, as a means of educating people into Christian practices, or after the fact, as an external aid and supplement at best or an irrelevant distraction at worst, to practices that might run well without it. Theological reflection instead arises within the ordinary workings of Christian lives to meet pressing practical needs. . . . (T)heological deliberation is a critical tool to meet problems that Christian practices, being what they are, inevitably generate.[10]

Tanner makes two significant points. First, she points out that Christian practices, precisely because they are open-ended and improvisational (good qualities in a complex and unpredictable world), "force" theological questions. In one congregation, for example, questions emerged during a conflict between military veterans and members who protested the Iraq war on the street corner in front of the church. For the participants in that instantiation of social witness, a very deep and practical theological question arose: shall we stop our protests out of compassion for our members who are hurt by it, or shall we honor the deep calling we feel to pursue peace and justice? (The protestors found it difficult to hold together their witness for peace and compassion for the veterans.) This practice of protest, related as it was to a social institution and to multiple traditions, eventually came to a moment in which a theological question presented itself. Practicing Christian faith in relationship to a living

---

10. Tanner also names the importance of theological reflection in adding religious depth to practices that otherwise mirror other, irreligious practices. Tanner, "Theological Reflection," 230.

community with sometimes contradictory values will, in and of itself, force questions that demand theological reflection.

Tanner's second observation about theological reflection within Christian practice is that it does not impose upon a practice from the outside, from a hierarchical or traditional authority, but that it "arises from within" practice. This second observation is related to the first: not only does the pressing *need* for theological reflection arise within practice, but the resources and possibilities for meeting this need are already resident in practice. The intrinsic character of theological reflection in social witness correlates well with MacIntyre's assertion that standards of excellence are *internal* to any given practice. In other words, practitioners of social witness know best what constitutes good practice—theologically, structurally, politically—and, if given the opportunity, can recruit that knowledge in service of strengthening the practice. In the case of theological reflection, persons already engaged in the practice are best equipped to discern its theological significance and meaning for Christian life. No arbitrary bar of theological excellence can do this.

While practices, including social witness, intrinsically bear within them both a pressing need and resources for theological reflection, they can be helped by more explicit attentiveness to these elements. To serve this purpose, there are many theories and methods of theological reflection that, when placed alongside the questions already present within social witness, might offer practitioners means by which they can engage these questions on a deeper level. Theological reflection can take any number of manifestations, some of which are more appropriate to social witness practice than others. Before I move on to presenting some of these descriptions of theological reflection, I should reiterate that they should not be understood as additional, *external* practices that exert control over social witness, but as *internal* means by which practitioners of social witness can surface and examine their own theological knowing and questions.

Practitioners of social witness, while rightly suspicious of recommendations for highly theoretical reflection, also voice questions, desires, and observations that bear theological significance. If either the practitioners themselves or the congregations and religious leaders to whom they relate ignore these opportunities, the potential for deepening, strengthening, and sustaining this practice of the Christian life are put at risk. The question that remains before us is, "How shall we do this?"

Defining Theological Reflection

What sort of theological reflection will deepen, strengthen, and sustain social witness practice? In this section, I elaborate on the method and content of theological reflection as it arises within and responds to the dilemmas raised in the practice of social witness. In short, the sort of theological reflection that I describe and advocate is a means by which social witness practitioners mine *both* their experience of social witness and the traditions and institutions in relationship to which they engage in this practice, with the expectation that both the logistics of the practice and practitioners' understandings of their participation in the Christian life are deepened. In the kind of theological reflection I propose, practitioners *themselves* become the object of reflection. In other words, theological reflection does more than identify and evaluate theological motivations and conclusions associated with the activities of a practice. It also leads practitioners to engage in a particular kind of self-examination, in which they consider how their experiences of social witness influence their self-understandings as Christians and, correlatively, how their identities as Christians influence their perception of what they are *doing* in social witness practice.

At the beginning of this chapter, I described theological reflection in the broadest possible terms: remembering experience in practice; identifying the connections with and challenges to theological knowledge via that experience; and imagining and implementing new ways to engage in practice. In his survey of styles of theological reflection, Robert Kinast also describes these three moments, which he names experience, theological correlation, and *praxis*.[11] This basic pattern of movement from practice to reflection and then back to practice matches the method inherent in practical theology. In both cases, practice is the starting and ending point. In theological reflection, experience is at the very core in the generation of theological knowledge, a methodological value that, in and of itself, distinguishes it from systematic theology. In the best cases, theological reflection invites a truly integrated and symbiotic relationship between action and thought. In *The Art of Theological*

---

11. Kinast, *What Are They Saying About Theological Reflection?*, 64–71.

Reflection, Patricia O'Connell Killen describes reflection in the following way: "Theological reflection is the discipline of exploring individual and corporate experience in conversation with the wisdom of a religious heritage. The conversation is a genuine dialogue that seeks to hear from our own beliefs, actions, and perspectives, as well as those of the tradition. It respects the integrity of both. Theological reflection therefore may confirm, challenge, clarify, and expand how we understand our own experience and how we understand the religious tradition. The outcome is new truth and meaning for living."[12]

Before I add more flesh to this outline, I want first to identify some of the significant issues at stake in defining theological reflection. Styles of theological reflection can vary widely, particularly the approach to relating experience and theological traditions. Attention to this particular issue will help us develop a clear definition of theological reflection and a description of its function before moving to concrete recommendations for its revitalization in social witness practice.

Despite a shared appeal to experience among diverse models of theological reflection, we can observe a number of trajectories in what Kinast calls this "general form of theologizing."[13] He writes that two characteristics help us to distinguish between what he describes as "styles" of theological reflection. The most obvious distinction that we might draw, he suggests, is among the types of experience chosen for reflection. We might reflect on pastoral or ministerial experience, cultural experience, experiences of marginalization, corporate experiences of the community of faith, or individual spiritual experiences, to name a few. In the case of social witness, in particular, practitioners would reflect upon (usually) corporate experiences of the encounter between Christian activists and social and political institutions.

Kinast goes on, however, to argue that the most important distinction among styles of theological reflection is "the way they correlate experience with the faith tradition."[14] Regardless of what sort of experience serves as the object of theological reflection, the process of correlation honors *both* experience and tradition, in contrast with "those who take their own experience as the sole norm of truth or those who insist on a

---

12. Killen and De Beer, *Art of Theological Reflection*, viii.

13. Kinast, *What Are They Saying About Theological Reflection?*, 64.

14. Ibid.

rigid conformity to a previous formulation of the faith."[15] Among methods of theological reflection that incorporate various means of correlation, however, we find a wide range of emphases upon experience and tradition.

In the mutually critical conversation that I have developed in this book, tradition is subject to correction by experience and other disciplines just as much as it corrects them. Within practical theology, as I noted in chapter 1, Don Browning has developed the perhaps best-known correlation method, which he calls a "revised" or "critical correlation method," building upon David Tracy's work on correlational theology. Browning proposes that the two poles of the revised correlation method, apologetics and confession, help persons of faith to reflect upon their experiences in light of the foundations of Christian faith. In a revised correlational approach to theological reflection, the practitioner relates to two "poles." In the confessional approach, experience must be reconciled to the tradition. In other words, experience has meaning insofar as it embodies the truth articulated in the narratives of Christian faith. In the apologetic approach, the tradition must be reconciled to experience. In other words, the tradition must be articulated in a way that makes it relevant to experience.[16] Particularly as Browning develops this approach, tradition seems to leave little room for argument—human life's deep theological essence is already settled and need only be discovered.[17] In other words, the tradition does not seem to change. Only the way in which it is connected to experience changes.

If theological reflection is truly intrinsic to something as unpredictable and complex as social witness, theological knowing cannot be as settled as Browning implies. Furthermore, theological reflection that amounts to a simplistic matching up of experience to the appropriate theological doctrines would not provide a nourishing component worth pursuing within social witness practice. If, however, theological reflection is supple and responsive to the contingencies of social witness practice, it will strengthen the entire complex practice—from the inside out.

In the context of social witness practice, the importance of this issue is difficult to overstate. While it is always appropriate for theological reflection within practices to incorporate the resources of tradition (in

15. Ibid., 68.

16. Browning, *Fundamental Practical Theology*, 44.

17. See Chopp, "Practical Theology and Liberation."

the sense that tradition is a living, embodied argument about what constitutes the good), the tradition is misused if it is formulaically applied to practice. Good theological reflection requires that we exhibit wisdom and sensitivity in negotiating how what we know in experience gives shape and life to what we know in tradition. For example, how might Southside Presbyterian Church's encounters with unjust immigration structures and practices inform how they understand the complexities of structural sin?

Bernard Lee writes that good practical theology makes use of the creative dialectic between *phronesis*, the knowledge of what sort of world we ought to be making together, and *praxis*, the means by which this knowledge is already working to make such a world a reality. *Phronesis* commonly is translated as "practical wisdom" and is a particular kind of intellectual virtue by which, in relation to the practical matters of life, we deliberate and seek the best way to pursue the good in social context. In no case, Lee argues, would *praxis* function apart from *phronesis*, or *phronesis* apart from *praxis*. They are "bound to each other."[18] The *phronesis/praxis* dialectic also occupies a place of privilege between *theoria* and *techne*, theoretical knowledge and technical practice. While the movement among *phronesis*, *techne*, and *theoria* is mostly fluid, there is one place where it is not—one would never move, in a *phronetic* practical theology, directly from theory to practice.[19] We must always pass through a middle, liminal space, in which we test and play with diverse arrangements of tradition and practice.

In this brief discussion of Lee's *phronetic* theology, we find important points of contact between it and the sort of theological reflection intrinsic to social witness. First, in privileging the place of *phronesis* in theological inquiry, Lee rejects the assumption that theoretical knowledge is more central or prior to any other sort of knowledge. Correlatively, the practice of social witness is not predicated upon an external, *a priori* theological position. Activists, for example, do not rely on formalized doctrinal mandates as they challenge structures of injustice and harm. Further, a rigid appeal to doctrinal theology would not lend itself to the practice of social witness, insofar as Christian activists are continually influenced by their relationships with one another, with the structures they seek to change, and with other activists who claim other or no religious

18. Lee, "Practical Theology as Phronetic," 1–2.

19. Ibid., 14.

tradition. Understood in this context, the theological traditions of sin and eschatology are best engaged as living and flexible languages. While particular traditions and histories give sin and eschatology structures of meaning, *phronesis* requires that we treat these structures of meaning with an improvisational spirit.

Second, *phronesis* demands a discerning spirit with regard to the concrete realities of our life together. Unlike Aristotle, his primary inter-locutor, Lee privileges *phronesis* above *theoria* for precisely this reason. While *theoria* involves the contemplation of ideal forms of goodness and truth, *phronesis* keeps us grounded and attentive to daily human living, in the interest of making small and constant decisions regarding what to do next: "But, the generalized understandings that inform *phronesis/ praxis* are about contingent, historical realities for which abstractions can never totally account. And when they do not, the virtue of *epieikeia* comes into play: knowing when exception to the generalization is re-quired by the concretely real."[20] Lee does not call for an abandonment of abstract, generalized understandings, but for the recruitment of *phronesis* in discerning when they are appropriate and when they must be modified in order to relate with authenticity to the practical contingen-cies of human life. In the context of social witness practice, the demand that theological reflection be supple in response to the twists and turns of concrete experience also rings true. For example, in the case of Southside Presbyterian Church's ministry with immigrants, practitioners found themselves confronting a diverse set of political and social structures of injustice: from companies that profit from the exploitation of migrant labor, to the criminalization of humanitarian assistance, to the complex web of the Immigration and Naturalization Service. The congregation has been able to negotiate these changes with flexibility and swiftness, an indication of a practical wisdom equipped to make decisions in the midst of practicing activism.

In Lee's description of *phronesis/praxis*, we can imagine how social activists might engage in theological reflection on the ground. Privileging *phronesis/praxis* does not mean rejecting "purer" theoretical reflection, but it *does* mean subjecting more abstract forms of theologizing to "on the ground" testing under the rubrics of moral formation and action. Elaine Graham, Heather Walton, and Frances Ward raise this issue well when they describe Browning's correlational approach: "And crucially

20. Ibid., 12.

the normative status of Christian theology remains unresolved within critical correlation. Does the gospel stand in judgement over all other insights into the human condition, which are at best proto-theological; or does the Christian tradition itself require correction and revision?"[21] In feminist models of theological reflection, the tradition does indeed require correction and revision. Feminist scholars might choose to retrieve, reconstruct or reject elements of the Christian tradition.[22]

Many feminists, as well as the broader category of liberation theologians, actually privilege experience over theological tradition: "This conviction is often expressed in the use of the Marxist term *praxis* (denoting the centrality of value-committed action), and the insistence that proper theological understanding cannot be formed independently of practical engagement. *Theology-in-action*, therefore, places primacy on *orthopraxis* (right action) rather than *orthodoxy* (right belief). This is more than simply another form of applied theology in which systematic and historical theology provide norms for pastoral care or ethics. Rather, here, practice is both the origin and the end of theological reflection."[23] Developing the *theology-in-action* method of theological reflection from the work of liberation theologians, Graham, Walton, and Ward describe Christianity's history of prophetic movement and interpretations of authentic discipleship. The prophetic tradition insists not on confessions of belief, but on action in solidarity with the suffering.[24] This method of theological reflection is predicated upon the assumption that God is active in history.

Theological reflection, of course, demands of activists a theological consciousness even *as they practice social witness*. The *theology-in-action* method fits well with the practice of social witness as I have described it above. In fact, it is meant to help those who are immersed in work for justice. The need for theological reflection comes as no surprise to those whose full-time vocation is working for social justice. The Open Door Community in Atlanta, for example, holds "clarification meetings" weekly, during which members of the community seek together to discern the causes of present sufferings and God's leading for the next steps.

21. Graham, Walton, and Ward, *Theological Reflection*, 168.
22. Ibid., 31–34.
23. Ibid., 170.
24. Ibid., 171–72.

The community also engages in daily reflection and frequent retreats away from the city on rural Dayspring Farm.[25]

The activists I met during my research, as well as the ones for whom I have developed this proposal, do not live at the Open Door. They live in retirement communities, in condominiums, and in rented apartments. They do not live in intentional communities in which the concern for social justice shapes every aspect of their lives together. I do think, however, that the emphasis on theological reflection within intentional communities can be instructive for them. While they might not be willing to expend a large portion of their already limited time for activism in retreat, we learn from intentional communities like the Open Door and some Quaker communities that theological reflection is what sustains and enriches social witness over time.

The practice of social witness can be strengthened by renewed awareness of the deep connections between theological reflection, building up the community of faith and social action. Graham, Walton, and Ward write, "Thus, the task of *forging Christian identity* and *building up the community of faith* involves taking a stand for human dignity and reconciliation in solidarity with those of all faiths and none who are similarly called to resist inequality, oppression and violence."[26]

Theology-in-action invites activists to engage in "behind the wall" discourse for the sake of "on the wall" discourse in solidarity with others who work for justice. *Theology-in-action*, beginning and ending in practice, creates a sort of spirituality of action, by which activists are equipped and formed by and for social witness. The exchange between experience and theological traditions is truly mutually critical, in that theology itself is transformed by its inseparable relationship with both action and spirituality.[27]

Theological reflection that generates a spirituality of social witness, in its best sense, contributes to the deep knowledge of participating in God's work for good in the world and confirms in practitioners the freedom gained by knowledge of grace and forgiveness. As Serene Jones puts it, we are both freed and encouraged by God's presence in the world. Just how this sort of theological reflection might come to be within the

25. The Open Door Community, "Street Teachers."

26. Graham, Walton, and Ward, *Theological Reflection*, 171. [Emphasis in original.]

27. Ibid., 185–86. For their description of *theology-in-action*, Graham, et.al., rely heavily on the work of Gustavo Gutiérrez. See Gutiérrez, *Theology of Liberation*.

context of social witness is the subject of the concluding section of this chapter. First, however, I will pause here to offer some methodological remarks on the value of this study for the larger family of practical theology.

A Note on the Implications of This Study for the Work of Practical Theology

As I have immersed myself in this work, I have developed a deeper and more nuanced understanding of the challenges and opportunities presented not only by the study of social witness practice, but also by the field of practical theology. As I draw on the ample resources provided for theological reflection by practical theologians in this final chapter, I also am left with some questions and hopes about the future of practical theology. For example, the work described in this book is heavily interdisciplinary, as I have so often noted. It draws on the work of several practical theologians, and it incorporates philosophical and social ethics, sociological theory, ethnographic study, classical and contemporary Reformed theology, process theology, feminist and womanist theology, and church documents. While I have danced with the methods of Don Browning, Rebecca Chopp, and others, the question remains: how, exactly, do these disparate disciplines come together in practical theology? This question is at the core of practical theology, and I do not dare assume to answer them here. The question alone clarifies the significance of Browning and others' experimentation with theological correlation. One question that might be asked of them is: what are other patterns of reflection, besides correlation, that might shape interdisciplinary work in practical theology?

Second, I want to note the peculiar way in which practical theologians may integrate ethnographic research into their work. Clearly, this study is not a reporting of the shape and practice of social witness, even among the subgroup of Presbyterian activists studied here. Instead, I have invited their voices into this bustling interdisciplinary conversation, and their participation has been invaluable in raising new questions, correcting assumptions, and breathing life—sometimes fire!—into the otherwise sterile categories. Finally, ethnographic research within practical theology is, perhaps, always action research. Insofar as action researchers always seek to improve that which they study, practical theologians who are committed to the deepening of practice share that goal.

Practical theologians ought not be shy about this purpose, particularly because ethnographic research with unpredictable subjects will ensure our humility in making constructive proposals!

Concrete Proposals for Theological Reflection in the Midst of Social Witness Practice

In the preceding pages, I illustrated both the challenges of introducing more explicit forms of theological reflection and the openings and possibilities for doing so. I described some theoretical models of doing theological reflection and showed how a theology-in-action approach lends itself in a particularly salient way to the enrichment of social witness practice. Drawing on the work of Graham, Walton, and Ward, I now turn toward concrete proposals for the shape, purpose, logistics, and process of theological reflection.

What Kind of Theological Reflection?

As I noted above, the activists themselves form part of what makes theological reflection difficult to accomplish within the context of social witness. Activists may be impatient with stepping out of the "active" mode; they may be hesitant to be perceived as proselytizing; they may doubt that consciousness of sin and the eschatology would encourage anything besides apathy and otherworldliness among activists. Their concerns are reasonable and require sensitivity to the particular needs that activists bring to any proposed method of theological reflection.

First, we must be clear that the proposals set forth in this project are meant to help activists develop a lively "spirituality of action" by which their already committed practice is strengthened and renewed. I do not propose, by any means, that social witness needs a more formal theological rationale in order to be justified as a Christian practice, but that theological reflection should serve to stimulate *phronesis*, lending deeper significance to the practice and inviting the practice to deepen Christian faith. In order to do this, theological reflection must be both mutually critical and mutually generative. In other words, the experience of social action should both challenge traditional theological assumptions as well as help generate new ones, in the same way that traditional theological discourse should both challenge the assumptions resting beneath social witness and generate new ways of engaging in the practice.

In order to do this, theological reflection must be adaptable to a variety of contexts. As I noted above, the many participants in social witness consider it an avocation: they do not live in intentional communities whose entire life together is shaped by social witness. In their case, the idea of setting aside a weekend or longer to separate themselves from activism in pursuit of theological reflection does not make sense, because their time for social witness is already limited, and they do not experience themselves as "fully immersed" in the practice. A theological reflection model appropriate to these forms of social witness practice must be adaptable to short-term, sporadic, and changing participation.

Second, we must respond to the anxieties among activists that theological reflection might lead to either (1) being mistaken for proselytizers or (2) apathy as a result of a focus on the role of sin and eschatology in the social sphere. In light of these concerns, the process of theological reflection briefly proposed here is particularly concerned with both explicit (but not necessarily public) reflection and specific ways of imagining the relationship between sin, hope, and social witness that encourage deeper and further action. Above, I discussed Brueggemann's concept of "behind the wall" discourse. Behind-the-wall discourse is explicitly theological, but not necessarily public in the sense that political discourse is public. In fact, as Brueggemann describes it, to engage in behind-the-wall discourse in a more public context is "dysfunctional,"[28] a diagnosis shared by many mainline Protestant activists. Correlatively, however, mainline activists sometimes mistakenly assume that conversation at the wall is the only discourse that has any import.[29] A process of theological reflection appropriate to social witness will disabuse activists of the assumption that theological reflection, if explicit, must also be conducted in the public sphere. As practitioners engage in theological reflection with more ease, however, components of theological reflection may begin to evidence themselves in more public spaces, albeit with great humility and space left open for wondering.

Secondly, in response to concerns that an emphasis on sin and eschatology will immobilize activists, theological reflection should draw specifically on the wealth of resources from Reformed, feminist, and process traditions, thus inviting us to consider the gifts of freedom and grace as they relate to any form of Christian practice. These resources

28. Brueggemann, "Legitimacy of a Sectarian Hermeneutic," 45.
29. Ibid., 61.

relate particularly to social witness practice, because without a deep knowledge of the complexity of and our complicity in sin and God's grace in response to it, our concrete failures might be attributed to a failure of will instead of the comprehensive condition of sin under which we live and work. These resources relate particularly to social witness practice, because without a deep knowledge of God's effective intent for the flourishing of the world and God's gathering our (admittedly limited) actions for the good into God's alternative future, we would surely be overcome by despair. For these reasons, the process of theological reflection proposed in this chapter invites very specific reflection upon sin and hope as they are evidenced in the Reformed and, to a lesser degree, process traditions. Before turning to the concrete steps of theological reflection, let us pause here to briefly consider its purpose and logistics in the context of social witness.

Getting to the Point: Purpose and Logistics

Activists like Nelson Tharp, who distrusts adding anything to social action that smacks of "preaching to ourselves," might not see any point in reflecting upon their practice of social witness. They do not see how theological reflection, in particular, advances the work that they understand themselves to be doing in the world. What if, however, the point is *not* political success, but deeper formation in Christian discipleship? Christian activists do maintain an aspect of personal and corporate identity that their secular partners do not share. Our identity is more than that of the "do-gooder," the identity assumed by the title character in the film *Amelie*.[30] Christian social activists, and what they do, are meant to be of a piece with the sort of world God is making among us. This means that political success, while a valid and important goal, is not all there is to Christian social witness. Theological reflection, when it is structured in a way that is appropriate to social witness, should urge activists to examine themselves as disciples, inviting them to ask not, "Is this successful?," but, "Is this faithful?"

Theological reflection may appear in a somewhat detailed and comprehensive form when deciding upon a strategy for action, when an issue first presents itself as an opportunity for social witness. As activists engage in letter writing, legislative visits, boycotts, and protests, theological

30. Jeunet, *Amélie.*

reflection might appear in a more abbreviated form. As Kathryn Tanner puts it, theological reflection is how we decide what to do next, given what we know at the moment.[31] The more frequently activists reflect theologically upon each aspect of a practice, the deeper their awareness of their identity as disciples and their participation in God's action in the world. In deciding when and how often to insert elements of theological reflection in practices of social witness, it is important to remember that the practice is not a single visit to a legislative office—it is the whole complex of activities associated with a particular social issue, including elements of theological reflection and worship. Finally, when (and if) a particular instance of social witness has reached some form of conclusion—when a desired bill is defeated, for example— activists can benefit from reflecting on the practice as a whole and their experience of it.

Having considered why and when to reflect theologically within social witness, we might also ask *who* does theological reflection. Of course, all practitioners are capable of reflection, and this affirmation is central to the liberation theological movement, which gives rise to Gutierrez's theology-in-action model. At the same time, however, one of the roles of the pastor is to *invite* practitioners into reflection. The pastor might be a part of the group engaged in witness, or she may be the pastor of a congregation in which some members engage in social witness. Her responsibility is to help all members seek faithful discipleship, including activists, who may be seeking ways to connect their activism with the broader Christian life. This role of facilitating theological reflection is, of course, different from proclamation: it is inviting and structuring the process (not content) of Christian formation among activists. To pastors whose role is to provoke and invite theological reflection, these concrete proposals are dedicated.

A Process for Theological Reflection in Social Witness, Briefly Proposed

All of the material above, addressing the purpose, style, and logistics of theological reflection, provide the frame for the process that I now briefly propose in conclusion. There are four "moments" in the process, all derived from the commitments gleaned from the interdisciplinary conversation elaborated above between Reformed, feminist, and process

---

31. Tanner, "Theological Reflection," 232.

theology; social movement theory; practice theory; and the experience of social witness as reported by some activists. The four moments are as follows:

- Experiencing activism and its immediate analysis;
- Taking a broader view via social analysis;
- Evoking theological awareness; and
- Renewing *praxis*.

In conclusion, I invite readers to consider how these moments might be captured in the midst of social witness practice and what other questions we might consider along the way.

Analyzing Immediate Experience

As practitioners engage in social witness, perhaps the foremost questions for them are "What is our goal?" and "Why are we seeking this?" These questions are important because they may surface very different interpretations of the practice among participants. In the Sanctuary movement, for example, some practitioners may have thought their goal was to save border refugees, one life at a time, while others may have thought that the goal was to bring to light flaws in United States immigration policy and apply pressure for legal change. In addition to surfacing goals for the practice, an immediate analysis also asks about the details of events. In the case of the protest of President Bush's visit to the Martin Luther King, Jr., Historic Site, for example, this kind of analysis asks questions such as: what was said? Who participated? What unexpected obstacles or opportunities did we find? What was the response? Did anything change as a result of our actions?

Questions pursued in an immediate analysis of an experience of social witness encourage us to examine the practice in its fullness, identifying the complex elements of it. This immediate analysis also is necessary to identify commonalities before moving into more abstract forms of analysis. Finally, beginning theological reflection with an immediate analysis of experience reveals the *praxis* orientation of this process. In other words, it is the whole practice, not its associated abstract theological concepts, that is at the center of our reflections.

ENGAGING IN SOCIAL ANALYSIS

While pastors might be tempted, when inviting activists into theological reflection, to move quickly into a theological analysis, pausing to first engage in social analysis serves to strengthen practitioners' understandings of the contexts of their witness. In social analysis, we ask questions such as: who are the persons affected by this issue? What structures of power are or would be impacted by our goal? And, what are the opportunities for action on this issue—what alliances can we build and where are the openings for change?

These questions are important because they help activists reevaluate the practice, adjusting their goals, strategies, and relationships. Emphasis upon social analysis keeps the practice grounded and responds to activists' wariness about seemingly abstract processes of thought. Furthermore, the inclusion and early placement also reaffirms the theological method developed throughout this project, which asserts that the fullest possible theological understanding is impossible without reflection upon concrete experience in practice. By placing social analysis alongside the immediate experience of social witness and before the evocation of theological awareness, this process of theological reflection opens up possibilities for new questions to emerge that invite theological analysis. If we were to begin with theological concepts and then seek to apply them to experience and our understandings of social structures, we might actually miss some of the new questions being posed by experience and social analysis to Christian faith.

EVOKING THEOLOGICAL AWARENESS

At the heart of the theological moment in this reflective process is Bernard Lee's question derived from a commitment to the development of *phronesis*: what sort of a world are we meant to be making? In the chapters above, I took two theological concepts as they relate to the "sort of world" we want to make—sin and eschatology—and wondered what sort of knowledge they might elicit about practitioners of social witness practice. With regard to sin and hope, practitioners of social witness might consider the following categories of questions. About the presence of sin and hope in current reality, practitioners might ask: How does present reality mirror or contradict our hopes for the world? Also, what inhibits our efforts to work toward this vision? In some way, practitioners should be invited to examine their own complicity in complex systems of sin and injustice, as well as their identification with particular understandings of God's alternative future.

About the relationship of theological traditions to the current state of affairs and experiences of social witness practice, practitioners might consider the following: What are the resources within our tradition, both written and experiential, that contribute to our understanding of this vision and to our understanding of how we fall short in service of it? Conversely, practitioners also should consider this question: What new thing do we know from our engagement in this particular instance of social witness that enriches, challenges, or confirms our understandings of our tradition? For example, practitioners might ask: Where do we see signs of the inbreaking of God's *basileia* in the midst of our practice? These questions about the relationship of theological tradition to practice draw very clearly on the mutually critical analysis model proposed by Rebecca Chopp, as described above.

Finally, about active theological discernment in the midst of practice, and in relationship to the questions discussed above, practitioners are challenged to consider these difficult questions: what is God doing in this situation? How is God present among us? What do we want to ask of God?[32] While these questions are not easily asked and even more difficult to answer, particularly for practitioners in the Reformed tradition, they are the orienting questions in Christian discipleship. If activists are to understand their practice as an important component of their relationships with God, we must always make room for seeking and being found by God in the present.

RENEWING PRAXIS

If the process of theological reflection stopped with this new theological awareness, then the fears of practitioners of social witness would be realized—the exercise would bear no practical fruits and would come perilously close to encouraging *only* self-satisfaction among activists. Instead, drawing on the foundational commitments of practical and liberation theology and all those other constructive theologies branded

32. It is important to distinguish these questions from the oft-asked question, "Where do you see God in this?" In contrast, the questions posed here invite both acknowledgments of God's perceived absence and yearnings for God's transformation of an unjust social order.

"contextual"—this process is not complete without a return to practice. I have described this moment as "renewed *praxis*," calling forth the intentional and reflective character of actions discerned and pursued within theological reflection. It may be that strategies change, or practitioners' understandings of God's action in the world demand new relationships, or simply that practitioners continue in their same struggle with the knowledge that they participate in the larger work of God within the world. In the words of the great hymn, practitioners of social witness who engage in theological reflection may find, simply, "Strength for today and bright hope for tomorrow."[33] Even if this were the only outcome of theological reflection within social witness, it constitutes renewed *praxis* in the deepest sense of renewal—having their needs for sustenance met, practitioners of social witness are strengthened in their continued seeking after the Kingdom of God. Once more, let us appeal to the words of the Confession of 1967: "With an urgency born of this hope the church applies itself to present tasks and strives for a better world. It does not identify limited progress with the kingdom of God on earth, nor does it despair in the face of disappointment and defeat. In steadfast hope the church looks beyond all partial achievement to the final triumph of God."[34]

May it be so.

---

33. Chisholm, "Great Is Thy Faithfulness."

34. Presbyterian Church (U.S.A.), "Confession of 1967," 9.55.

Appendix

Ethnographic Sample, Research Methods, and Themes

As NOTED IN THE INTRODUCTION, THE STUDY OF RELIGIOUS PRACTICE
and practical theology is most fully engaged when it contains an ethnographic component. Encountering actual practitioners, observing their
practice, and talking with them about their experiences brings to life
otherwise abstract theories of practice and social action. Readers will
have noticed that data gathered via ethnographic research is reported
throughout this project, illustrating and challenging theoretical and
theological categories.

Over the course of a year, I studied two groups engaged in social
witness practice within the Presbyterian Church (U.S.A.). Though I
found myself yearning to meet more of these Presbyterian activists, I
intentionally selected a narrow sample for this highly interdisciplinary
project. I engaged in participant observation on six occasions and interviewed eight subjects, in addition to collecting and examining documents relating to the subjects' practice.

More specifically, I conducted observations and interviews (supplemented by documentary analysis) with participants in monthly denominational briefing and lobbying events in Washington DC, as well
as Greater Atlanta Presbytery's annual "Rally Day" at the Georgia State
Capitol. I have supplemented the data gathered during those events with
data gathered during a preaching conference on "truth-telling." Since
practice is always to be understood as embedded in and in relation to
institutions and communities, the Presbyterian Church (U.S.A.) presents
a complex context in which to examine social witness, as does the larger
reformed tradition of which it is part.

The two forms of social witness practice that I studied are the
Presbyterian (U.S.A.) Washington Office's monthly "Second Tuesday"
education and lobbying program and the Presbytery of Greater Atlanta's
"Rally Day at the Capitol." In both instances, participants attend a "brief-

ing" session on policy issues such as living wage ordinances, the environment, foreign policy, and religious freedom. Following the briefings, participants make lobbying visits to their legislators to discuss these, or other, issues. While there are a number of subtler, congregationally-based, and less programmed instances of social witness practice, I have chosen these two crystallized forms of this practice because of their clarity of purpose, relative stability, and highly organized programs. This provides a clear and defined picture of social witness and an opportunity to study the presence, absence, and/or character of theological reflection within the practice. These instantiations of social witness occur on higher organizational levels (presbytery and denomination), thus inviting reflection on how these bodies might provide resources for congregations, pastors, and other individuals in their own practice. Finally, these crystallized forms draw a particularly committed group of participants, offering a sample that yields some insight as to how these practices flourish and are best sustained over long periods of time.

In addition to these two crystallized forms of social witness practice, I also conducted research at a denominational conference called "Reclaiming the Text." Often called the "preaching" conference, the theme for the 2005 conference was "Telling the Truth in a World of Denial," and in the description for the conference, the planning committee revealed their normative assumptions about the role of the preacher in practices of social witness: "It is the job of the preacher to be the point person for truth telling that exposes deadly denial and voices an alternative. This vocation of the church and its pastors will be explored by focusing on the text and how it mediates to us a voice other than our own." At that conference, I met many pastors who are invested in various forms of social witness. Through sermons, workshops, and informal conversations, I listened for instances of and discourse about theological reflection in relation to social witness practice. It was interesting to compare the role of theological reflection in this conference, where it is an explicit goal, to its role in the two previously described forms of social witness, where it may be more assumed than explicitly engaged.

Initially, I selected three subjects within the Presbyterian Church (U.S.A.), two pastors and the director of the Washington Office of the Presbyterian Church (U.S.A.), because of their public roles in leading practices of social witness. One pastor, John Fife, is well known among Christian activists for his role in the Sanctuary Movement of the 1980's.

I interviewed him during the preaching conference on truth-telling. The other pastor, Caroline Kelly, serves a downtown Atlanta congregation (across the street from the state capitol, in fact) and chairs the Presbytery's public policy committee. In this role, she also coordinates the Presbytery's annual lobbying day at the state capitol. The director of the Washington Office, Elenora Giddings Ivory, oriented me to the office's work and introduced me to other staff members, as well as welcomed my participant observation during the monthly briefings and lobbying visits. (I interviewed two of those staff members.) Elenora served in that capacity for eighteen years, and has since accepted a position with the World Council of Churches directing the program called Public Witness: Addressing Power and Affirming Peace.

To some degree, this was a snowball sample. The three initially-selected interview subjects made suggestions for events to attend and other persons to interview. I thus attended and conducted participant observation during four "Second Tuesday" briefings in the Washington Office and the annual "Rally Day at the Capitol." From these events, I located and invited (by email) more interview subjects. Between eight and ten of the persons I contacted indicated interest in participating in the project and I scheduled interviews with three of them. The three subjects identified in this manner were long-time participants in programs offered through the Washington Office, and they graciously invited me to worship with them, to share two meals with them, and to accompany them on a visit to their congressional offices. I also interviewed one of their pastors.

My research in all of these contexts is comprised of participant observation, interviews, and documentary analysis. In participant observation during these events, I looked for several things:

- Discourse: How do participants name and describe what they are doing? Do participants use the term "witness?" How so? Do they explicitly define it? How do they use scripture in formulating and engaging in witness? How do theological concepts like hope, sin, and calling emerge in discourse?

- Practice: Is there a sense that "internal goods" are gained via practice? What are the standards of excellence in operation? What activities happen within and give shape to the practice—song, prayer, discernment, marching? Is there some common, ongoing sense of motivation? To some degree, observation of practice is limited in its capacity to measure internal dispositions and experience, but a researcher can listen for verbal articulation of goods or standards, and also look for clues to emotional investment, community building, and religious meaning.

- Biography: Who participates in these events? What sorts of experiences have they had in the past that might predispose them to this kind of practice? How do the participants relate to each other?

- Resources: In the formulation and execution of social witness, how do theological, political, economic, and social knowledge inform the practice? Are different resources employed at different stages? Does theological reflection happen at particular points, or is it a continual process?

Participant observation is indispensable for studying practice, since many practices are experienced without explicit articulation. Interviews would not be sufficient on their own, since much of the lived theology of social witness is likely to be implicit. There are, however, important insights that can also be gained *only* via interviews with participants in the practice. During the interviews, I asked questions like:

- I'd like to know about how you got involved in this sort of activity. Tell me a little bit of your story.

- Tell me about your experience with social witness. Why don't you start with a particularly memorable experience?

- What have been some of the disappointments you've encountered, and how did you deal with those?

- What do you think has sustained this particular form of social witness over time? What sustains you in your participation in it?

- How do you think social witness is understood in congregational life? Do you bring your experience with this activity into your congregation? Does your congregation engage in practices like this? What does that look like?

- (For pastors) How do you understand your role as pastor, as it relates to social action?

Finally, a full ethnographic investigation of these practices takes into account all the written and spoken materials that, along with activities, constitute the practice. In fact, it sometimes is through documentary analysis that theological framing appears most explicitly. Through documentary analysis, I examined how the practice of social witness is communicated in and augmented by documents such as newsletters, confessions, email briefings, and sermons.

This project was conducted in a post-positivist frame, with a critical theoretical impulse. This means that, while I used theory to design my research questions and to organize and analyze my data, the encounter with the lived experience of the practice sometimes challenged this theoretical framework. For example, one theoretical assumption I brought to the project was that the work of denominational "Washington offices" was known among clergy, but that lay persons were less informed about not only the nature of this work but even about the very existence of the offices.[1] This assumption was quickly challenged by the first briefing I attended at the Presbyterian Washington Office, where there were *no* pastors, only committed lay persons!

The critical theoretical impulse means that my findings also yield some insights that can challenge, strengthen, and propose change to the practice of social witness. In the end, these findings helped me to make critical constructive proposals regarding the logistics of the practice, the role of theology within the practice, and our understandings of traditional reformed theological doctrine.

Implications of Ethnographic Research for This Study and Future Work

The first thing that must be said about the ethnographic research used in this study is that it is intentionally small in scope. As such, it serves a mostly illustrative purpose, breathing life, and thus living questions, into otherwise abstract categories and concepts. It also lights the path for future work. Let me name just three of the many implications drawn from the preliminary findings from this study: the very real resistance among activists toward reflective modes of social witness practice; the hopes and challenges faced by pastors who seek to minister with and

---

1. Laura Olson has studied the changing relationship between clergy and denominational Washington offices. See Olson, "Mainline Protestant Washington Offices and the Political Lives of Clergy."

among activists; and the need for a tested model of theological reflection that speaks to the needs of social witness practitioners.

First, as described in chapter 6, I found that these particular practitioners of social witness exhibit a high level of impatience with abstraction in all its forms, including theological. This tendency most certainly manifested itself in interviews. Recall Nelson Tharp's lament when asked about the possibilities for more reflection among activists: "(I)t's good, in the sense that it re-inspires you to get out there and work. But it bothers me that we spend so much time talking to people who are already convinced." It also was on display to a large degree during some of the briefings. The image that immediately comes to mind is of the participant who rustled his papers with exasperated sighs when asked to stay for "just two minutes" for a closing prayer. While we cannot draw generalized conclusions about activists' receptivity to theological reflection from this small sample, we do find here a clue to the need for such reflection to be highly contextualized. In other words, the data gathered in this project suggests that an action-reflection model, while a step in the right direction, may not be integrated enough to be sustained by activists. It seemed, during my research, that even a *suggestion* of what appeared to be abstract or reflective thinking quickly raised anxiety levels. Pausing from the *real* work of activism quickly meets with resistance.

Second, I encountered a wide range of perspectives among pastors in response to questions about what it means to be a pastor to social activists. John Fife described a very symbiotic relationship among ministries of charity with border migrants, congregational worship life, communal discernment, and the pursuit of social justice in Arizona. Caroline Kelly, who serves in downtown Atlanta, expressed some concern for how the desire to do good connects with faithfulness in Christian life and how already overworked activists can be convinced to return to the critical work of reflection. And Dorothy Boulton, pastor to Nelson and Ellen Tharp, raised questions about how she must be pastor to all members of the congregation, of which social activists are a minority. As I spoke with the three of them, it became clear that pastoral responsibility for the Christian nurture of activists is highly contextual. One repeated theme, however, was the need, often unfulfilled, to more closely weave the work of social witness into the tapestry that is the whole Christian life. Social witness both draws its strength from and brings its prophetic voice to bear upon the whole constellation of beliefs and practices that make up the Christian life.

Now, we have come to that third implication of my preliminary findings—the need for tested models of theological reflection appropriate to the needs of social witness practitioners. Given what appears to be a tendency toward impatience among activists with regard to all things deemed abstract or self-serving, on the one hand, and pastors' identification of the need to more closely connect social action with other practices of the Christian life, on the other, how are we to bridge the gulf between the seemingly contradictory needs identified by pastors and activists? I have outlined in the preceding chapter, in a necessarily abstract form, a process and rationale for theological reflection in social witness practice. This proposal must be tested among real groups of social witness practitioners, however. Insofar as it is only a proposal, it contains vagaries and perhaps even inconsistencies that will be discovered as we actually try to incorporate the model into social witness practice. Similarly, the proposal will be strengthened by the insights of social witness practitioners as they seek to engage in forms of theological reflection that are contextual, integrative, and responsive to the particular challenges faced by activists. While this project, and the ethnographic research contained herein, means to identify challenges and possibilities for theological reflection within social witness practice, it also calls for a subsequent project, in which methods of theological reflection are tested and evaluated within the context of social witness.

Bibliography

Abbott, Jennifer, and Mark Achbar. *The Corporation*. USA: Zeitgeist Films, 2004.

Ammerman, Nancy, Jackson Carroll, Carl Dudley, and William McKinney. *Studying Congregations: A New Handbook*. Nashville: Abingdon, 1998.

Bass, Dorothy. "Congregations and the Bearing of Traditions." In *American Congregations*, edited by James P. Wind and James W. Lewis, 2:169–91. Chicago: University Of Chicago Press, 1994.

Bass, Dorothy C. "Introduction." In *Practicing Theology: Beliefs and Practices in Christian Life*, edited by Dorothy Bass and Miroslav Volf, 1–9. Grand Rapids: Eerdmans, 2002.

Bass, Dorothy C., and Craig Dykstra. "A Theological Understanding of Christian Practices." In *Practicing Theology: Beliefs and Practices in Christian Life*, edited by Dorothy Bass and Miroslav Volf, 13–32. Grand Rapids: Eerdmans, 2002.

Bauckham, Richard, and Trevor A. Hart. *Hope Against Hope: Christian Eschatology at the Turn of the Millennium*. Grand Rapids: Eerdmans, 1999.

Bauer, Walter. "μαρτυρεω." In *A Greek-English Lexicon of the New Testament and Other Early Christian Literature*, edited by F. Wilbur Gingrich and Frederick W Danker, translated by William Arndt, 492–3. 2nd ed. Chicago: University of Chicago Press, 1979.

Becker, Penny Edgell. *Congregations in Conflict: Cultural Models of Local Religious Life*. New York: Cambridge University Press, 1999.

Bellah, Robert N. *Habits of the Heart: Individualism and Commitment in American Life*. Berkeley: University of California Press, 1985.

Boff, Leonardo, and Clodovis Boff. *Introducing Liberation Theology*. Maryknoll, NY: Orbis Books, 1987.

Bourdieu, Pierre. *The Logic of Practice*. Translated by Richard Nice. Stanford, CA: Stanford University Press, 1992.

Bowman, Donna. "God for Us: A Process View of the Divine-Human Relationship." In *Handbook of Process Theology*, edited by Jay B. McDaniel and Donna Bowman, 11–24. St. Louis: Chalice, 2006.

Brown, Robert McAfee, editor. "Kairos: Challenge to the Church." In *Kairos: Three Prophetic Challenges to the Church*, 17–66. Grand Rapids: Eerdmans, 1990.

Browning, Don. *A Fundamental Practical Theology: Descriptive and Strategic Proposals*. Minneapolis: Fortress, 1991.

Brueggemann, Walter. "The Legitimacy of a Sectarian Hermeneutic." In *Interpretation and Obedience*, 41–69. Minneapolis: Fortress, 1991.

———. *The Prophetic Imagination*. 2nd ed. Minneapolis: Fortress, 2001.

Calvin, John. *Institutes of the Christian Religion*. Edited by John T. McNeill. Translated by Ford Lewis Battles. The Library of Christian Classics. Philadelphia: Westminster, 1960.

Carroll, Jackson, and David A. Roozen. "Congregational Identities in the Presbyterian Church." *Review of Religious Research* 31 (1990) 352–69.

Chaves, Mark. *Congregations in America.* Cambridge: Harvard University Press, 2004.

Chawla, Navin. *Mother Theresa.* New York: Vega, 2002.

Chisholm, Thomas Obadiah. "Great Is Thy Faithfulness." In *The Presbyterian Hymnal*, No. 276. Louisville: Westminster John Knox, 1992.

Chopp, Rebecca. "Practical Theology and Liberation." In *Formation and Reflection: The Promise of Practical Theology*, edited by Lewis S. Mudge and James N. Poling, 120–138. Minneapolis: Fortress, 2009.

"Coalition of Immokalee Workers (CIW)," 2010. Online: http://www.ciw-online.org/.

Crawford, Elaine Brown. *Hope in the Holler: A Womanist Theology.* Louisville: Westminster John Knox, 2002.

De Gruchy, John W. *Confessions of a Christian Humanist.* Minneapolis: Fortress, 2006.

Dykstra, Craig. *Growing In The Life Of Faith: Education And Christian Practices.* 2nd ed. Louisville: Westminster John Knox, 2005.

———. "Reconceiving Practice." In *Shifting Boundaries: Contextual Approaches to the Structure of Theological Education*, edited by Barbara G. Wheeler and Edward Farley, 35–90. Louisville, KY: Westminster John Knox, 1991.

Epstein, Barbara. "The Politics of Moral Witness: Religion and Nonviolent Direct Action." In *Peace Action in the Eighties: Social Science Perspectives*, edited by Sam Marullo and John Lofland, 106–24. New Brunswick, NJ: Rutgers University Press, 1990.

Farley, Edward. *Ecclesial Man: A Social Phenomenology of Faith and Reality.* Philadelphia: Fortress, 1975.

García-Rivera, Alex. *The Community of the Beautiful: A Theological Aesthetics.* Collegeville, MN: Liturgical, 1999.

Geertz, Clifford. "Religion as a Cultural System." In *The Interpretation of Cultures*, 87–125. New York: Basic, 1973.

Gerlach, Wolfgang. *And the Witnesses Were Silent: The Confessing Church and the Persecution of the Jews.* Translated by Victoria Barnett. Lincoln: University of Nebraska Press, 2000.

Goldstein, Valerie Saiving. "The Human Situation: A Feminine View." *The Journal of Religion* 40:2 (1960) 100–112.

Graham, Elaine L. *Transforming Practice: Pastoral Theology in an Age of Uncertainty.* Eugene, OR: Wipf & Stock, 2002.

Graham, Elaine L., Heather Walton, and Frances Ward. *Theological Reflection: Methods.* London: SCM, 2005.

Green, Fred Pratt. "How Clear Is Our Vocation, Lord." In *The Presbyterian Hymnal*, No. 419. Louisville: Westminster John Knox, 1992.

Gutiérrez, Gustavo. *A Theology of Liberation: History, Politics, and Salvation.* Translated by Caridad Inda and John Eagleson. Maryknoll, NY: Orbis, 1988.

Haberer, Jack. *GodViews: The Convictions that Drive Us and Divide Us.* Louisville: Westminster John Knox, 2001.

Harper, Frederick Nile. *Urban Churches, Vital Signs: Beyond Charity Toward Justice.* Eugene, OR: Wipf & Stock, 2005.

Hauerwas, Stanley. *Dispatches from the Front: Theological Engagements with the Secular.* Durham, NC: Duke University Press, 1994.

———. *The Peaceable Kingdom: A Primer in Christian Ethics*. Notre Dame, IN: University of Notre Dame Press, 1983.

Hilton, Robin. "Exclusive Premiere: New Avett Brothers Video." *NPR: All Songs Considered (The Blog)*, 2010. Online: http://www.npr.org/blogs/allsongs/2010/07/14/128511595/exclusive-premiere-new-avett-brothers-video.

Huffaker, Lucinda A. "Feminist Theology in Process Perspective." In *Handbook of Process Theology*, 11–24. St. Louis: Chalice, 2006.

Illegal Immigration: Border-Crossing Deaths Have Doubled Since 1995; Border Patrol's Efforts to Prevent Deaths Have Not Been Fully Evaluated. Government Accountability Office, 2006.

"Interface Sustainability," 2008. Online: http://www.interfaceglobal.com/Sustainability.aspx.

Jasper, James M. *The Art of Moral Protest: Culture, Biography, and Creativity in Social Movements*. Chicago: University Of Chicago Press, 1999.

Jasper, James M., and Francesca Polletta. "Collective Identity and Social Movements." *Annual Review of Sociology* 27 (2001) 283–305.

Jenkins, Richard. *Pierre Bourdieu*. Key Sociologists. New York: Routledge, 1992.

Jeunet, Jean-Pierre. *Amélie*. Miramax Films, 2001.

Johnson, James W., and John R. Johnson. "Lift Every Voice and Sing." In *The Presbyterian Hymnal*, No. 563. Louisville: Westminster John Knox, 1992.

Jones, Serene. *Feminist Theory and Christian Theology: Cartographies of Grace*. Guides to Theological Inquiry. Minneapolis: Fortress, 2007.

———. "Graced Practices: Excellence and Freedom in the Christian Life." In *Practicing Theology: Beliefs and Practices in Christian Life*, edited by Dorothy Bass and Miroslav Volf, 51–77. Grand Rapids: Eerdmans, 2002.

Katzenstein, Mary Fainsod. *Faithful and Fearless: Moving Feminist Protest Inside the Church and Military*. Princeton, NJ: Princeton University Press, 1999.

Kearns, Laurel. "Saving the Creation: Christian Environmentalism in the United States." *Sociology of Religion* 57 (1996) 55–77.

Kelsey, David. "Some Kind Words for Total Depravity." Lecture presented at the Institute for Reformed Theology, Richmond, VA, 1999.

Killen, Patricia O'Connell, and John De Beer. *The Art of Theological Reflection*. New York: Crossroad, 1995.

Killian, Lewis M., and Ralph H. Turner. *Collective Behavior*. 2nd ed. Englewood Cliffs, NJ: Prentice-Hall, 1972.

Kinast, Robert L. *What Are They Saying About Theological Reflection?* WATSA. Mahwah, NJ: Paulist, 2000.

King, Martin Luther, Jr. "Letter From Birmingham Jail (1963)." In *A Testament of Hope: The Essential Writings and Speeches of Martin Luther King, Jr.*, edited by James M. Washington, 289–302. New York: HarperCollins, 1986.

———. "Remaining Awake Through a Great Revolution (31 March 1968)." In *A Testament of Hope: The Essential Writings and Speeches of Martin Luther King, Jr.*, edited by James M. Washington, 268–78. New York: HarperCollins, 1986.

Lee, Bernard J. "Practical Theology as Phronetic: A Working Paper from/for Those in Ministry Education." *Association of Practical Theology Occasional Papers* 1 (1997) 1–16.

MacIntyre, Alasdair. *After Virtue: A Study in Moral Theory*. 3rd ed. Notre Dame, IN: University of Notre Dame Press, 1984.

Marshall, Ellen Ott. *Though the Fig Tree Does Not Blossom: Toward a Responsible Theology of Christian Hope*. Nashville: Abingdon, 2006.

Martin, Joan M. "A Sacred Hope and A Social Goal: Womanist Eschatology." In *Liberating Eschatology; Essays in Honor of Letty M. Russell*, edited by Margaret A. Farley and Serene Jones, 209–26. Louisville: Westminster John Knox, 1990.

Marx, Karl. *The German Ideology: Including Theses on Feuerback and Introduction to the Critique of Political Economy*. Great Books in Philosophy. Amherst, NY: Prometheus, 1998.

May, Gerald G. *Will and Spirit: A Contemplative Psychology*. San Francisco: HarperOne, 1987.

McCarthy, John David, and Mayer N. Zald. *The Trend of Social Movements in America: Professionalization and Resource Mobilization*. Morristown, NJ: General Learning, 1973.

McDonald, Timothy. "He Came Not to Praise King But. . . ." *Los Angeles Times*. Los Angeles, CA, January 19, 2004. Online: http://articles.latimes.com/2004/jan/19/opinion/oe-mcdonald19.

McFadyen, Alistair I. *Bound to Sin: Abuse, Holocaust, and the Christian Doctrine of Sin*. Cambridge Studies in Christian Doctrine 6. New York: Cambridge University Press, 2000.

McKnight, John. "Why 'Servanthood' Is Bad : Are We Service Peddlers or Community Builders?." *The Other Side* 31:6 (1995) 56–59.

"Mission Zero," 2010. Online: http://missionzero.org/about.

Moltmann, Jürgen. "The Diaconal Church in the Context of the Kingdom of God." In *Hope for the Church: Moltmann in Dialogue with Practical Theology*, edited by M. Douglas Meeks and Theodore Runyon, 21–36. Nashville, TN: Abingdon, 1979.

———. "Hope." In *The Westminster Dictionary of Christian Theology*, edited by Alan Richardson and John Bowden, 270–73. Philadelphia: Westminster John Knox, 1983.

———. *Theology of Hope: On the Ground and the Implications of a Christian Eschatology*. Translated by James W. Leitch. 5th ed. San Francisco: HarperSanFrancisco, 1967.

Morris, Aldon D. *The Origins of the Civil Rights Movement: Black Communities Organizing for Change*. New York: Free Press, 1984.

Niebuhr, Reinhold. *The Nature and Destiny of Man: A Christian Interpretation*. Library of Theological Ethics. Louisville: Westminster John Knox, 1996.

Oberschall, Anthony. "Mobilization, Leaders, and Followers in the Civil Rights Movement." In *Social Conflict and Social Movements*, 204–13. Englewood Cliffs, NJ: Prentice Hall, 1973.

Olson, Laura R. "Mainline Protestant Washington Offices and the Political Lives of Clergy." In *The Quiet Hand of God: Faith-Based Activism and the Public Role of Mainline Protestantism*, edited by Robert Wuthnow and John Hyde Evans, 54–79. Berkeley: University of California Press, 2002.

Pagnucco, Ron. "The Political Behavior of Secular and Faith-Based Peace Groups." In *Disruptive Religion: The Force of Faith in Social Movement Activism*, edited by Christian Smith, 205–22. New York: Routledge, 1996.

Parker, Evelyn L. *Trouble Don't Last Always: Emancipatory Hope Among African American Adolescents*. Cleveland: Pilgrim, 2003.

Pauw, Amy Plantinga. "Some Last Words About Eschatology." In *Feminist and Womanist Essays in Reformed Dogmatics*, edited by Amy Plantinga Pauw and Serene Jones, 221–24. Louisville: Westminster John Knox, 2006.

Peek, Charles W., Mark A. Konty, and Terri E. Frazier. "Religion and Ideological Support for Social Movements: The Case of Animal Rights." *Journal for the Scientific Study of Religion* 36 (1997) 429–40.

Peters, Rebecca Todd. *In Search of the Good Life: The Ethics of Globalization*. New York: Continuum, 2004.

Plantinga, Cornelius. *Not the Way It's Supposed to Be: A Breviary of Sin*. Grand Rapids: Eerdmans, 1995.

Presbyterian Church (U.S.A.). "A Brief Statement of Faith." In *Book of Confessions*. Vol. 1. The Constitution of the Presbyterian Church (U.S.A.). Louisville: Office of the General Assembly, 2004.

———. "Directory for Worship." In *Book of Order*. Vol. 2. The Constitution of the Presbyterian Church (U.S.A.). Louisville: Office of the General Assembly, 2004.

———. "The Confession of 1967." In *Book of Confessions*. Vol. 1. The Constitution of the Presbyterian Church (U.S.A.). Louisville: Office of the General Assembly, 2004.

Ray, Stephen G. *Do No Harm: Social Sin and Christian Responsibility*. Minneapolis: Fortress, 2003.

Ruether, Rosemary Radford. "The Theological Vision of Letty Russell." In *Liberating Eschatology; Essays in Honor of Letty M. Russell*, edited by Margaret A. Farley and Serene Jones, 16–25. Louisville: Westminster John Knox, 1990.

Salgado, Sebastião. *Migrations: Humanity in Transition*. New York: Aperture, 2005.

Schleiermacher, Friedrich. *The Christian Faith*. Edited by H. R. Mackintosh and James S. Stewart. Edinburgh: T. & T. Clark, 1989.

Schüssler Fiorenza, Elisabeth. "To Follow the Vision: The Jesus Movement as Basileia Movement." In *Liberating Eschatology; Essays in Honor of Letty M. Russell*, edited by Margaret A. Farley and Serene Jones, 123–55. Louisville: Westminster John Knox, 1990.

Smith, Christian. "Correcting a Curious Neglect, or Bringing Religion Back In." In *Disruptive Religion: The Force of Faith in Social Movement Activism*, edited by Christian Smith, 1–27. New York: Routledge, 1996.

———. *Resisting Reagan: The U.S. Central America Peace Movement*. 1st ed. Chicago: University Of Chicago Press, 1996.

Snow, David. *Collective Identity and Expressive Forms*. Irvine, CA: Center for the Study of Democracy, 2001. Online: http://escholarship.org/uc/item/2zn1t7bj.

Stout, Jeffrey. *Democracy and Tradition*. Princeton, NJ: Princeton University Press, 2004.

———. *Ethics After Babel: The Languages of Morals and Their Discontents*. 1st ed. Princeton, NJ: Princeton University Press, 2001.

Stroup, George W. *Before God*. Grand Rapids: Eerdmans, 2004.

Suchocki, Marjorie Hewitt. *The Fall to Violence*. New York: Continuum, 1995.

Tanner, Kathryn. *Jesus, Humanity and the Trinity: A Brief Systematic Theology*. Minneapolis: Fortress, 2001.

———. "Theological Reflection and Christian Practices." In *Practicing Theology: Beliefs and Practices in Christian Life*, edited by Dorothy Bass and Miroslav Volf, 228–42. Grand Rapids: Eerdmans, 2002.

Taylor, Verta, and Nancy Whittier. "Analytical Approaches to Social Movement Culture: The Culture of the Women's Movement." In *Social Movements and Culture*, edited by Hank Johnston and Bert Klandermans, 163–87. Minneapolis: University of Minnesota Press, 1995.

The Open Door Community. "Street Teachers," n.d. Online: http://opendoorcom munity.org/street_teachers.htm.

Townes, Emilie M. "'The Doctor Ain't Taking No Sticks': Race and Medicine in the African American Community." In *Embracing the Spirit: Womanist Perspectives on Hope, Salvation, and Transformation*, 179–95. Maryknoll, NY: Orbis, 1997.

Tutu, Desmond. *No Future Without Forgiveness*. New York: Doubleday, 1999.

Wyman, Jr., Walter E. "Sin and Redemption." In *The Cambridge Companion to Friedrich Schleiermacher*, edited by Jacqueline Mariña, 129–50. New York: Cambridge University Press, 2005.

Yarger, Lenore. "Holy Communion: By Building Relationships Across National Borders, John Fife and His Congregation Are Challenging the Market Economy." *The Other Side* 33 (1997) 22–25.

Young, Josiah. "'Good Is Knowing When to Stop': Dénucléation and the End of Privilege." In *In Search of the Common Good*, edited by Dennis P. McCann and Patrick D. Miller, 211–27. New York: T. & T. Clark, 2005.

Zald, Mayer, and Roberta Ash. "Social Movement Organizations: Growth, Decay, and Change." *Social Forces* 44 (1966) 327–41.

Subject Index

Author and Name Index